CASPAR LEE

by Caspar Lee and Emily Riordan Lee

(My mom)

LEARNING CENTRE
CLASS NO: 920 LEE
ACC NO: 171629

MICHAEL JOSEPH
an imprint of
PENGUIN BOOKS

Contents

INTRODUCTION
by Caspar Lee

Hi, my name is Caspar Lee and today I found out my mom has written a completely unauthorized biography. About me. And she's landed a deal with Penguin book publishers. I don't understand how this is legal? Thinking about it there was that time when she asked for my signature... I thought it was just because she is a big fan of mine... But I'll definitely pay more attention to what I'm signing in the future!

At the last minute, I have managed to somehow get my hands on a copy so at least I get the chance to have my say and tell the real story*.

Caspar Lee

CASPAR KEY

I love this

I don't like this

I'm embarrassed...

* I love you, Mom! ♡

CHAPTER ONE

How Caspar tried TO KILL HIS MOTHER

Caspar tried to kill me. He really did. I'm not joking. And to lay that charge on your son is quite a serious thing. And all because of his head. It was (and still is) just too darn big. (Nice, Mom. Really nice. Already making fun of a newborn baby and we're only on page one. This is going to be tough).

Prior to his arrival on this planet in 1994, I was so looking forward to meeting the wee chap. I had a suitcase packed full of "Petit Bateau" babygros, ready in the car to go to the hospital. It also contained a plethora of natural remedies like arnica, lavender, StressLess, CrampEase, homeopathic this and Ayurveda that. (No wonder I'm so f**ked up!) I was rather an alternative type when it came to childbirth, and everything else really. I tried to have Theo at home, but ended up in hospital with all the bells and whistles and every type of pain relief possible! But this time, with child number two, I had opted for a hospital birth. Just before my time came, I arrived home from some antenatal yoga class to find a window of our car smashed in and the suitcase gone. Not exactly a thief's best booty, a suitcase full of fluffy nappies and nipple shields (Ewww!) but the shock I got was enough to get me going.

> I felt like I was starring in "Casualty" as they were struggling, for real, to save my life.

My husband Jon was in bed suffering from possible bird flu, so my wonderful friend Hilary took me in hand and got me swiftly to St Mary's Paddington in the middle of the night. I'm not going into the details of Caspar's arrival but all I can say is that it didn't go to plan. The fact that his head was very big didn't help, (Again with the head?) and I remember, just after his delivery, being completely surrounded by medics, drips, needles, monitors and bleepers. I joked with them saying I felt like I was starring in "Casualty" as they were struggling, for real, to save my life.

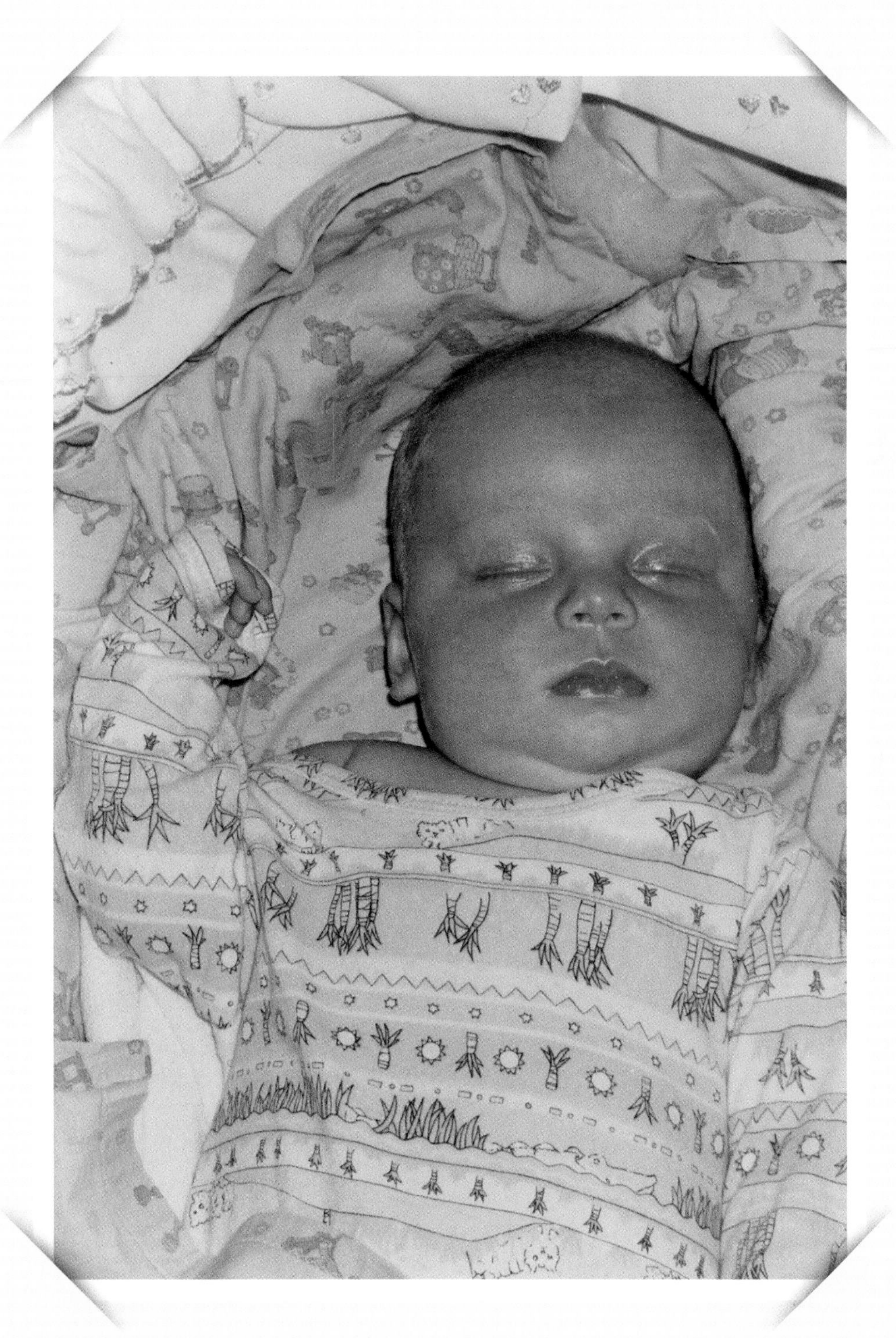

I come from England and so do my forefathers they were mostly farmars and fighters.
England.
If you go even further back some of them were in Queen Boodika's army.
My mom had trouble giving birth to m
becouse my head was to big.
But
I came
event
out.
HERE I AM.

As my world dimmed I remember being blissfully happy that our baby was fine and I wasn't at all concerned about passing on myself. It was all very surreal. Jon (covered in a face mask and gown) held our beautiful new born while Hilary held my hand and tried not to faint at the sight of buckets of blood on the floor.

We spent a good eight hours recovering in the birthing theatre, before being moved to the public ward, but since I was only half-conscious, everything was a bit of a blur. A lot of noise, mostly from talking nurses, prevented sleep and the next day they discovered something was wrong with our beautiful baby. (Aside from my gigantic head?) His eyes weren't opening properly and motherly panic set in. The high of giving birth and the near death experience quickly gave way to uncontrollable sobbing . The paediatrician arrived and confirmed a serious bacterial eye infection, which meant that both Caspar and I would be required to remain in hospital for at least two weeks. I was too weak to stand up, and I felt

I was a happy todler. I went to Joycebroadhead and had lots of iends. I also used o fall in the ool while iding my ittle plastic notorbike.

I am a normal kid, in a normal school with great friends.

One day I hope to have a succesible bussiness.

Further evidence of Caspar's massive head:

"My mom had trouble giving birth to me because my head was to (sic) big".

---

as though the ground had been taken from under me. My baby was sick and I was filled with despair.

But fortunately this horrible episode didn't last long at all. The outcome was good. More than good. Our medical insurance kicked in and we were promptly moved to the luxury of the "Lindo Wing". So Caspar spent the first two weeks of his life in the manner to which he would have liked to have become accustomed – a five-star private hospital suite where Prince George and Princess Charlotte also began their lives. I'm sure I've heard of them ... The nursing was superb. There was no noise audible from the nursing staff, as I had a private room. I had my baby boy next to me during the day, and at night I had long, blissful sleeps (with the help of tranquillizers and a fine gourmet dinner), while Caspar was whisked away to the nursery surrounded by other gurgling babies.

Buckets of blood...

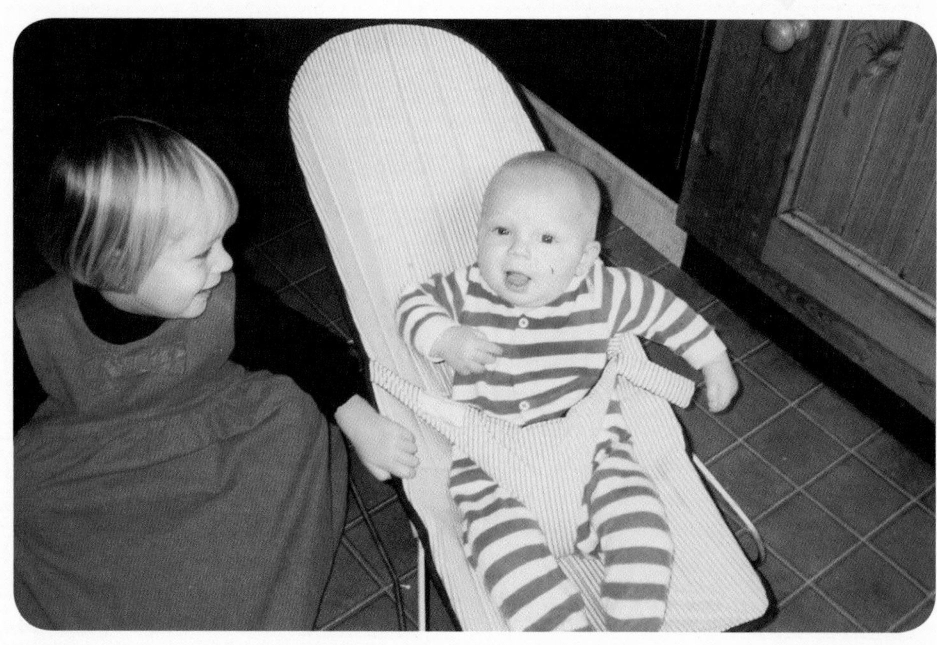

Caspar is the one in the stripey baby-gro. Theo is with him.

Dad, of course, was running around with his video camera filming everything in sight, knowing one day we'd all like to watch how the big-headed one started his days.

On the third day, his sister Theodora, aged three, arrived to inspect Caspar for the first time and it really was a precious moment. It was definitely love at first sight, and the ecstatic smile on her face when presented with a brand new ironing board (Caspar's gift to her) was enough to convince me of her undying sisterly loyalty for life. Clearly I didn't choose that present, which is why it was the first and last sexist gift I've ever given. She would spend ages ironing all the babygros and dressing him up like her dolly. So far so good. I was a good boy, no bother at all, unlike my sister who screamed her head off most of the time, when she wasn't kicking and stamping her feet.

It was definitely love at first sight, and the ecstatic smile on her face when presented with a brand new ironing board (Caspar's gift to her) was enough to convince me of her undying sisterly loyalty for life.

We both recovered in a leisurely way, with many friends and family coming to visit. Theo inspected the blob in the basket on a daily basis, and prodded him with keen interest, hoping he might squeak. She opened all his presents hoping they might be for her, threw a few tantrums when they weren't, and then continued with the ironing (poor little girl). Caspar, in the meantime, was such a good boy and was fully compliant with all things a baby was meant to be. (*Blushing*)

So there was a happy ending to the first few weeks of the life of big-headed Caspar.

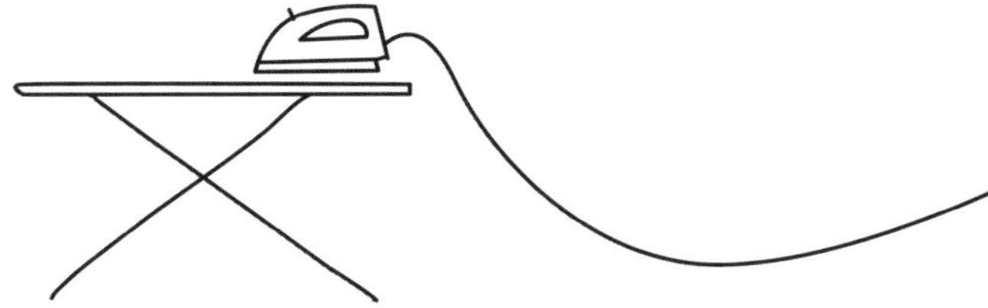

CHAPTER TWO

On the Move

When I became a mother I gave up working in television in Soho. *Is TV that thing you had before YouTube, Mom?* I used to production manage TV commercials, music videos and documentaries. There were extremely long hours involved. I also gave up wild champagne evenings in private members clubs, and endless boozy "working lunches" and the occasional work trip to Paris. *I can't imagine you being that cool, Mom. Are you sure this isn't a figment of your imagination?* It was a big change in my life.

The place where I worked was owned by the Irish band U2, and most of U2's early videos were produced in that building. I remember there was great excitement and secrecy when Caspar's uncle, Meiert Avis, directed the U2 video "Where The Streets Have No Name". No one was allowed to know anything about that video beforehand, for fear of police cancelling the roof-top gig in downtown Los Angeles, California, but we all knew something big was happening. And it did. It's now one of the most iconic music videos ever made.

Caspar's favourite food was bananas

and ice cream!

Soho Square was a happening place. On our floor we produced mostly TV commercials, and at midday every day one of the company directors would announce "It's time for a glass of champagne!" and the afternoon would officially begin with a glass of bubbly. *I really don't believe any of this.* After the birth of Theodora, I can't say I didn't miss the rock 'n' roll life. I was an all or nothing kind of person, a bit excessive you might say. But children brought about the biggest change in my life, for the good. I was a parent now. *Parents don't make fun of the size of their children's heads.* For the first time in my life I had a responsibility. I gave up drinking champagne at lunchtime and working late, because I had made a decision: I wanted to give my kids the best upbringing I could possibly give them.

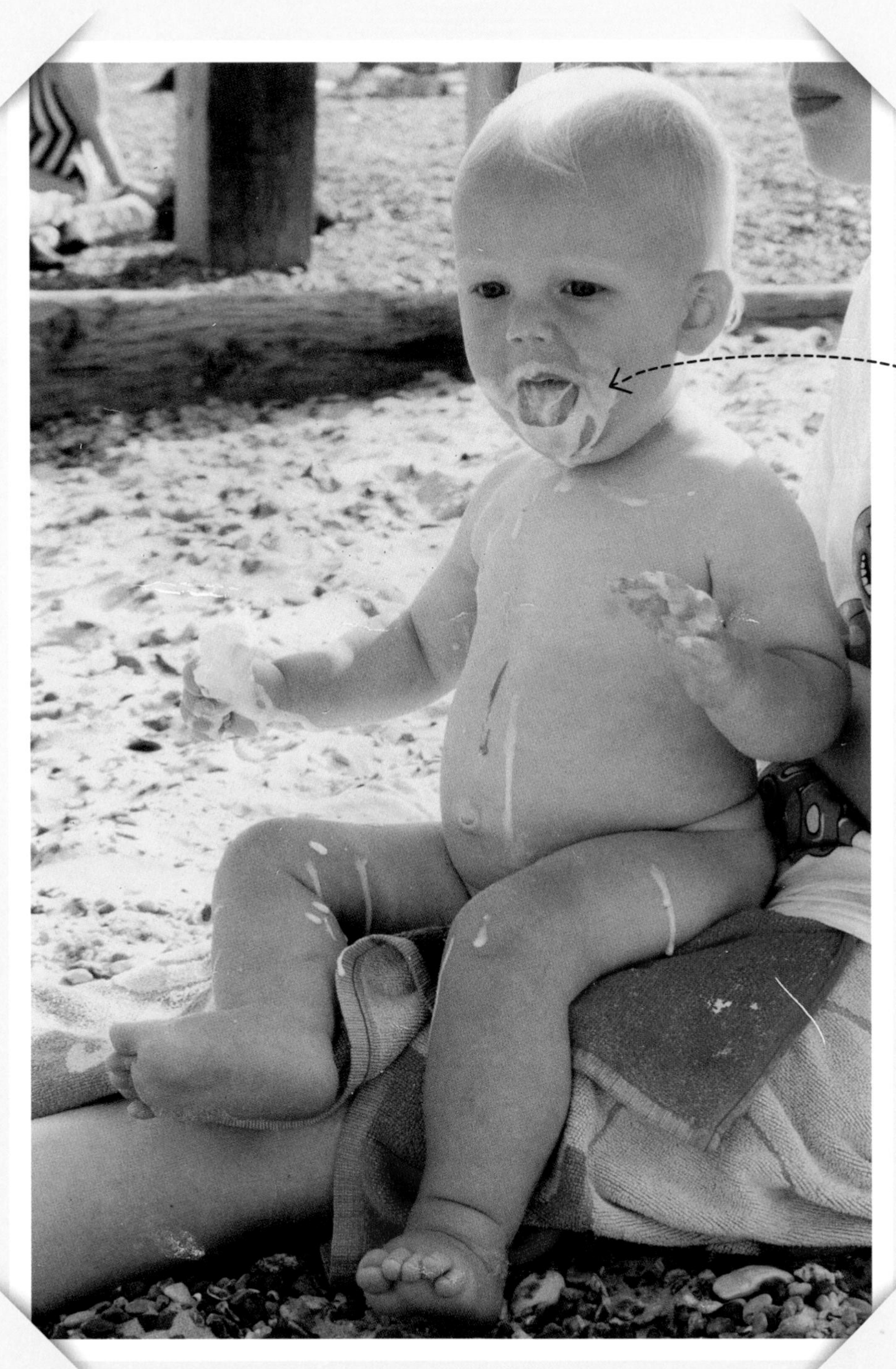

I look like a panting puppy

CUTE

~~Chubby~~ **Caspar:**

"Cherub like..."

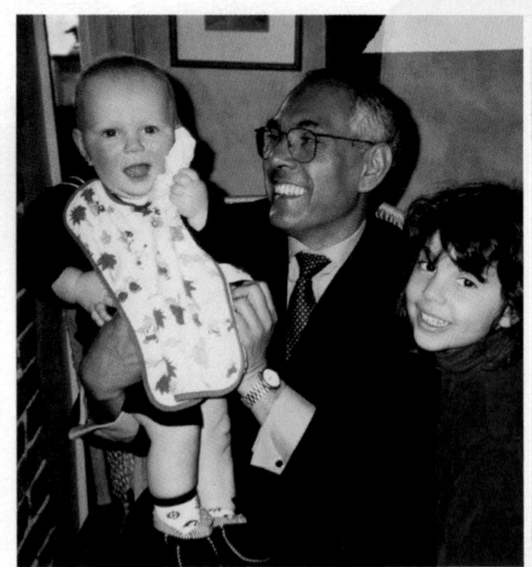

The day of my christening

We were somewhat nomadic as a family, and the move to Suffolk was the start of a long journey from place to place. Before Caspar was born we had decided to sell our large house in London and downscale to the countryside. Jon was between jobs, working on and off as a TV commercials producer in London, in a time of frequent redundancies in the early nineties. We were looking for a new kind of life, and besides we had always enjoyed our weekend jaunts to Suffolk.

I would be a full-time mum, making jam, **I've never seen you make jam in my life** growing vegetables, **Ditto** cooking up a storm, **OK, yeah, I've seen you cook** and taking the children to the seaside, **Where you used to make me run around completely naked. Brilliant** while Jon would continue to work and commute to London. Anyway, I had grown to hate the London playgrounds, the underground, and the hoards of people. Being a parent in London was so different to the kind of life I was used to! Negotiating the tube with a double buggy was no fun. There were also the problems of "schools" and "catchment areas" (every parent's nightmare) to consider. If you weren't living in the right area then your kids only got into crummy schools. And we were definitely not in the "right" area. By comparison, Suffolk had many good schools and it had the Seale-Jones's.

Now the Seale-Jones's (Victoria Seale and Trevor Jones) had been friends of ours for many years. I had gone to school with Vic, and she and her partner Trevor had a daughter called Emily, named after me, and a son called Caspar. So to make things a little more complicated, we called our new boy Caspar. **Thank God he wasn't called Joe. That's a terrible name.** From then on when we were in their company, the "Caspars" were referred to as Big Caspar and Little Caspar, and the same with the "Emilys", which was all very well until Caspar Lee grew a lot bigger **Insert obvious head joke here** than Caspar Seale-Jones and we just had to give up, hoping that no one took offence.

Caspar thrived and was the easiest baby on earth. He became cherub-like in his chubbiness.

We moved to Suffolk when Caspar was barely three weeks old. We bought a beautiful sixteenth-century house in the small ancient village of Laxfield, with windy stairs and doorways that were so low you had to stoop to get through. We continually banged our heads. It was an exciting time for us creating a nest for our children. We tore up flooring, repainted everything and created an enormous playroom for the kids... Caspar thrived and was the easiest baby on earth. He just smiled and drank and ate everything he was given with no complaints. His favourite food was bananas, and he loved elderflower cordial. He became cherub-like in his ~~chubbiness~~. CUTENESS.

Caspar was christened in the local village church and Trevor Jones became his godfather, and has remained a model godfather ever since. On the day, Caspar cried a little... probably because he was forced to wear a beautiful sailor suit.

Uncle Christopher at his wedding, with Caspar and Theo.

Note the sailor suit that reduced me to tears...

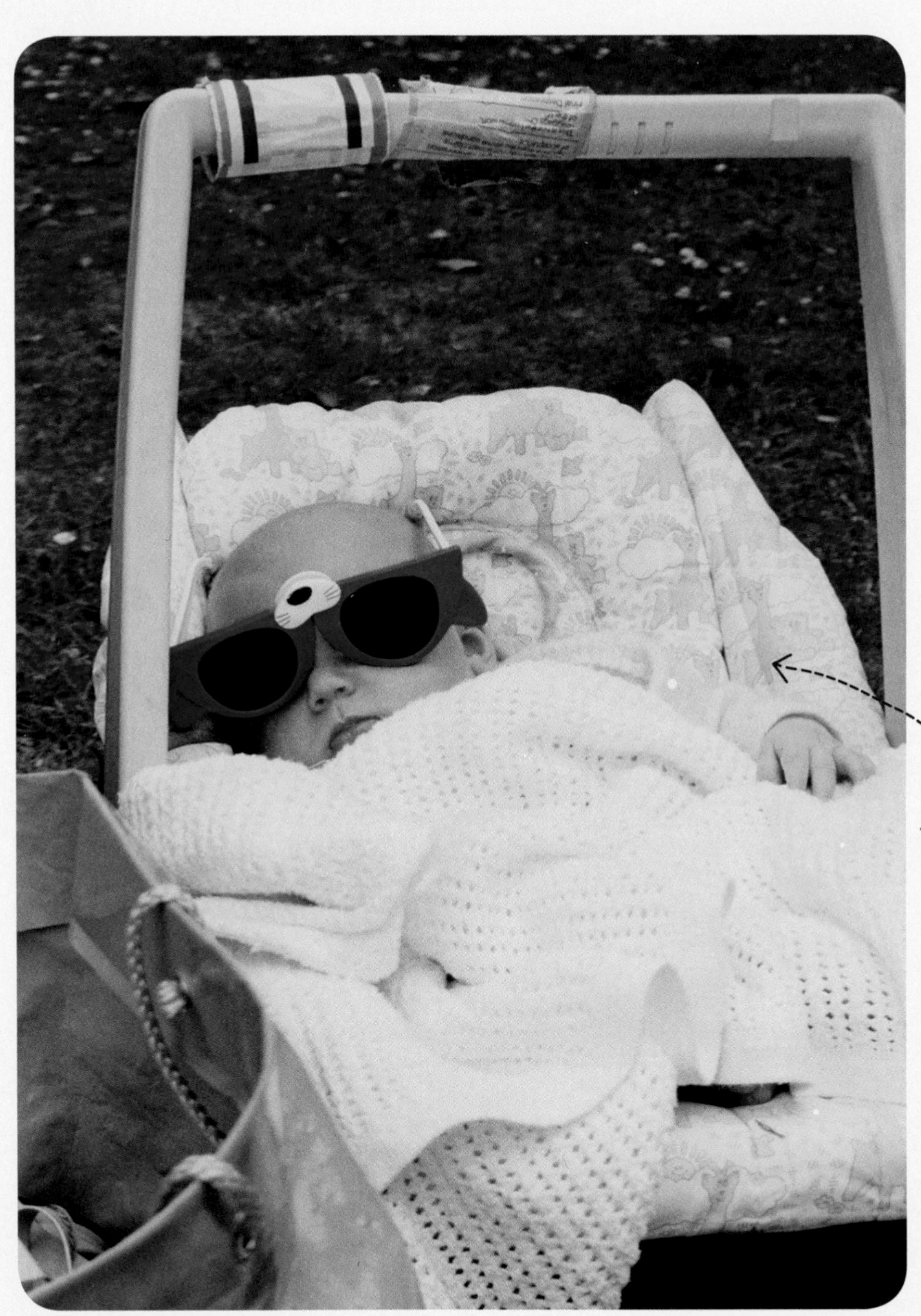

I've always been a cool dude.

Caspar was adored at the local nursery, where he made lots of new friends and began to pick up new words fast.
As I said, genius.

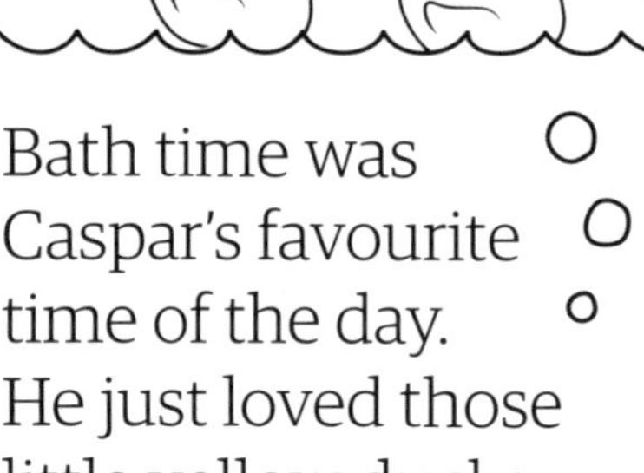

> Bath time was Caspar's favourite time of the day. He just loved those little yellow ducks bobbing around bubble bath islands.

In the meantime, life in the playroom took on a new dimension with him and Theo. She would spend hours pushing him very fast in his baby walker, seeing how quickly he could get from one side of the room to the other without actually falling out. He looked like a crab, all bandy-legged, scuttling swiftly across a sand marsh. Theo had created a racetrack. It was terrifying to watch and Caspar just used to roar with laughter, repeating the word "more" over and over. The word "more" became a bit of a mantra for him. Whatever it was that he enjoyed, he always wanted "more". *This isn't a bad thing.*

Bath time was Caspar's favourite time of the day. He just loved those little yellow ducks bobbing around bubble bath islands and floating matchboxes filled with imaginary people (matches). It was heavenly but not all roses. A period of unemployment had sadly set in for Jon. Moving to the country had not been the best idea for him. It was difficult to get back into the world of advertising without late-night networking, which usually meant hanging around Soho restaurants and clubs until very early in the morning. And we as a family could no longer afford to do that. We ate into our savings and scoured the weekly advertising magazine *Campaign,* hoping something would turn up. But being 40, and "in between" jobs in advertising, was not a good thing for a CV. *This is the first time I've actually heard about this. You guys were always great at sheltering us from the tough times. Thanks for being such great parents.*

Apart from job worries, I loved the time in Suffolk. We entertained our friends a lot around a long oak table in front of a fire and I developed a deep love of cooking. *I really do miss your cooking. Especially your banoffee pie.* My father came frequently from Ireland to visit the children, and thought we were far too easy going with them. Theodora was certainly becoming a bit wild, and I don't think he thought it a good idea that they both still slept in our bed. *I still remember you gently scratching my head to send me to sleep!* I was a "spoiler" definitely; anything they wanted I would try and provide, and this sometimes put me at odds with my husband. I loved dressing them in the nicest clothes, and would scour the second-hand shops for "designer" children's wear. My addiction to clothes shopping had transferred to the kids.

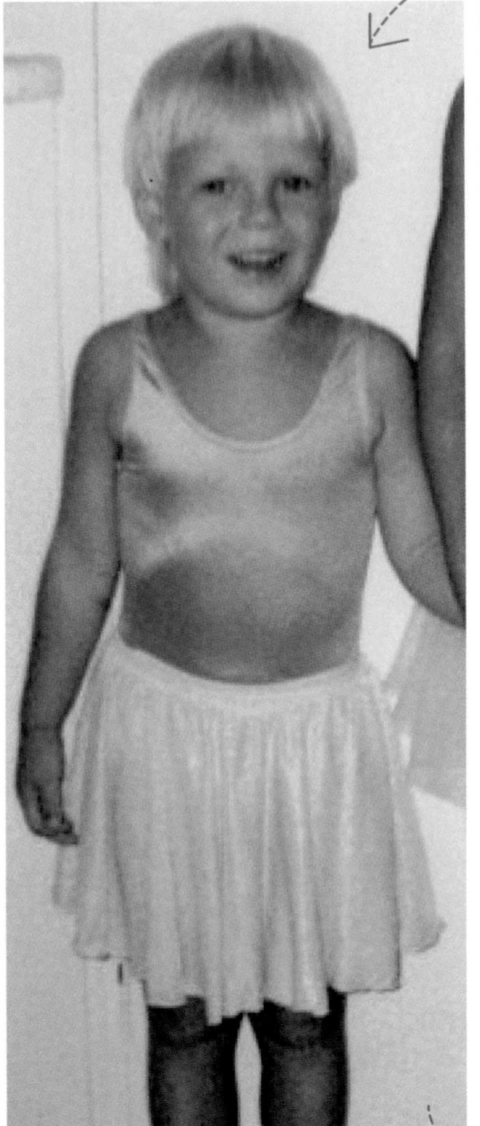

Mom, are you responsible for this haircut?

Caspar's first introduction to ballet *Surely you mean rugby, Mom?* began in Suffolk at the age of about 15 months. Theodora had taken it up, along with every other activity the village had to offer. I used to bring Caspar along to watch her and he wouldn't sit still for one minute. He had to be part of it all himself. They had a performance in the village hall with all the parents watching and I remember him escaping from me, screaming in delight and charging into the show, disrupting the concentration of all the three and four year olds. *You know me, I love to be the centre of attention.*

"Mom, look at me. Look what I can do!" Caspar yelled.

"Oh no, here we go, now what?" were the grim thoughts that crossed my mind, as all the other parents watched in horror. A twirl followed by a big grin, and then another twirl. And then a quick run around all the ballet dancers who hadn't a clue what was going on. I could feel a certain amount of "evil eyes" being flung in my direction for not disciplining this wild toddler *Erm, sorry, Mom* and when I did finally grab him he screamed his head off, and I had to make a quick exit from the hall with his legs kicking. This little fella of mine knew what he wanted from a very early age *A good way to meet girls!* and he was as strong-willed then as he is now.

OMG

"Mom, look at me. Look what I can do!" Caspar yelled… A twirl followed by a big grin, and then another twirl. And then a quick run around all the ballet dancers who hadn't a clue what was going on.

A few years later he was trying on leotards!

HARROW COLLEGE
Learning Centre

CHAPTER THREE

Bonny Scotland

We lasted a year and a half in our Suffolk house and I was loath to leave. It was perfect. I had put my heart and soul into the place. We had created a family home, which I was truly happy in. The children were settled and we had made loads of new friends, but Jon was offered a job in Edinburgh, which it would have been unreasonable to turn down. And besides, Scotland was beautiful and we could just rent and keep our lovely Suffolk home for later.

So off we went house hunting again. I still didn't want to live in a city and money was tight. We found a shepherd's cottage high up on the moors, overlooking Loch Lomond, on the estate of the 8th Duke of Montrose – miles from anywhere. We needed a 4x4 to get there as the road was so bad, and I'd always liked the idea of owning an off-road vehicle such as a Mitsubishi Shogun. It was also partly compensation for leaving our beautiful house in Suffolk. Caspar loved that car; most of all beeping the horn and flashing the lights, and singing "Baa, Baa, Black Sheep", which was enough to scare the scraggly sheep way up the mountainside, enabling a swift passage over the pot-holed track.

It was damp but we arrived in summer, so who cared? We were eaten alive by a plague of Scottish midges, and Caspar was covered in pimply bumps.

One day Caspar honked the horn so much it got stuck and let out this terrifying high-pitched blare, which along with his "beautiful" singing was enough to send the poor "baa baas" scurrying away at an alarming speed.

Everyone thought we were mad to even think of living in such a place. **You were.** "Did we not know it would be cut off by snow in the winter?" people would tell us. It was damp but we arrived in summer, so who cared? We were eaten alive by a plague of Scottish midges, and Caspar was covered in pimply bumps. We only had two bedrooms, but we only really needed one as Caspar and Theo continued to sleep in our bed with us. **That reminds me of the grandparents in Charlie and the Chocolate Factory.** LOL.

During our time in Scotland we made many happy family memories. We climbed nearby mountains with Caspar in a backpack, while Theo continued tantrum-ing her way around local supermarkets, demanding everything in sight. By comparison, Caspar was a placid blob of a boy. She tormented her brother, but they loved each other all the same.

?????

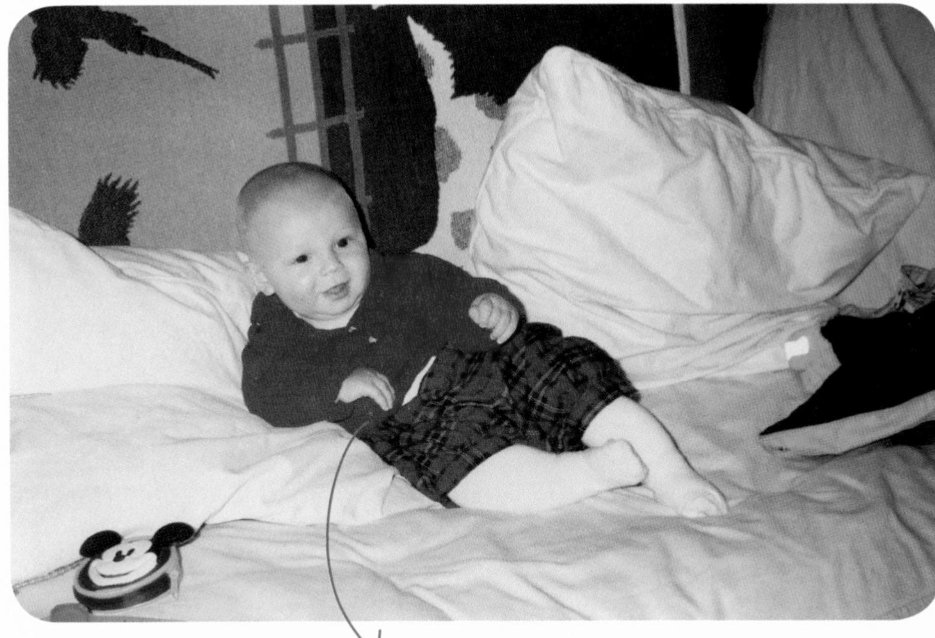

Tartan pants!

Caspar loved nothing better than piggybacks.

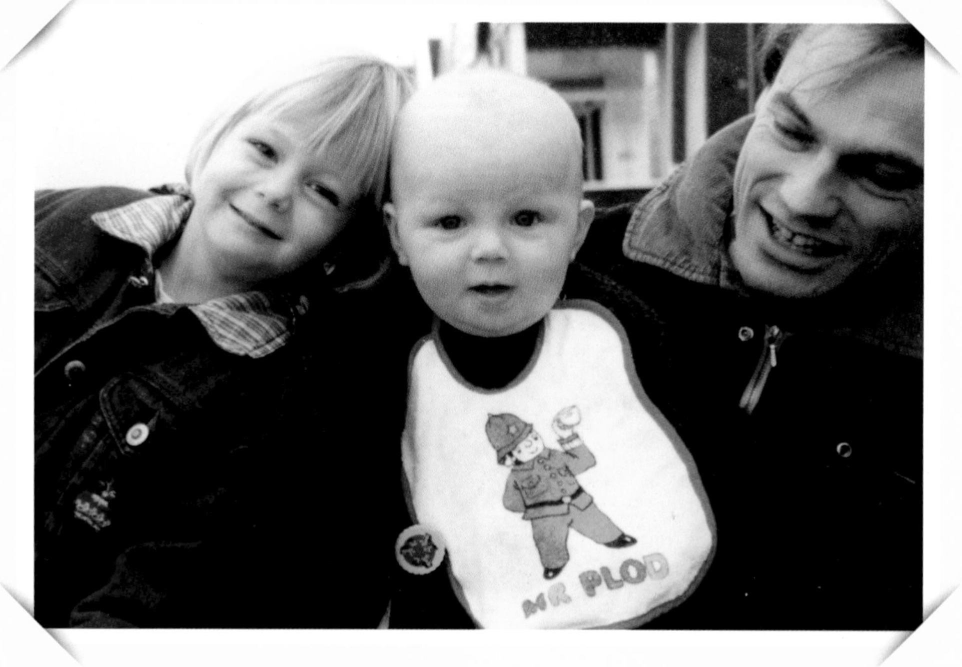

We enrolled Caspar in a nursery school, where larger-than-life Scottish comedian Robbie Coltrane (Hagrid in the Harry Potter movies) used to arrive with great aplomb in a vintage Buick, dropping off his son, Spencer. Caspar loved the drama of Spencer's arrival and departure, as he later came to love Hagrid. *Harry Potter*, by the way, was about the only book Caspar ever managed to read cover to cover. **That's not true, I used to read Tintin. But I do love Harry Potter, they're the best books ever... except this book, obviously.**

We explored the Scottish Highlands, sleeping in lighthouses, *Sadly, Hagrid never appeared at any point to tell me I was wizard* trudged across windswept bogs and cycled in sideways rain in the Inner Hebrides, with Caspar in the back carrier. We tried to find Nessie in Loch Ness, and of course Theo spotted him when Caspar's back was turned. Theo enjoyed teasing her brother more and more every day.

Our Scottish sojourn came to a quick and calamitous end when Jon's Glaswegian producer decided to make cutbacks. Our company car was taken away and the lease on our cottage was terminated. By the time the winter chill was beginning to settle in we packed our bags once more, and Jon made the decision to abandon the fickle world of advertising once and for all. We would leave the wilds of Scotland and think up some other brilliant way to earn a living. In other words, we were in deep trouble. Two little kids and nowhere to go.

What would we do, where would we go? Great Britain wasn't so great. We had been dealt a bad hand. The prime of our lives was turning into a nightmare of "Family Support" offices and retraining schemes.

> We explored the Scottish Highlands with Caspar in a back carrier.

My cousin very kindly offered us a cottage on their estate in the Lake District and said I could work in a restaurant there until we found our feet. It was a very kind offer and we did consider it. The other option was to move to Ireland and live with my Dad, but that wouldn't have worked because we still had to find jobs and we didn't want to live off welfare. We had to think of something that would be best for the kids, and England and Ireland were going through a tough time due to the recession. My father, much as he'd have loved us to be with him, came up with a brilliant plan. Why not sell our house in Suffolk and use the money to set up a guesthouse or business in South Africa, where property was cheap compared to England and pounds went much further?

I loved the idea. My mother was from South Africa after all, and from all our previous visits there I considered it to be one of the most beautiful countries on earth. And the schools were brilliant, and cost very little. We were sold.

CHAPTER FOUR

An African ADVENTURE

Nelson Mandela was elected President of South Africa just two weeks after Caspar's birth. It was a time of extraordinary change and there was both tension and excitement in South Africa. No one in their right mind dreamt of emigrating to South Africa at that time, but Caspar's grandmother grew up there and, besides, we felt like we had no other option. I was excited to be part of the post-colonial "New South Africa". We would never have lived there under apartheid, where people were segregated according to the colour of their skin, and where the colour of your skin determined your right to vote, be educated, or be offered a job. Freedom of movement was also restricted if you were not white.

We flew into Johannesburg, the country's capital city, with Caspar and his fluffy blanket (adorned with elephants) from which now he was inseparable, and took refuge in this rather daunting metropolis with Uncle Simon and Auntie Marie. One of the least safe cities in the world.

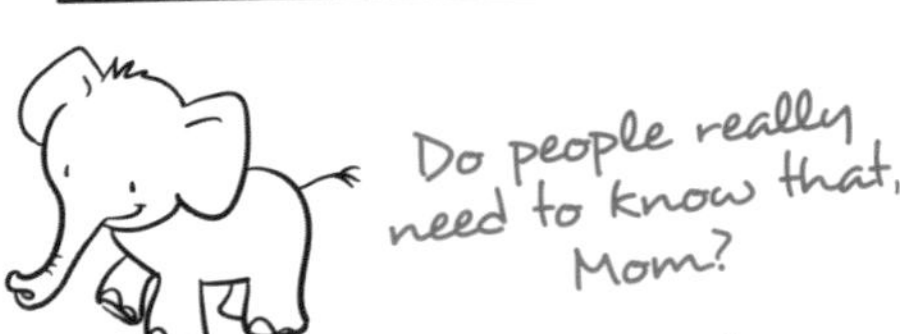

Do people really need to know that, Mom?

Their house was enormous compared to our shepherd's cottage on the moors of Scotland. It had a large swimming pool that the kids took an immediate liking to, and meals were prepared by the cooks. The breakfasts were particularly spectacular, with all sorts of beautiful tropical fruits adorning the table, and you could have eggs and bacon, or anything else for that matter. Caspar ate and ate, and became blobbier and blobbier by the day. Blobbier and cuter, I'm sure. He was in his element with all the attention from Marie, and all the floating about with his ring and armbands in the swimming pool. It felt like arriving in a grand hotel, which was some change indeed. Housekeeping was no longer an issue; no more beds to be made or plates to be scrubbed. We also no longer felt cold - South Africa is sunny pretty much every day of the year.

We flew into Johannesburg, the country's capital city, with Caspar and his fluffy blanket (adorned with elephants)

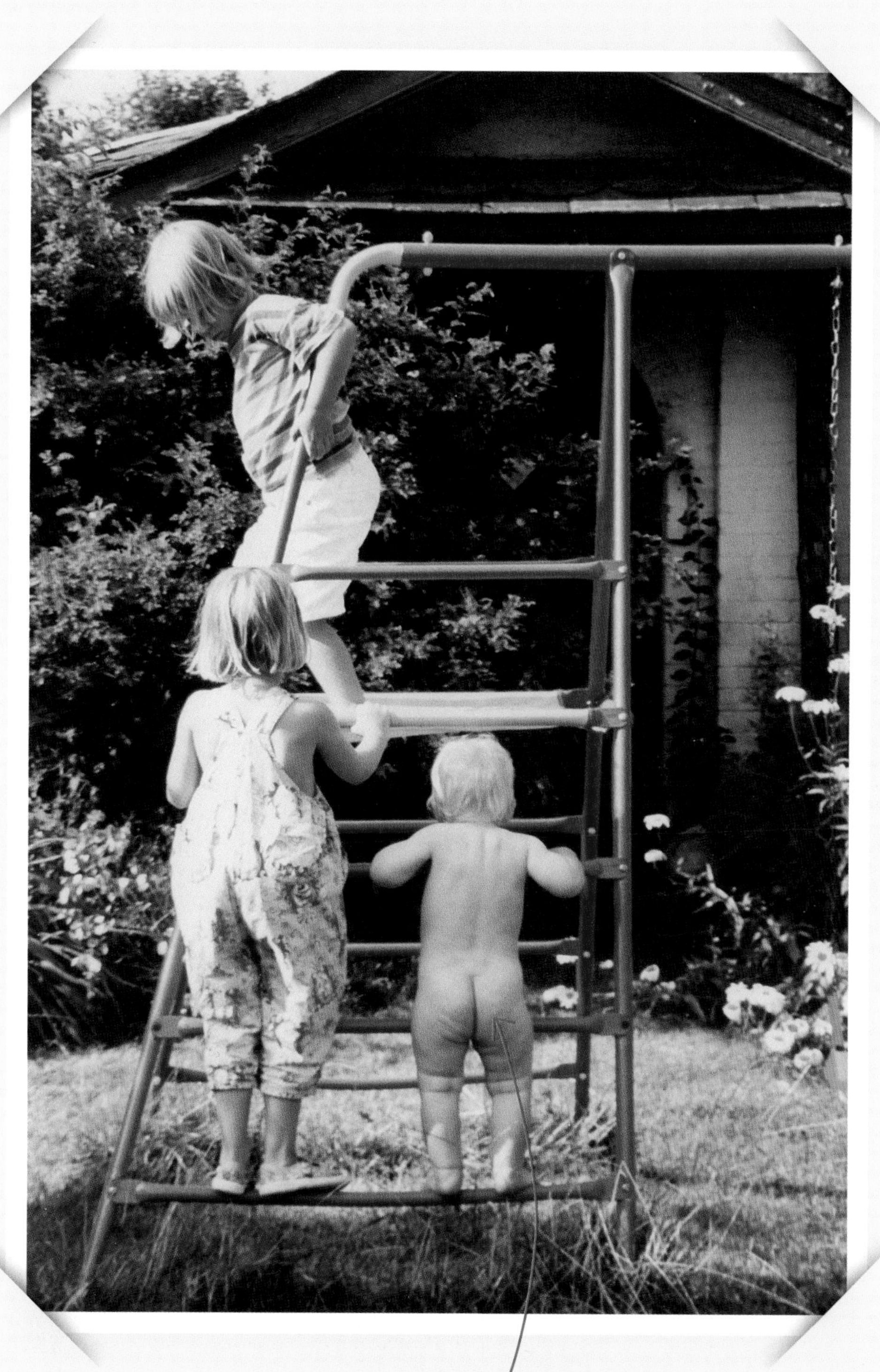

Dat ass doe

Ladies' man from day one

Sophie and Caspar on the swing at Simon and Marie's house.

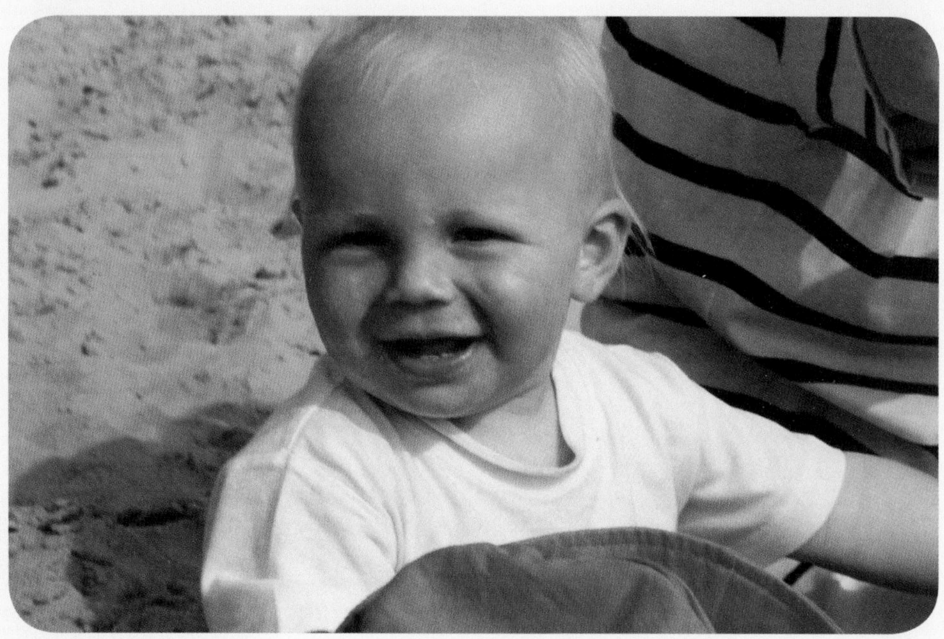

Marie loved kids, and ours were no exception. She bought them toys and took them shopping. Both she and Simon were so generous in opening their house up to us and it was wonderful to get to know our young cousins, Keesje and Lalage, who were in primary school at the time. We were made to feel like one big family.

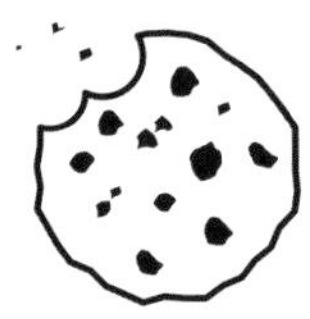

[Sophie] would ply [Theo and Caspar] with biscuits and tell them all about the Zulus.

Marie, always one to spoil Caspar and Theo rotten, bought Caspar a remote controlled ear-flapping beagle, which scared the living daylights out of Simon and Marie's three huge dogs, Rhodesian Ridgebacks, don't you know! much to Caspar's delight. At bed time Theo would often sneak off, dragging her brother along with her, to the tiny cottage in the garden that was lived in by Sophie, the cook and housekeeper. She would ply them with biscuits and tell them all about the Zulus. The unruly Theo and Caspar were not used to formal bed times and this arrangement suited us all.

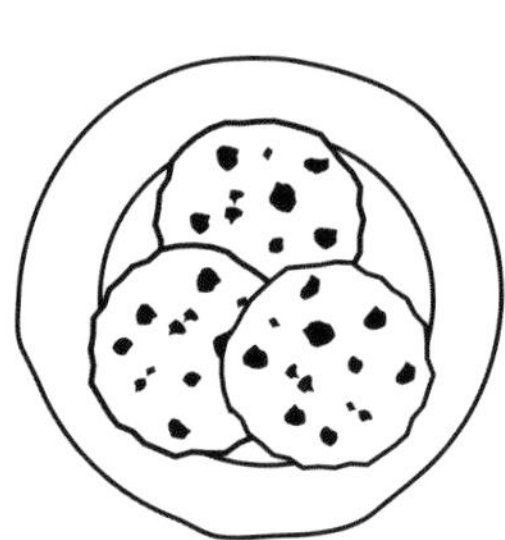

The sun shone, and Caspar loved all the new attention. Six million YouTube subscribers can't be wrong! Marie took him everywhere. He adored her and when she was too busy, Sophie took over.

In the meantime, Jon and I had decided to save the family from ruin by selling our home in Suffolk and buying a restaurant in rural KwaZulu-Natal. This area is a little safer than Jo'burg, but still not ideal. However, at the time I had no idea. My parents were very protective of us. I was sad to see our beautiful old home disappearing, and the thought of never being able to afford to go back to England ever was quite daunting, but we had to get on with life and do the best we could at that time in our lives. And weighing up all our options it seemed we had made the right decision. My cooking skills were going to be our saving grace, and a tin-roofed settlers house, plus a glorious two-acre garden for the kids to run wild in, came with the package.

When Caspar was barely two and Jon had gone back to Scotland to sort out the sale of our house, I bundled the kids, and what possessions we had, into an ancient VW Beetle held together by silicone, and headed off on a 280-mile journey from Jo'burg to KwaZulu-Natal. The car was piled to the ceiling with children's clobber. Our emerald green Beetle, not quite the Shogun I hoped for, was delightfully idiosyncratic, and all we could afford at the time. I was very fond of it though, and loved the bright colour. I was on my own with the two kids, starting our new adventure, and we all sang "The wheels on the bus go round and round" Reminds me of driving around with Joe for the movie! to pass the time. All was hunky-dory, between the singing and bottles of juice, until we hit a tumultuous thunderstorm.

Rain turned into a clatter of golf ball-sized hailstones, and the windscreen wipers broke. Lightning eclipsed the huge lorries trundling past. We could barely see.

"Mom, I need to pee, right now," said Theo.

"Me too," said Caspar.

I could barely see out of the windscreen. I was worried about a head-on collision and my kids needed to pee.

"Caspar," I interjected. "You've got a nappy on, remember?"

"But I don't like my nappy!" *Come on now, do people really need to know this, Mom? Is there nothing you won't hold back?*

"Mom, I'm bursting." Theo, again.

Toilet ↓

"I told you both to stop drinking juice!" I said with desperation in my voice.

"I can't wait, Mom!" screeched Theo as she crossed her legs into a shape that resembled pool noodles.

"There's a plastic bucket on the floor there. Use that!" I roared.

I could barely see out of the windscreen. I was worried about a head-on collision and my kids needed to pee. There was much scrambling around in the back. There were no seat belts of course, as they didn't work. But somehow, and I was never too sure how, Theo managed to relieve herself, and Caspar reconciled himself with his nappy.

On no account could I stop because:

A. If you stopped on the side of the road in South Africa you stood a very good chance of getting hijacked.

*Holy s**t!*

B. I couldn't see out either side of me with all the luggage.

C. And besides, if I did stop the car probably wouldn't restart.

It was miraculous that we arrived alive. The driveway at our destination had turned into a river and the Beetle was swept along in a torrent towards the house, where, on arrival, the brakes decided to fail and we crashed into the front door. *You know me, I like to make an entrance!*

None of us were hurt or anything, and all Caspar wanted to do was get out of the car and have "more" juice. The kids were thankfully unaware of the danger they had been subjected to. This marked our arrival in KwaZulu-Natal. As it turned out, it was a relatively tame start to the crazy times that lay ahead.

Our host, Gill Rouillard, and her daughter Mandy, met us with open arms and were aghast at the sight of this beaten-up Beetle, with its plastic bin bags piled to the roof, on their doorstep. It wasn't quite what they had in mind when they kindly offered us temporary accommodation for a month or so before we moved into our house. They ushered us in from the bog outside, past a pack of very large and terrifying dogs, sat us down in front of a roaring log fire and gave us a delicious lunch. Caspar had lots of cake and thankfully his juice bottle was replenished. *This makes it seem like all I did when I was a baby was drink juice. Non-stop. And clearly I quite liked cake too.*

We chatted for hours, and discovered that Gill had been at school in Johannesburg with my mother, who sadly passed away when I was quite young. Gill remembered her quite well. I was amazed and entranced. What a coincidence. I immediately felt at home and at one with this wonderful lady. Life has its miraculous moments, and this was definitely one of them.

It was miraculous that we arrived alive.

I couldn't be more relieved to have finally arrived; this was my idea after all, and our little cottage, which was to be our temporary home, was delightful. A few days later, Theo celebrated her fourth birthday under a large oak tree. Gill decided that a girl as tenacious as Theo deserved a fancy garden party, china plates and all. She invited a few other girls from the neighbourhood and we all sat graciously around the beautifully arranged table and ate cucumber sandwiches.

The Blob

When Caspar arrived on the scene he took one look at the pile of presents and thought it amusing to spill his apple juice all over them.

I'll never forget that birthday. Here we were in the middle of nowhere, with Jon away in England packing up the house, knowing no one, and these wonderful people were throwing a party for a little girl they barely knew.

Theo screamed, "Those are my presents!"

Caspar bellowed, "Where's mine?" then began to cry. But the soggy wrapping paper actually made them easier for Theo to open so she was thrilled. And I couldn't believe she actually allowed her brother to help her open them. *I was being helpful and teaching her about sharing.*

I'll never forget that birthday. Here we were in the middle of nowhere, with Jon away in England packing up the house, knowing no one, and these wonderful people were throwing a party for a little girl they barely knew. I was introduced to other mums and we became part of the family. When we weren't socializing, I spent time developing my cooking skills and used Gill and Mandy as my guinea pigs. It was a nice way of paying back their wonderful hospitality. Sticky toffee pudding definitely got the thumbs up from everybody, but they weren't so sure about the rather too adventurous Crocodile goulash.

Thankfully I have no recollection of this, but sticky toffee pudding will always get a thumbs up from me.

I have a lot to thank Gill and Mandy for, and will never forget their kindness, and we spent as much time as we could with them during our stay in the Natal Midlands.

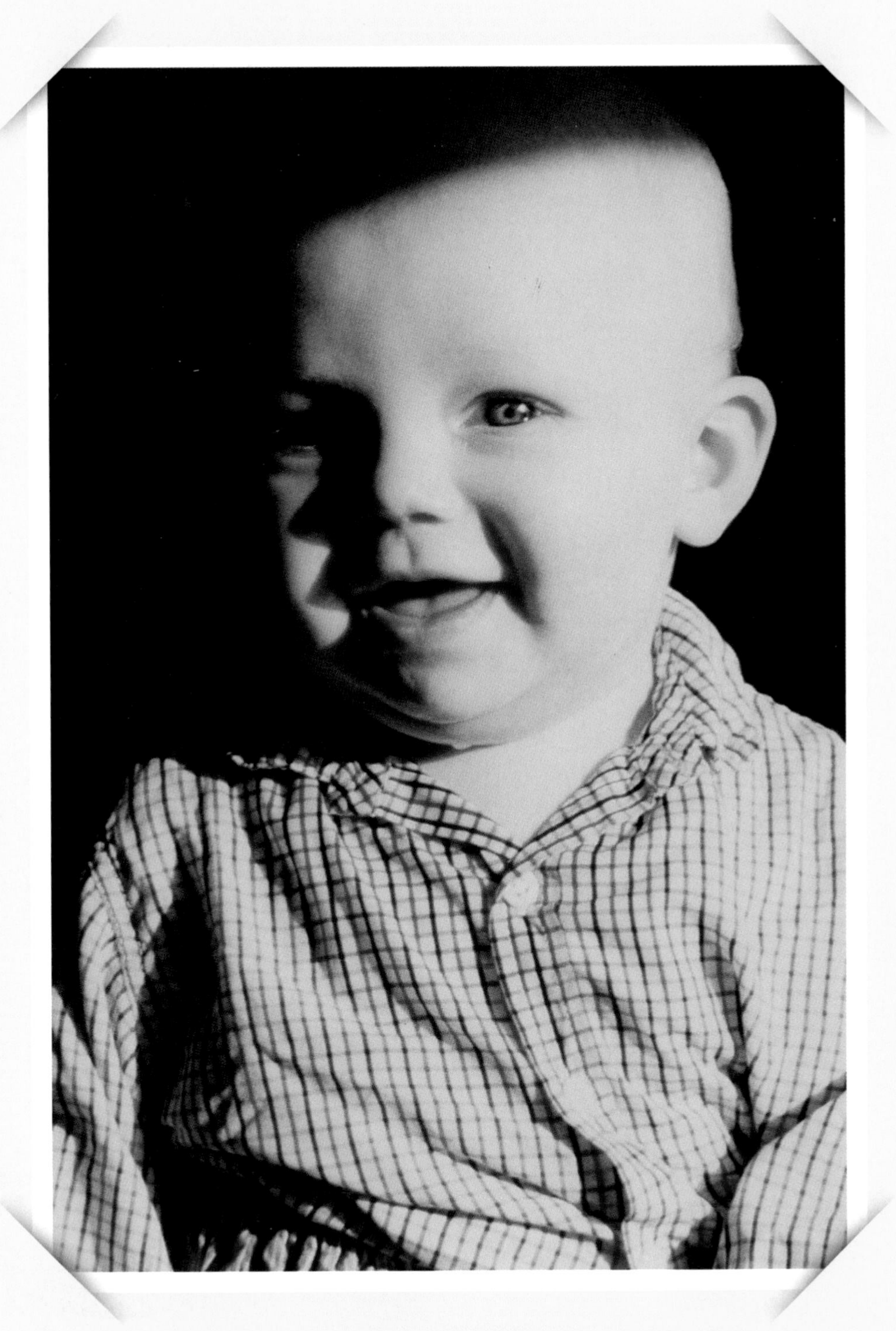

CHAPTER FIVE

Storm Troopers

My desire to bring up the children in "way-out" places continued with our move to Fort Nottingham. I wanted to give my children an unforgettable childhood, an adventure. It couldn't have been more remote. Surrounded by mountains, horse-filled meadows, and a big African sky: it was paradise. The nearest town was an hour away (yay!) and the bumpy road was mostly dirt (even better).

We moved in a week before Easter weekend, which was to be the busiest time of the year for the restaurant. The settlers bungalow, right next door, when we first decided to buy it, was filled with beautiful antique furniture, crackling fires and the smell of ground coffee. Freshly cut flowers in beautiful vases festooned the bedrooms and the yellowwood floors were brightly polished. It had a beautiful tin roof that added to the romance. Our predecessors were definitely schooled in the business of selling, and we fell for it.

> I wanted to give my children an unforgettable childhood, an adventure.

On our arrival the place had been stripped bare. There wasn't a curtain in sight. Our Zulu housekeeper and cook, Mildred, who lived in a smoke-filled rondavel (an African hut) in the garden was nowhere to be seen. She had been abandoned by our previous occupants who apparently had not paid her for weeks, so she'd travelled back to her homestead. But we found her soon enough through what was known locally as the Bush Telegraph (word of mouth) – not quite high speed internet, but very effective in the middle of rural Africa. She was delighted to have her job back and though she hardly spoke a word of English she understood us quite well. She took an immediate liking to the kids *I'll be honest – I reckon she must have preferred me.* and introduced Caspar to the chickens, which were wandering in and out of her hut.

I miss Mildred. She was like a second mom to me. I don't remember her too well but my mom has told me stories about how lovely she was.

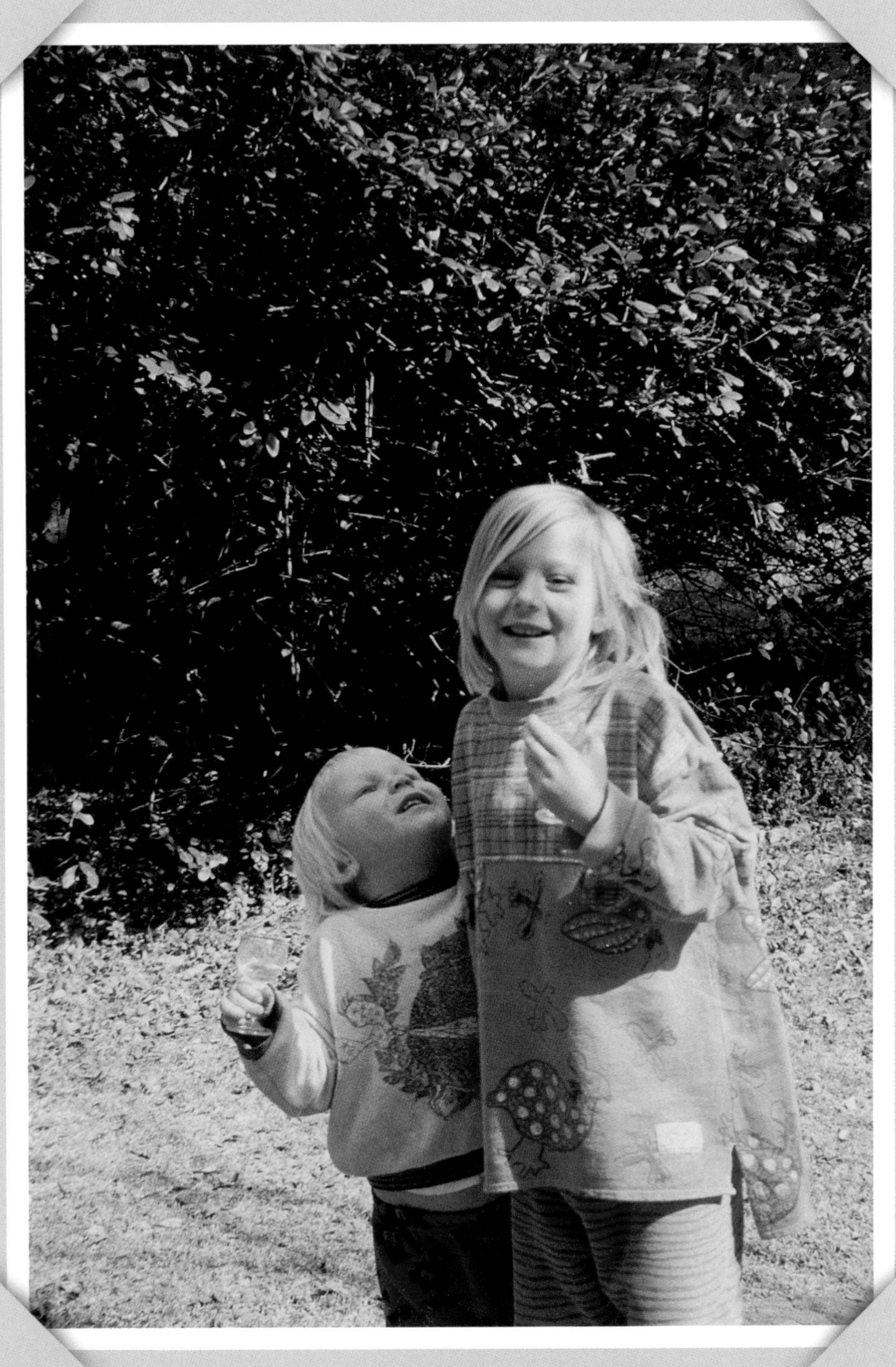

Can't believe you used to let us turn up
like that during the day, Mom!

Mildred always made yummy cakes.

Mildred (far right), Thandi, Caspar and Theo.

Theo and Caspar.

On our first night a massive thunderstorm welcomed our arrival. The heavens opened up to reveal several holes in our tin roof. We lay on the floor in sleeping bags surrounded by buckets to catch the rain, and as the power went off I clutched my children, wondering how we were going to survive the night, the next day and the future in this upmarket cattle shed. Caspar was frightened of the loud bangs, which were coming at closer intervals. We told him it was God having a party for us. The terrifying thunderclaps were just champagne corks popping in heaven and the luminous flashes were heavenly disco lights, co-ordinated by a host of angels. *Would a genius seriously believe all of that? Heavenly disco lights?! I guess I was only two...* He seemed to accept this while I lay there, riddled with fear that the house was going to be struck and we were about to die. I was also extremely anxious about my imminent foray into working at a restaurant, which was already fully booked for the weekend.

Caspar was frightened of the loud bangs, which were coming at closer intervals. We told him it was God having a party for us. The terrifying thunderclaps were just champagne corks popping in heaven and the luminous flashes were heavenly disco lights...

Melta, our nanny, also came to stay. Melta was a stunningly beautiful lady, with great poise and dignity, and the kids absolutely adored her. Anytime Caspar cried she'd hoist him up on her back and envelop him tightly in a blanket, African style. It had an extraordinarily calming effect on him and his tears would be replaced, almost instantly, by a deep comforting sleep. She had a calming effect on us all during this rather stressful time.

We had a slightly eccentric nanny and kitchen helper called Lindy who was a bit jealous of Melta's looks, and possibly her role in the household too. They kept their distance from each other. Melta had her own bedroom in the house, while Lindy lived in a rondavel in the local village. Melta was dignified, Lindy was more eccentric. She'd say "yes" to everything we asked her, grinning vacantly, whether she understood us or not, which she mostly didn't. Lindy spent much of her time tickling Caspar. She thought if she made him screech he would be happy. Caspar, however, made it quite clear he preferred being with Melta, which only added to Lindy's woes.

Sadly this is the only time I've ever had girls fighting over me.

And then there was the gardener. He had a great liking for drink and "daggha" (marijuana), which was freely available in our little hamlet. He arrived on our second morning with bloodshot eyes, and by lunchtime he'd gone missing. We found him out for the count, snoring under a bush. On discovery he hoisted himself up, staggered out and carried out a good afternoon's work.

The next day, he was so out of it Mildred thought he had been demonized by spirits of his ancestors. His eyes rolled back, pupils disappearing into the eye socket, and he shook all over. We thought he was dying. He demanded to be taken to a witchdoctor, but instead we called an ambulance and took him to hospital where he sobered up over a couple of days, and they couldn't find a thing wrong with him. Our main concern was to keep him away from the restaurant guests. And, of course, the wine cellar. **Very wise.**

> [I wanted the kids to have] a carefree upbringing up in the wilds of Africa as bare-footed nature lovers.

How we managed to get through that Easter weekend, Lord only knows. I cooked all day and all night, while Jon cleaned up the gardener and taught him to lay tables. While Theo sat in the corner of the kitchen making figures out of dough, under strict orders of silence, Caspar was off on Melta's back visiting the local tribal village, where he received much attention. He cried every time he caught a glimpse of me and called out "Mommy, Mommy" with his arms reaching out as though the world was coming to an end. But he forgot all about me as soon as Melta was on her way.

And so the restaurant was born. We got rave reviews, and most of our customers drove from Durban, which was a good two hours away. If this was the way things were going to continue, we were made. Caspar was put down for Michaelhouse, the Eton of South Africa **Basically, it was super posh** – again, schools were a primary concern! – while Theo was all set for St Anne's, the sister school. In the meantime, the kids would have a carefree upbringing up in the wilds of Africa as bare-footed nature lovers.

★★★★★

What is that on my head?!

CHAPTER SIX

Restaurant ADVENTURES

After a few months we discovered our numbers didn't tally with the restaurant figures provided to us by our predecessors. We were in a desperate situation financially. While we started off with a bang, as winter came our customer numbers dwindled, which forced us to close during the week.

Jon found advertising work in Johannesburg, and each week he travelled seven hours, in the depths of the night, on a Greyhound bus, to arrive bleary eyed at his Jo'burg office on Monday mornings. He came home at weekends, only to turn himself back into the maître d'. I don't know how he survived.

Thanks, Dad. I can't believe how much you sacrificed for us. You were both always there for us and we were so lucky to be so well looked after. I'm feeling so much gratitude right now!

I was left on my own with the kids in an area that was not as safe as we'd first thought. Again. Farm murders were rife. We installed bars on the windows, and had a farm radio linked to all the local farms in case of an emergency. All the local farmers had guns for protection, often AK-47s, but we had nothing. *Luckily I don't remember any of this. Theo and I were always made to feel safe.*

> He'd scramble into Charlie's bus, with his lunch box filled with peanut butter sandwiches.

I tried to ignore all the violence and racial tension and busied myself with taking Caspar to his new nursery and Theo to pre-school. It was an exciting day when Caspar, aged two, was allowed to go to Charlie's school, run by a delightful lady called Charlie, in the magnificent grounds of Michaelhouse, and I was full of joy at the thought that one day he would attend this incredible school. It was miles away from where we lived, so after a while I used to deposit him in our nearest village, Nottingham Road, about half way, where he'd scramble into Charlie's bus, with his lunch box filled with peanut butter sandwiches.

Hit the thumbs up if you are enjoying this book. Oh, wait...

Caspar at Joyce Broadhead.

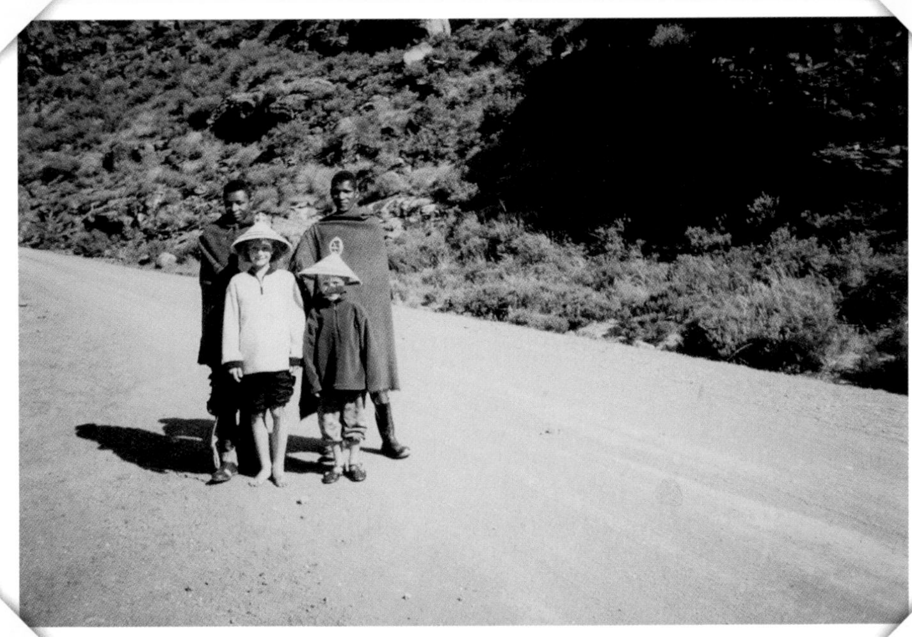

Caspar and Theo in Lesotho, wearing Lesotho hats.

Caspar loved Charlie and Charlie loved him and he always sat in the front seat right next to her with the biggest dimples on his face. I was so proud of this little fella going off on his own at the age of two with such a spirit of adventure. He hasn't changed! *I'll still be the same when I'm 93… I hope!*

In the afternoons Theo and Caspar would run wild around our two-acre garden with Bella, our beloved boxer, and Cicely, the crazed Jack Russell, who was later diagnosed by a dog psychologist with severe OCD. Cicely was about as nutty as any dog could get. She'd run round and round in circles, howling in the highest pitch possible, and then launch herself into the air, grab on to any tree branch in biting distance, and dangle like a bat swinging in the wind. Crazy as they were we loved our dogs. We also loved our chickens, which began to disappear one by one. We were never quite sure whether they had become dinner in next door's homestead, or whether Bella was snacking on them. ***You can't blame poor Bella! Although she did look a bit shady at times.***

Mildred's hut, where there was always something intriguing brewing on an open fire, became Caspar's hideout during the endless games of hide and seek. It was so dark in there he was easily hidden. He always won, because Theo didn't really like going in there. His other favourite place, equally obnoxious to Theo, was the "long drop", an outdoor loo with a very long drop. I was terrified that Caspar would fall in and drown in a sea of muck. *I've always liked living on the edge.*

Cicely was about as nutty as any dog could get. She'd run round and round in circles, howling in the highest pitch possible, and then launch herself into the air, grab on to any tree branch in biting distance, and dangle like a bat swinging in the wind.

In the meantime, the aforementioned gardener (whose duty it was to sweep and clean the restaurant) was slimming down our fine wine cellar at an alarming rate. We were useless at stock control generally, but this was blatantly obvious. He had to go. It turned out for the best as he was replaced by Jablan, who was young, fun and was endlessly patient at playing kids' games.

I was always happy and excited when Jablan was around. I used to try and impress him when we were playing games. He was the big brother I never had. He stood up for me if Theo was being mean, and I have really great memories of hanging out with him.

I asked the hairdresser
to make my hair like spaghetti.

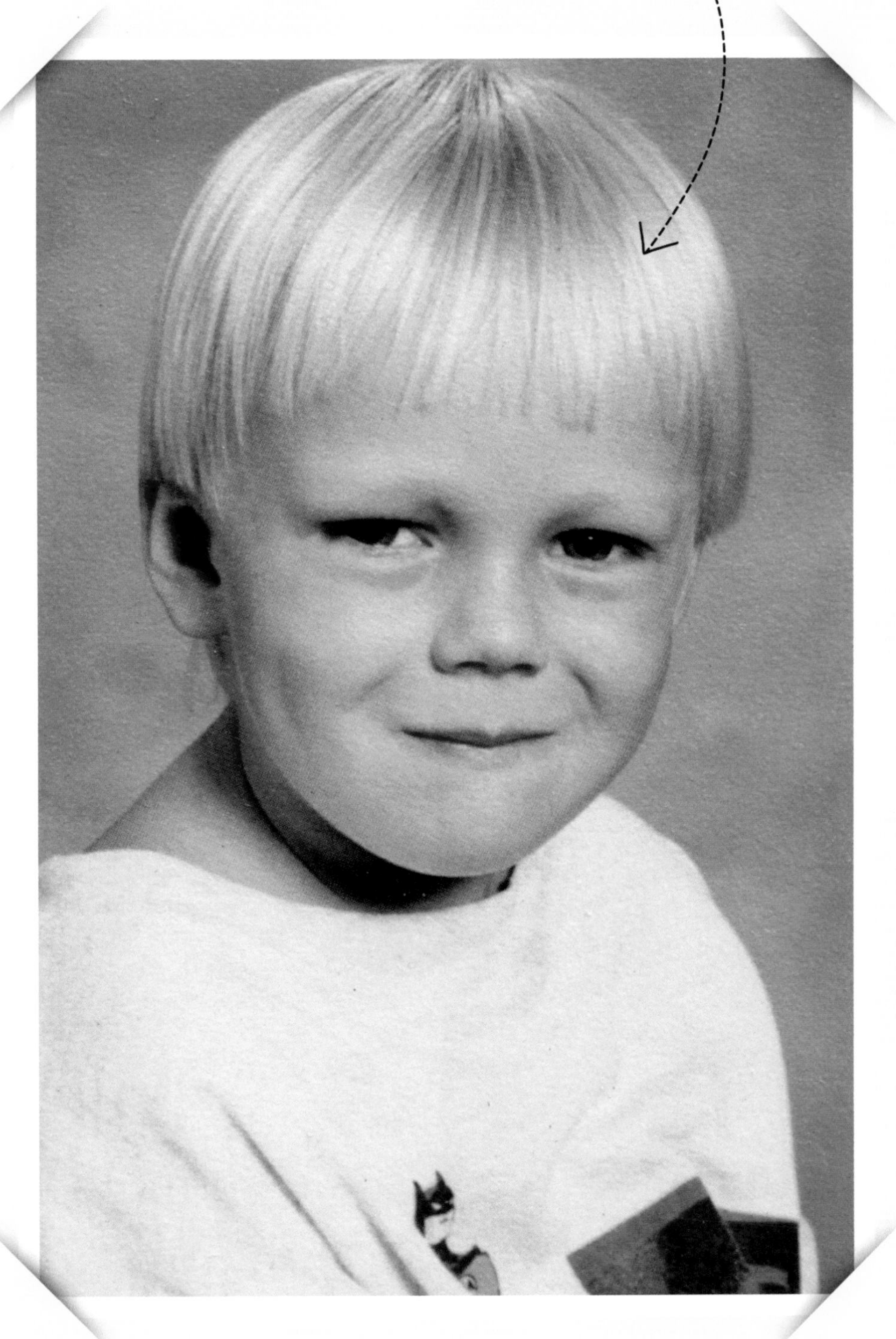

Me and Dad. I seem to have snacked on my hand

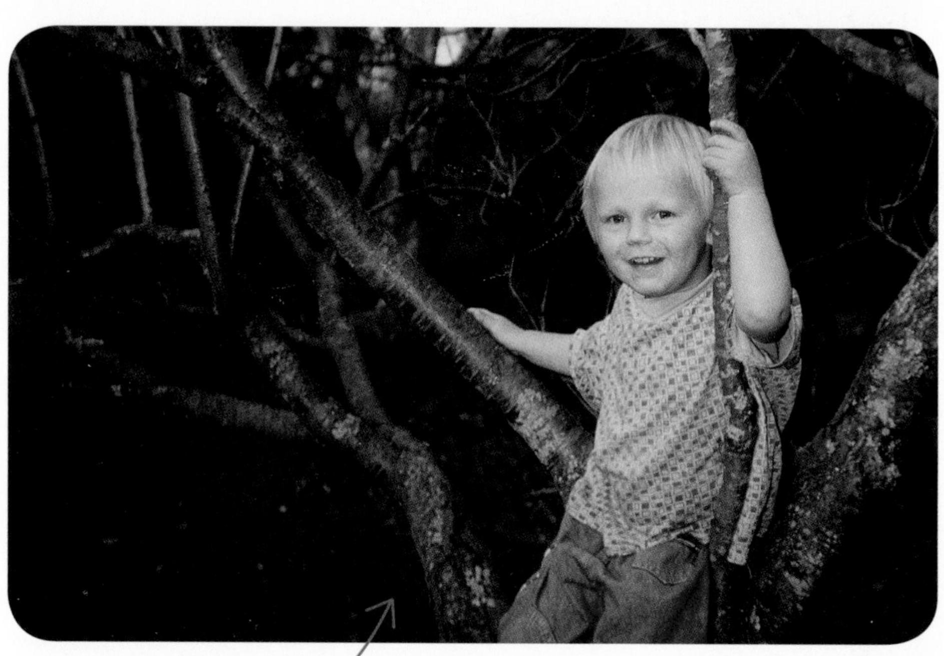

Me, Tarzan

Melta also left. We were never too sure of the reason, but we suspected it was because of Lindy, who was nanny number two. They fought. Melta started to sleep a lot, which we put down to sadness at being away from her family. Tragically she died of AIDS a few years later. It was so sad. At that time one in four people in South Africa was suffering from the dreaded disease, and KwaZulu-Natal had one of the country's highest incidences of AIDS.

Life in Africa did indeed have its ups and downs. And we are only just getting started...

Caspar really missed Melta, as we all did, but luckily Jablan took over her role, as well as the gardener's. He was a busy young man simply working in the garden and the restaurant, but he also took on the role of nanny and the kids' chief entertainment officer.

He built a tree house for them with a long rope where they played Tarzan and Jane. **Funnily enough I got to be Tarzan.** Jane was very bossy and poor Tarzan had to put up with a lot. Tarzan wasn't supposed to cry however much Jane tormented him, and when Caspar had clearly had enough Jablan would come to the rescue and comforting hugs would be provided. And then, when the tears had subsided, he wanted "more", and the game would start all over again. *I told you Jablan was an absolute hero. Me? Not so much.*

The evenings were taken up with stories and books. Caspar had several favourite books. We'd cuddle up, the three of us in the bed with *Meg and Mog*, a book about Meg, a witch whose spells always seemed to go wrong, and Mog her cat, and their friend the Owl. It was mildly scary for the children, but nothing compared to the real ghosts that regularly visited us in the middle of the night. I'd often be woken by loud thumping noise coming from the attic that sounded like our stored furniture being rearranged. Added to this were strange hissing and squeaking sounds. I'd try and dismiss it as trees brushing against the tin roof in the wind, or rats scuttling above us, but it occurred regularly even when the nights were still. I would lie there terrified. Theo and Caspar were blissfully unaware of these nocturnal visitors, and I had many sleepless nights. **I know you really think there were ghosts there, Mom, but I still don't believe in them.**

Life in Africa did indeed have its ups and downs. And we are only just getting started...

CHAPTER SEVEN

Music, Maestro

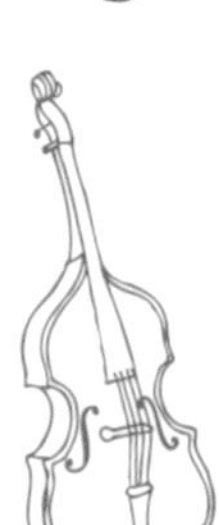

My father Rick (Caspar's grandfather) came from Ireland to stay with us in South Africa, and not long afterwards decided he liked the climate and being with us so much he would establish himself there on a more permanent basis.

He moved in next door and Caspar would go there and listen to classical music – Schubert's "Adagio (Nocturne) in E-flat" mostly – through an old pair of Bose headphones. I don't know whether it was Schubert or the headphones that transfixed Caspar most, but in either case his grandfather was highly impressed with his grandson's ability to concentrate.

I have mentioned I was amazing, right?

Rick also brought a brand new computer for the children, which Caspar couldn't wait to get his grubby hands on. With the computer came a heap of CD-ROMs designed for early childhood learning, which served to prove his "ever so clever" grandson was intellectually way ahead of his years. So Caspar began his computer career at the age of two, and every few years his very generous grandfather would replace it with the latest model. He considered computers "highly important".

So Caspar began his computer career at the age of two, and every few years his very generous grandfather would replace [his computer] with the latest model. He considered computers "highly important".

I couldn't agree more.

Jon and I thought it was a scandalous waste of money and preferred the more simple pursuits of Lego and Play-Doh, but little did we know how right he was. So there we were living in the depths of the African bush, away from all mod-cons, bringing up our children in nature as it were, but we still had the latest technology.

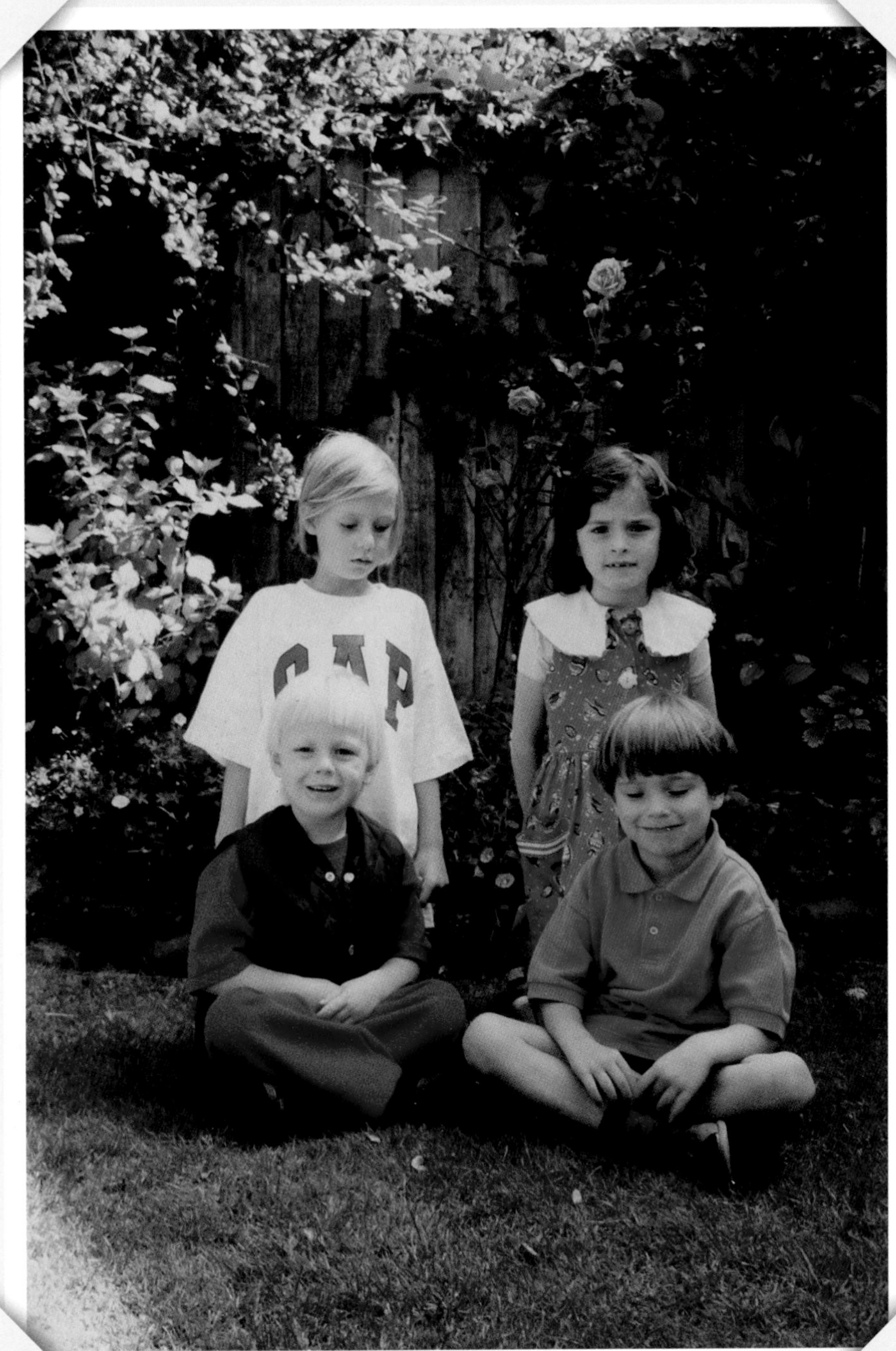

Caspar and Theo with their English cousins Isabella and Christoph in London.

Godfather Trevor with Caspar in Fort Nottingham.

I really do believe Caspar would not be where he is today without Rick's obsession with the importance of computers from a very early age. *Thanks, Rick! Who would have thought your obsession all those years ago would later become mine, and that I'd go on to make a career out of it?*

Now, there were other things about Rick that Caspar was not so fond of, and one of those concerned breakfast cereal. Rick was a firm believer in never giving children a choice. In other words, Rice Krispies should be the only cereal on offer. Our breakfast table would have Cheerios, Coco Pops, Muesli and Rice Krispies. Caspar's decision-making skills would be put to the test on a daily basis. He might start with Cheerios, and then decide he didn't want the Cheerios after all, and change to Coco Pops. I had to use my cereal negotiating skills to keep equilibrium, but I'd often fail and a lot of shouting would ensue. Rick would arrive, remove all the cereal boxes from the table saying, "What is all this noise about?" in a rather authoritative way, and Caspar would start bellowing, "I don't like you, Grandad!" ***I really liked cereal.*** Then I would be accused of spoiling my kids rotten. Back in the day when Rick was a child he was brought up to "be seen and not heard", and was told to "think of the poor starving children in China" when he didn't finish his meals.

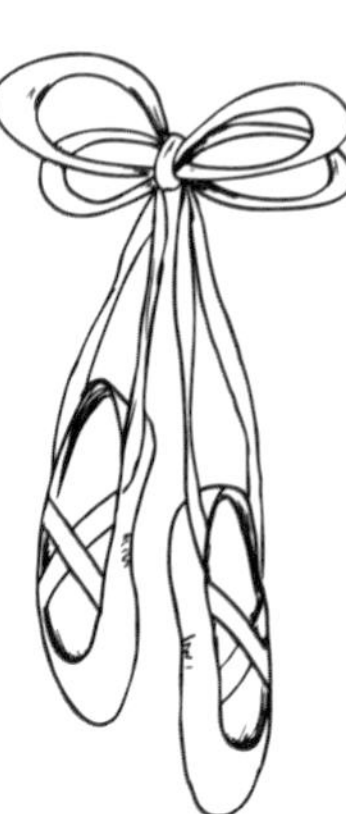

It's true. I wasn't much good at discipline. It was cuddles and embraces from me when tears and anger arose. We tried "time outs" occasionally when things became dangerously overheated, but it never worked because I was too impatient. I preferred bribes. "If you do this you can get that" was my way. And, of course, Caspar never forgot the "that". ***What kid would? It was always a good way to get new ballet shoes! I'll explain this later...***

> Our breakfast table would have Cheerios, Coco Pops, Muesli and Rice Krispies. Caspar's decision-making skills would be put to the test on a daily basis.

"But you said, Mom!" was one of Caspar's favourite accusations, which lasted throughout his childhood. Rick would tell me, "Don't ever promise anything!" But it rang on deaf ears. On so many occasions I'd spend hours running around fulfilling these promises, riddled with guilt. Here was I, a working mum, not spending enough time with my children, and giving in to every whim.

You had to do what you had to do. Yes, maybe we could be bratty a lot, but at the end of the day what you said still went.

Caspar and Bella were the best of friends. She'd even let him ride on her back.

Rick helped us so much in those early days in Fort Nottingham. Our VW Beetle, which had had three new engines in the space of a year in a vain attempt to keep it on the road, was replaced by a Golf. He reroofed our house. He entertained the guests at the restaurant, and while he was in his little cottage next door, he wrote. Rick was ambitious for his grandchildren and would have liked them to be as academically acclaimed as he was. He was great at reading them stories and poetry and really believed Caspar's listening to Schubert could turn him into a concert pianist. **Little did he know I just liked the luxurious feeling of the Bose headphones.** He was also great company for us while Jon was away in Johannesburg.

However, Rick made it quite plain that he didn't like the dogs. He thought that Cicely and her howls were ridiculously distractive, and the constant barking was not good for the children's psyche... or ears. Bella would jump up on Caspar and knock him over, and this was downright dangerous. Not to mention all the dreadful diseases Bella might carry on her slobbery tongue when she licked Caspar's face with frenzied excitement. But I was amazed that, when Bella ate a wasp and her whole face swelled to the size of a large balloon, Rick took her off to the vet. He saved her life. Caspar and Bella were the best of friends. She'd even let him ride on her back without ever giving him the slightest scratch. **Bella was a great dog.** Above is a very lifelike picture of how I looked hitching a ride on her back.

Bella had other less admirable traits, however. Caspar arrived one day in the restaurant holding two rotting deer hoofs. The stench was terrible, but he was delighted with his find. Bella was close behind wagging her bottom. I put two and two together and realized that our beloved boxer, playmate to the kids, had taken to going hunting at night, and was a murderess. Maybe Rick was right after all? Maybe dogs were not such a great idea. **Not such a good idea – too much temptation to eat the local and abundant wildlife.** But we badly needed Bella for security. In the end we fenced her in, but still the hooves would arrive in the morning. And we never – on all our treks up the mountain – found the rest of the deer.

Poor Bella. Maybe she was just really hungry? It does make me wonder about those missing chickens more than ever.

This photo was taken just before Cara tragically blew the house down with one puff

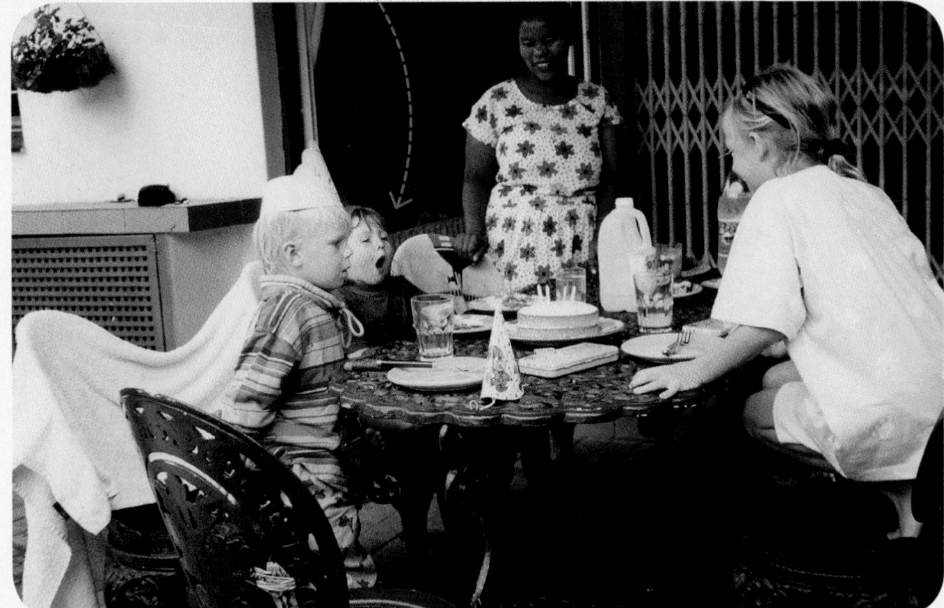

Caspar, Cara, Theo and Dawnby in Durban.

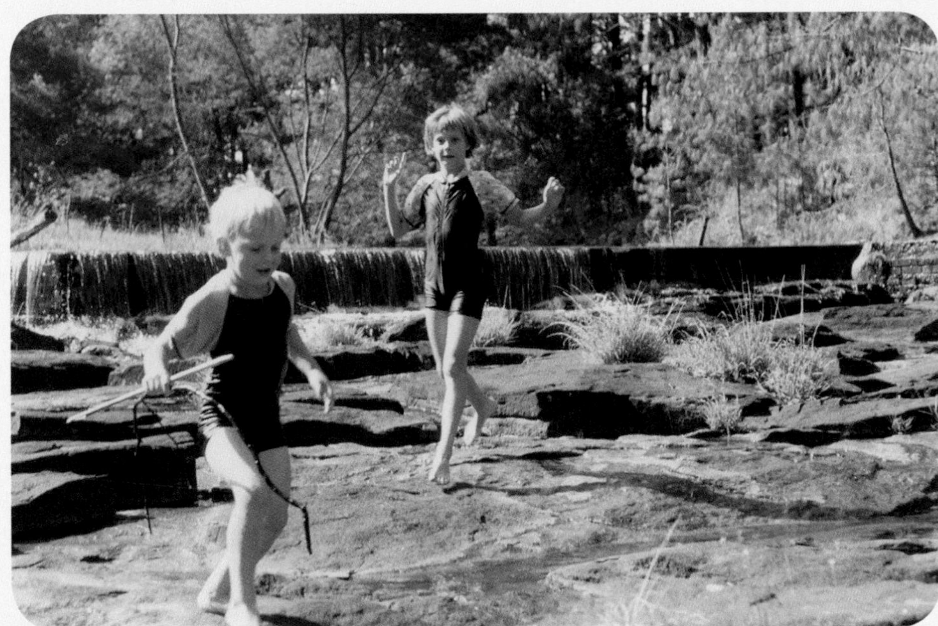

Theo and Caspar playing at a waterfall in Fort Nottingham.

CHAPTER EIGHT

Let It Snow

Our first winter in Fort Nottingham brought with it a snowfall unlike any seen before. Caspar woke up to a completely white landscape and we couldn't believe we were still in Africa. Caspar had never seen snow before and he, Theo and Jablan built the biggest snowman, placing Caspar's favourite French beret on top, *I didn't want him to get cold. Let's also gloss over the fact I owned a beret* while Bella danced around barking like mad at this strange new creature.

The power went off for several days, and there was no access to the shops. Several people tried to come to the restaurant from Durban to see the snow, but got stuck on the way. The kids were delighted; no school, and all-day attention from Mum and Dad. Snowballs appeared everywhere, and ended up everywhere, but mostly down your back! The house was awash with melting slush.

The kids' life was idyllic. Theo was three years older than Caspar ***And she still is!*** and everything she managed to do he would want to copy. ***Apart from wearing dresses. The beret was bad enough*** She became "teacher" and bossed him about from dawn until dusk. She'd ride around on her Barbie bicycle tormenting him with her skills – cycling without her hands on the handle bars, of course. Caspar hated his Batman bike with its training wheels, so one day Jablan decided to take them off. Caspar was only three at the time. Theo thought the best way for him to learn to ride on two wheels was to push him down a steep hill, which she did with great relish. So he flew down, legs askew, and landed head first in a bush at the bottom. He was so delighted to have managed a whole 50 metres on his own that he didn't cry, and instead ran to the restaurant for me to come and witness another attempt. It was a milestone in Caspar's life and remains his earliest memory.

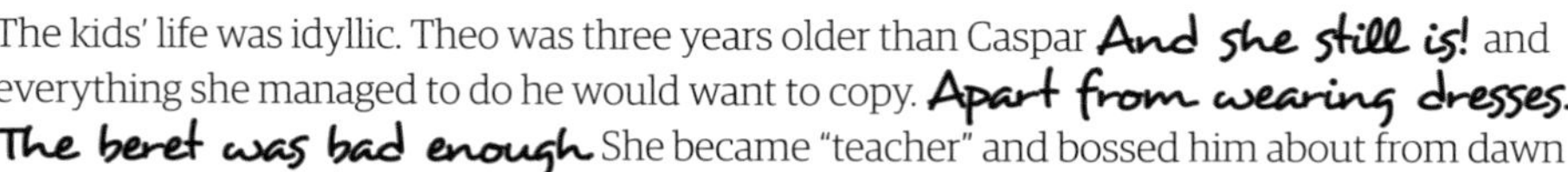

Caspar woke up to a completely white landscape and we couldn't believe we were still in Africa.

This is still so clear. I had to wait for Mom to finish baking a cake before she could give me her full attention. I was so frustrated! It's the only time I've ever wanted her not to bake a cake

I rubbed a balloon on my head a minute before this picture.

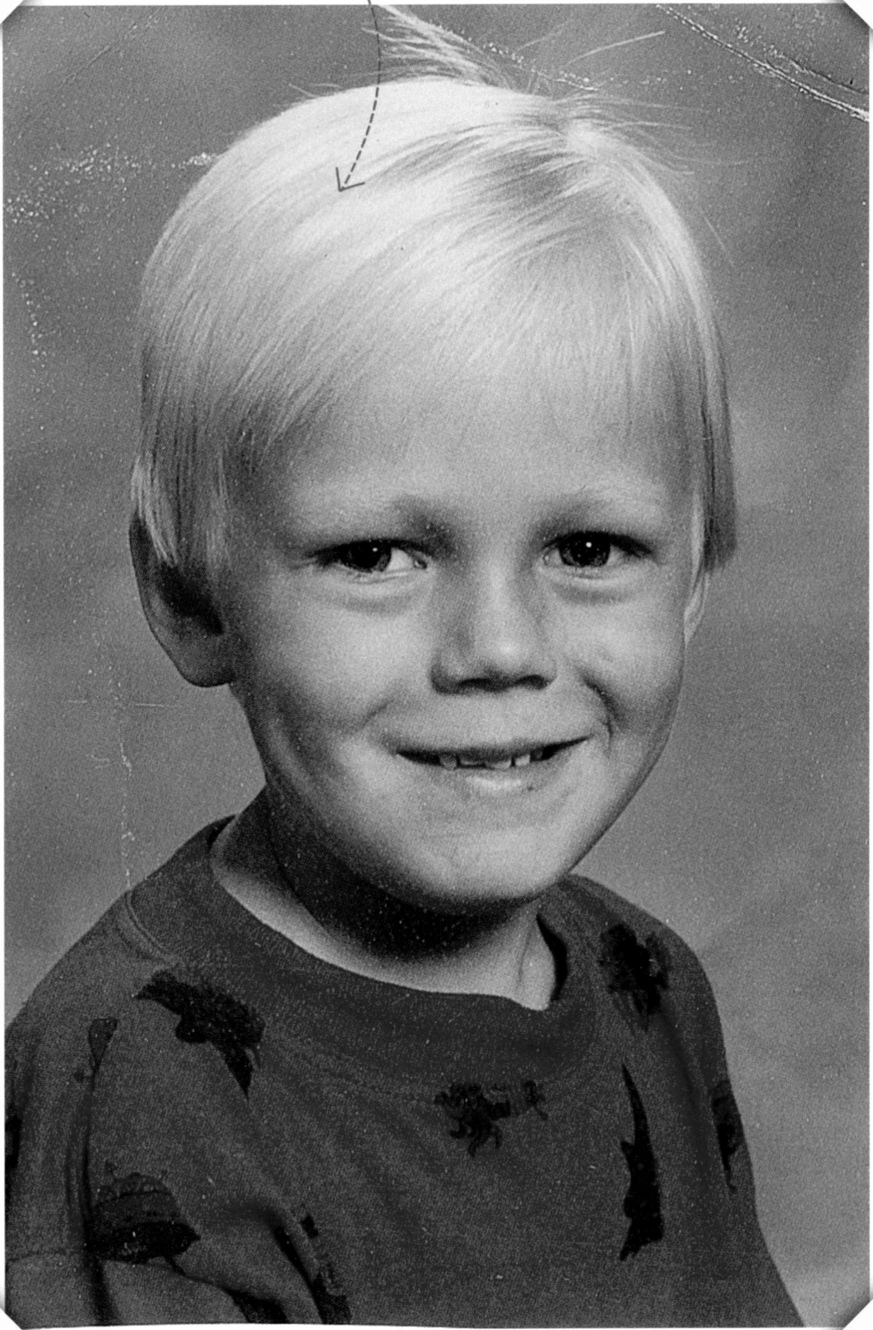

After that there were several "more" attempts (typical Caspar), and soon the two of them were racing around the garden, with Bella in tow.

Theo and Caspar also decided to build their own "swimming pool", and together with Jablan they dug a big hole in the garden and filled it with water. The sight of these loonies wallowing around in a bath of mud shrieking with joy at their new pool was hilarious. **It was definitely more of a pond. Mainly because it was so dirty we would have caught something if we'd properly swum in it.**

Caspar's first "challenge" - something that he has become famous on YouTube for in recent years - was a game invented by Theo to do with Marmite. She brewed up a strong concoction, which consisted of more Marmite than water. Jon and I weren't there at the time but she challenged him to drink it down in one go, telling him he would be rewarded with three Wine Gums on completion of the task. I don't know how he drank it, but he did, and ended up getting sick a few times in the loo. **I hated it for years afterwards, but I suppose I could just about stomach it now after all of the pranks I've had to go through with Joe.**

We had some very interesting neighbours too. The Fox's had a stud farm and barns full of hay that Jablan secretly introduced the kids to. They were wonderful people, but Mrs Fox, who could be a bit severe at times, was not at all happy when she discovered Caspar and Theo leaping from one bale to another causing havoc... and a mess! She shouted and waved her wooden walking stick in the air, frightening the daylights out of them. She reported it to us asking, "How could you have allowed this to happen?" and we took the blame to save Jablan's honour. It didn't stop the kids going back, however, as it was their favourite bit of dare-devilling. Jablan just had to make sure Mrs Fox was not around.

That was such a brilliant game but we were always terrified of getting caught by Mrs Fox. She was the first person I was properly scared of. She reminded me of Mrs Tweedy from Chicken Run. Thankfully Jablan was a great lookout so she didn't catch us again

Caspar's first "challenge" - something that he has become famous on YouTube for in recent years - was a game invented by Theo to do with Marmite. She brewed up a strong concoction, which consisted of more Marmite than water.

Marmite – Inbox
From: Theo
Subject: Marmite
Date: 20th October 2015 04:45:34 GMT
To: Mom
Hide
Save
Quick Look

Hi Mom

Thanks for sending me this chapter, but I do think you've painted me as a bit of a meanie. Caspar and I were, and still are, very best friends and my "challenges" back then were merely a way to make him more tolerable to hang out with. Our games always meant well, apart from the Marmite incident, of course. Oh, and the Gardener incident too. They knew never to ask me for water because lo and behold there would always be salt at the bottom of the glass. Why was I so obsessed with ruining drinks?!

Maybe you should add in the story where Caspar and I mutually decided to fake being sick so we could stay at home and I could teach him to count using marbles.

We found a thermometer in your cabinet and put it under hot water to show you how sick we were, and you believed us. Well, you pretended to at least.

Anyway, I better get back to work! Keep up the good writing, just less of the stuff about me being mean, OK?

Theo
XXXXXXXXX

I still feel a sense of distrust that I'm not sure I'll ever be able to move on from. Of course, I love you as a sister, Theo, but once someone tricks you into drinking something with Marmite in, you can never fully put your faith in them again. But, OK, you were a pretty good sister otherwise and I have been very nice about you in other parts of the book

The customers at the restaurant mostly sat outside and our kids played with their kids. They'd form little troupes and play all sorts of games while their parents drank merrily. Lunches would stretch out all day. Our customers loved the laid-back atmosphere, the beauty of the garden, and the freedom to let their children run amok. We began to make friends with regulars who travelled from Durban. The Blanckenbergs became our best friends, and their daughter, Clarissa, was the same age as Theo. Pete Blanckenberg arrived in a bright red Porsche one day, which was a very exciting sight for young Caspar to behold. While Pete and his wife, Sharon, were enjoying my culinary delights, Clarissa was playing with Theo and Caspar in the Porsche. **It was the first time Id ever seen electric windows and I played with them for hours on end. Still do!** They somehow managed to start the engine and release the handbrake; off the three of them went before shuddering into a tree a few metres away. Caspar was in the driving seat – of course! He came running into the restaurant crying, "Teedora made me do it!" We were horrified. What would our new friends think? **Forget your new friends – what about me?** Our kids had damaged their Porsche. Hells bells! It worked out OK in the end, except for poor Clarissa, who got a good telling off. Thankfully Caspar has taken no further interest in Porsches. Not strictly true. I love cars these days, so if anyone would like to give me a Porsche, get in touch!

They somehow managed to start the engine and release the handbrake; off the three of them went before shuddering into a tree a few metres away.

Caspar found the pronunciation of his sister's name quite a challenge. She was known first as "Teedora" and then it became "Feedora", like Indiana Jones's hat. Caspar couldn't quite manage to twist his tongue around the "H", but when he finally succeeded, after much practice, he was thrilled, and she became known as Thedora. Until this very day Caspar still hasn't managed to call her Theodora! **You know me, I like to be different.** Our "idyllic" life didn't come without its down periods. Soon after the snow had melted and we were back in business, we were woken in the middle of the night by people trying to break their way into our house. Window panes were being smashed by large rocks, and I immediately thought we were going to be just another South African farm murder statistic. It was terrifying. I was literally trembling with fear. While Jon went to confront the intruders (he was so brave), I got on to the farm radio and transmitted an emergency message. The kids slept through all of it. **I probably wouldn't have been that much help anyway, to be fair.**

The SOS message was effective. Within ten minutes two farmers arrived with AK-47 machine guns. Shots were fired up in the air and our attackers fled. It was the sound of police walkie-talkies in the kitchen at three in the morning that finally woke the kids up. I think Caspar thought it was some elaborate game involving cops and robbers as he sat on the superintendent's knee having his juice while the rest of us drank bucket-loads of sugary tea. I was still shaking all over. It was a close shave, and I really did believe we were lucky to come out alive. **This makes me feel so brave.**

I truly was a
good buoy

Around this time there was also a spate of burglaries in the restaurant. On one particular morning I arrived with Mildred to get the day's cooking under way only to find the kitchen door off its hinges and the remnants of a massive party scattered inside. Wine and beer bottles were strewn everywhere, and the gas hob had been left on. A mighty feast had been consumed and the drinks cellar had been emptied.

Caspar and Theo were enthralled as they watched this crazy looking man dipping a mop into a bucket of his "magic potion".

A neighbour of ours suggested we bring in the help of a witch doctor. *Mom, this is not normal.* He was expensive but we were promised he could cast a spell on our premises that would terrify all future burglars. *Please tell me you didn't fall for this?*

The witch doctor arrived *Oh, you did* in a Mercedes Benz, dressed in animal furs with feathers in his hair, an hour before a busy Sunday lunchtime. He was in such high demand that we had no choice but to let him get on with what he had to do in spite of the imminent arrival of our customers.

Caspar and Theo were enthralled as they watched this crazy looking man dipping a mop into a bucket of his "magic potion", which smelt of – and most definitely was – paraffin. He doused the whole exterior of the house and restaurant with this stuff while performing a hypnotic dance, with much wailing, muttering and rolling of the eyes. *Even at that age, I would have found this completely ridiculous!* He then lit three candles in the restaurant and instructed us to keep them alight for a week. Before we knew it he was back in his expensive car and on his way, with a lot of money in his pocket. We were told that all the local thieves would be terrified of the spells that would be cast upon them if they approached our premises again. As far as I remember I think it lasted about a month until we were burgled again. *I hate to say I told you so.*

It was around this time in 1997 that Mildred became quite an accomplished chef and created a wonderful loaf of bread, which she called "fashion bread". It consisted of butternut, white flour and yeast, and became our signature loaf. Caspar adored it straight out of the oven covered in lashings of butter, which melted instantly. His other favourite treat was sticky toffee pudding covered in toffee sauce *Still is!* with a Mont Blanc-sized topping of whipped cream, for which the restaurant became famous. Every evening when the guests had gone we'd sit down with the kids and eat the leftovers and the pudding would be produced (but only after a large plate of broccoli had been consumed).

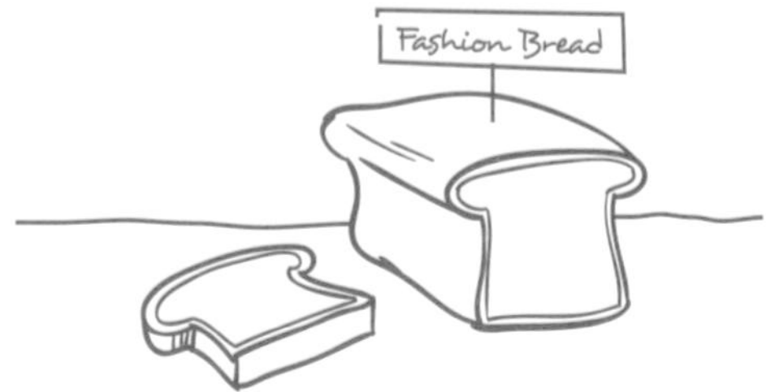

Mildred, Jon and I worked excessively hard to make the restaurant a success. We'd begin the day at 6.30am and often wouldn't leave the restaurant until 7pm. At one time we noticed how thin poor Mildred was getting and that she had this awful rasping cough. She was a small lady and never complained and we often put it down to a touch of the flu. But the cough was resistant to all our home remedies, and we began to worry that it might be serious and life-threatening. We persuaded her to come with us to Durban to see our wonderful doctor and get herself tested. It transpired she was suffering from tuberculosis (TB). We managed to find her a bed in the nearby hospital, which wasn't an easy thing to do. So many people had TB in South Africa back then. It was mostly AIDS related, and the hospitals were brimming over. We knew she wouldn't stand a chance of surviving if she didn't go to hospital and were very lucky to get her in there.

We were also worried about the children because they hadn't been vaccinated at that point, but we were relieved to hear TB is quite hard to catch.

After this string of unfortunate incidents, Rick decided that we were living in an area that was far too dangerous and persuaded us to think about moving to Durban. The plan was to live in Durban during the week and drive up to Fort Nottingham at weekends to run the restaurant until it could be sold. After a couple of trips to the city, a wonderfully balmy and tropical mini-metropolis, we found two lovely houses right next to each other and – much to the delight of the kids – both had swimming pools. **I remember feeling like all my birthdays had come at once.** Jablan would come with us, as well as Mildred's daughter, Ntombi. Caspar and Theo loved Jablan so much and by now he was very much part of the family.

(whispering to Theo)
Your flowers wouldn't exist without my water, bitch

EASY BANOFFEE PIE

INGREDIENTS:

450gms digestive biscuits
225gms butter
2 tins condensed milk
500gms cream
3 bananas
1 bar Lindt dark chocolate

1. Crush the biscuits into fine crumbs.
2. Melt the butter and add to biscuit mixture.
3. Line the bottom of a baking tin and place in the fridge to harden up.
4. Place the tins of condensed milk in a large pot of boiling water, and boil gently for 2½ hours, making sure the tins are covered in water at all times.
5. Allow to cool and then spread the toffee all over the base.
6. Slice the banana and place on top of the toffee.
7. Whip the cream and spread over the bananas.
8. Top with grated chocolate.

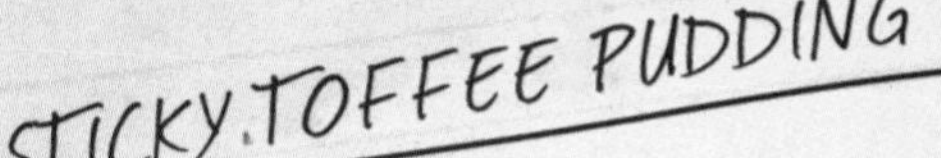

STICKY TOFFEE PUDDING

INGREDIENTS

200gms stoned dates
1 tsp vanilla essense
¾ teaspoon bicarbonate of soda
75 gms butter
130gms castor sugar
3 eggs, beaten
175 gms self-raising flour

TOFFEE SAUCE:

30 gms pecan nuts
175 gms soft brown sugar
120 gms butter
5 tablespoons double cream

1. Pre-heat oven to 350F/180C
2. Chop the dates and then pour 175mls boiling water over them to soften them.
3. Add the vanilla essense and bicarbonate of soda.
4. In another bowl, beat together butter and sugar until light and pale.
5. Add the beaten eggs, gradually, stirring gently.
6. Gently fold in the sifted self-raising flour, using a metal spoon.
7. Fold in the date mixture including the water.
8. Divide the mixture into eight little containers.
9. Place them on a baking tray and bake in an oven pre-heated to 350F/180C and cook for 25 minutes.
10. Remove from oven and allow to cool slightly before sliding a pallette knife around the edges of the puddings to gently release them.
11. Allow to cool on a wire mesh.

SAUCE:

1. Mix together all the sauce ingredients in a pan and heat gently until all the sugar has melted.
2. Pour over the puddings and serve with pouring cream.

YUMMY YUMMY YUMMY

CHAPTER NINE

Car Trouble

The first thing we noticed on arrival in Durban was the weather. Durban has a warm subtropical climate that was very different to Fort Nottingham. Although it was only two hours drive away, we moved from an often rainy and cold English-type climate to a land of palm trees, high humidity and endless glorious sunshine. And, best of all, we were beside the sea.

Jon carried on working in Johannesburg during the week, but now an extra leg was added on to his journey. We still had the restaurant to run at weekends, so on Friday nights he'd change out of his smart office clothes and head off to Jo'burg's very dangerous downtown to catch the overnight Greyhound bus to Durban, disguised in a tatty black overcoat, hoping he wouldn't be relieved of his computer when he nodded off. Dad, you're a proper legend.

Then, early Saturday morning, as soon as he'd arrived, we'd all pile into the car and drive to Fort Nottingham, to be there in time to serve lunch to our guests. Caspar hated car journeys, and there would be lots of tears. The conversation would often go like this:

CASPAR: "Mom, do we have to go?"
(Tears)

ME: "Yes, darling, you know it's not far!"

CASPAR: "Mom, I'm hungry."
(Out with the crisps)

CASPAR: "Mom, I'm thirsty."
(Out with the Appletiser)

CASPAR: "Are we there yet?"

ME: "We've only just left."

CASPAR: "But you said it wasn't far."

ME: "It isn't far, don't worry, Caspar."

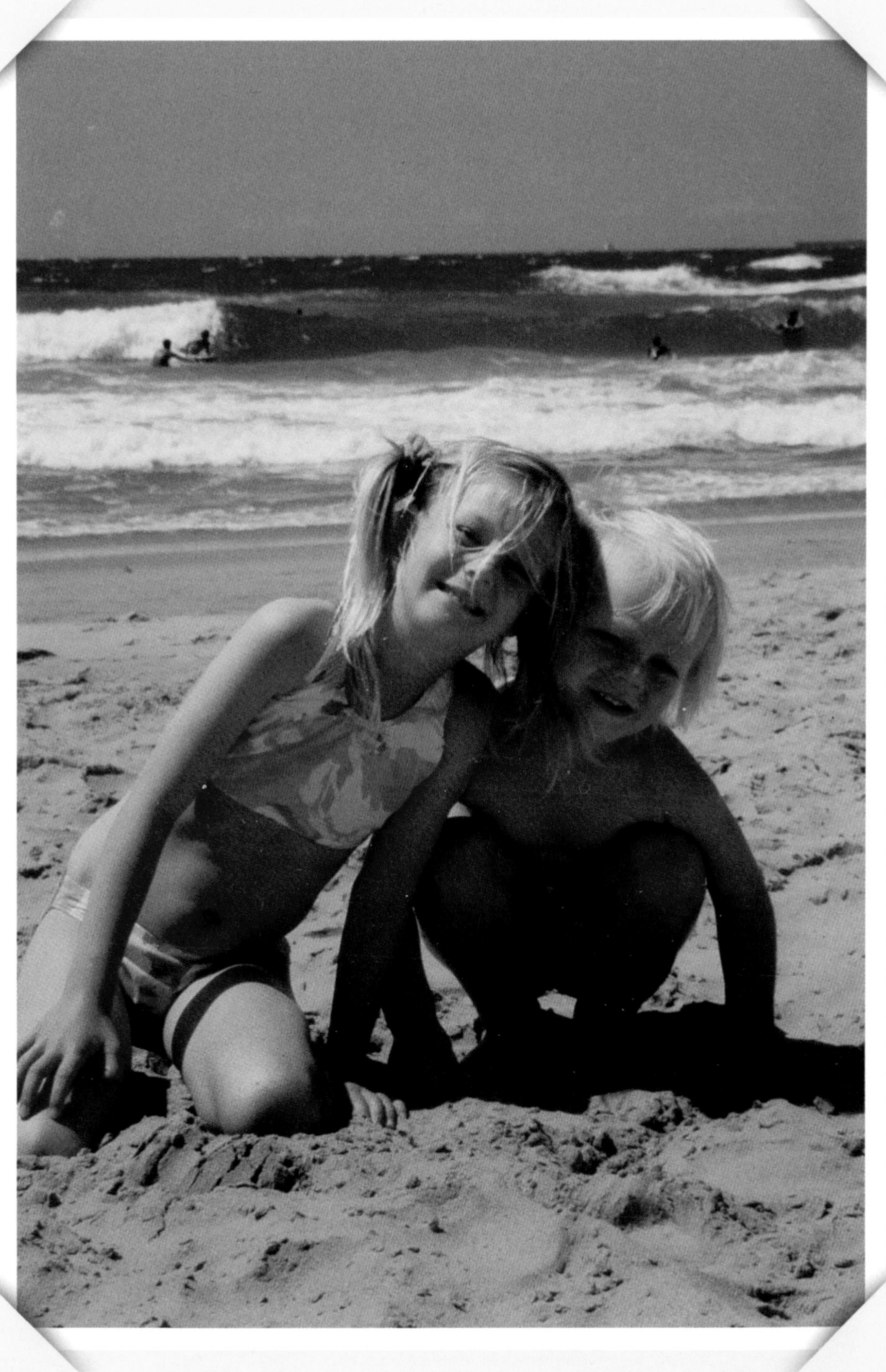

Don't be fooled by the happy smiles.
Theo and I were probably arguing about
sand castles seconds later

CASPAR: "So if it isn't far, how come we're not there yet?"
(Pause)

CASPAR: "Teedora hit me."
(More tears. Dad turns the music up full blast and the dog goes bananas barking)

THEO: "Shut up, Caspar, you hit me first."

ME: "Hush now, guys! You know it's going to be such fun when we get there."
(More wails)

CASPAR: "But, Mom (biggest wail), you're always working. You never play with us."

ME: "Darling, we have to work to buy you things and pay for school."

CASPAR: "What are you going to 'get' me?"

ME: "Nothing, unless you shut up!"
(Peace descends)

CASPAR: "Mom, what are you going to get me?"

ME: "A surprise."
(Big grin quickly followed by...)

CASPAR: "I want it NOW."

ME: "You're going to have to wait."

DAD: "You can't just promise him things to shut him up. He's got to learn to behave."

CASPAR: "I want it NOW. Mom SAID."
(Wails again)

DAD: "No, she didn't."

ME: "Yes, I did."

THEO: "Can I have a surprise too?"

ME: "Surprises will happen when we get there, but only if you're both as good as gold."
(Look of extreme exasperation from Jon.)

> Caspar… discovered that you could buy 50 Chappies (the most disgusting bubble-gum in the world) for one rand. I always loathed that bubble-gum… there'd be bits everywhere, and Caspar would often excitedly swallow the stuff.

And so on. Car journeys with Caspar always tested us to the limit. If he wasn't asleep, he'd be full on Caspar, and we'd arrive at our destination not in the best of humour to entertain our customers. **What do you expect when you promise a present and then don't deliver? I'm still scarred.**

By lunchtime Jon would have swapped the "Dad" role to that of a highly entertaining maître d'. He'd write down the orders on the paper tablecloths and then would rip them off, laughing that we'd run out of order pads. He'd wax lyrical about the "cold Senegalese" soup, and how the recipe was discovered on the ceiling of an old establishment in downtown Dakar. He had an anecdote for everything and his management skills were eccentric… but they worked. Looking back now he was definitely "Caspar Senior" – quirky, playful and as entertaining as some of Caspar's best videos. **If only YouTube had been around then, eh?**

Empty wine bottles and bits of left over sticky toffee pudding would be scattered around a mini-mountain of paper slips next to the electronic paying device, which was continually offline due to thunderstorms. I'm amazed we ever got paid, to be honest. There was always a lot of waiting, and expectation as to what disaster would befall us next. When customers walked out, Jon would pretend to be delighted but was anxious about losing business deep down. But as far as Jon was concerned, the fact they had walked out and didn't like our food/atmosphere/chaos, or Caspar and Theo running around, meant they weren't the type of clientele we wanted to cater for after all. This was "slow dining" with Basil Fawlty at the helm. I think our regulars came for the drama every bit as much as the dining experience.

During all this kerfuffle in the restaurant Caspar would be claiming his surprise, which invariably consisted of a few rands (South African currency, known as ZAR) to spend at the mobile sweet shop. A battered old van would arrive to provide the local community with a huge variety of cheap sweets and crisps. It was a big event for the village kids, and they all congregated around it. Caspar always liked to make his money go as far as possible (and still does), and to his delight he discovered that you could buy 50 Chappies (the most disgusting bubble-gum in the world) for one rand. Caspar was generous and he'd always give some of his sweets away to the other little boys and girls. I always loathed that bubble-gum; there'd be bits everywhere, and Caspar would often excitedly swallow the stuff. **Yeah, I may have enjoyed them a bit too much.**

My big head meant it was diffi-cult to stand straight

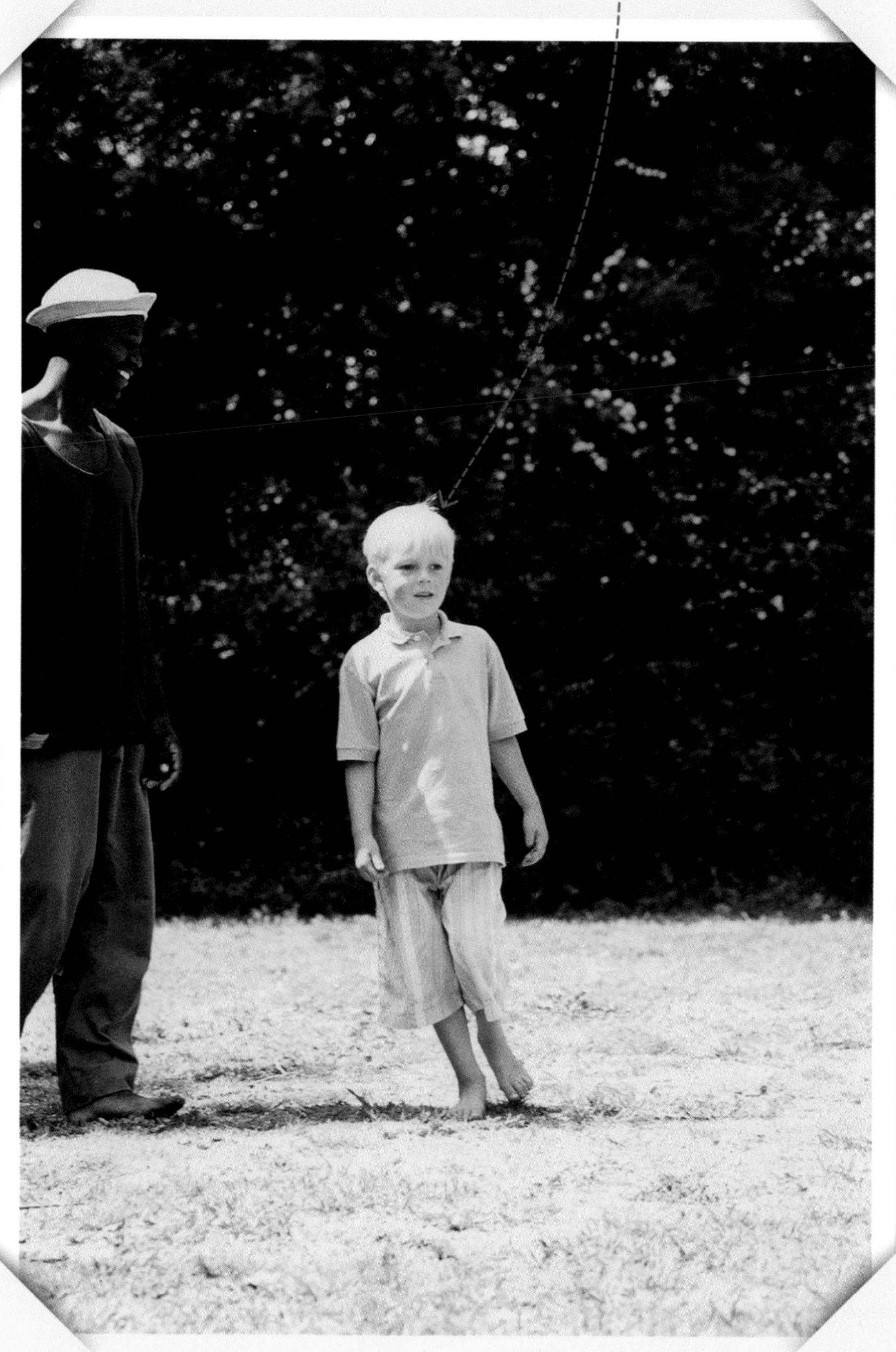

Caspar and Jablan at Fort Nottingham.

Cricket is so exciting, look how much fun I'm having

Caspar, Daniel and the boys of Fort Nottingham.

It was during this time Caspar and Theo didn't see their Dad during the week, which was sad for them and for him. Theo had a particularly close bond to her Dad and hated to see him go, but Caspar was young enough not to be too affected by it. At weekends Jon was working often too. He was juggling his life seven days a week to keep the family afloat. Still to this day I don't know how he managed without going crazy.

Neither do I. The more I hear about how hard he worked, the more grateful I am to him. I like to think he's passed some of that work ethic on to me and I hope I always have the drive to work hard as he did.

At weekends Jon was working often too. He was juggling his life seven days a week to keep the family afloat. Still to this day I don't know how he managed without going crazy.

Glad I wasn't the only one smiling!

Caspar and Daniel with the local boys at Fort Nottingham.

Caspar was generous and he'd always give some of his sweets away to the other little boys and girls

I've always been a fan of symmetry

CHAPTER TEN

Water Babies

Our life in Durban took on a whole new dimension. After much inspection of all the pre-schools on offer, Caspar settled into Joyce Broadhead, a pre-primary school. Tree Tops, next door, was a posh school that guaranteed a place in Durban "high society", but since we hadn't put him down at birth, no amount of persuasion could get him in. It was like being back in London! Even in Durban, competition for getting into the right schools was rife. Caspar had to opt for second best, which turned out well. As soon as he arrived at Joyce Broadhead we realized it was the place for him! He settled in to cuddles from his new teacher, and he never looked back. No tears, no promises and lots of juice. I remember playing kissing catches there, which is also known as kiss-chase. I used to lose on purpose.

> It was like being back in London! Even in Durban, competition for getting into the right schools was rife.

In those days, Durban was still very colonial. Most white families had live-in maids. While their children were at school, mums enjoyed tennis teas, hard-to-get-into book clubs, and discussions about their offspring's latest sporting achievements. And then there was the home interiors one-upmanship.

I remember (while waiting in the car park to pick up the kids) numerous discussions about cushion covers and bedspreads. But in our house there were no cute Peter Rabbit duvet covers, because a certain someone found Beatrix Potter "boring". Caspar was into Barbie. TOO MUCH INFORMATION, MOM! Do you want me to be single forever?

Moving to Durban was quite a shock after the wilderness of Fort Nottingham, and initially we didn't really fit in. Our beautiful bijoux cottages, which we had bought on impulse with Rick's kindness, turned out to be in a mostly Indian quarter. (Durban, incidentally, has the largest population of Indians in any city outside of India.) The sweet smell of curry wafted down the street, while at night drunks wandered the pavements shouting out obscenities. The shopping mall at the end of the street was a concrete mess (a definite no-go area), and although our part of town wasn't considered the safest, it had its own strange kind of exotic charm. But it definitely didn't feel like the Africa we knew. **I thought it was normal to have electric fences and bars on the windows. I used to touch the electric fences for fun to see if I got a shock. It's ridiculous to think of how unsafe it was.**

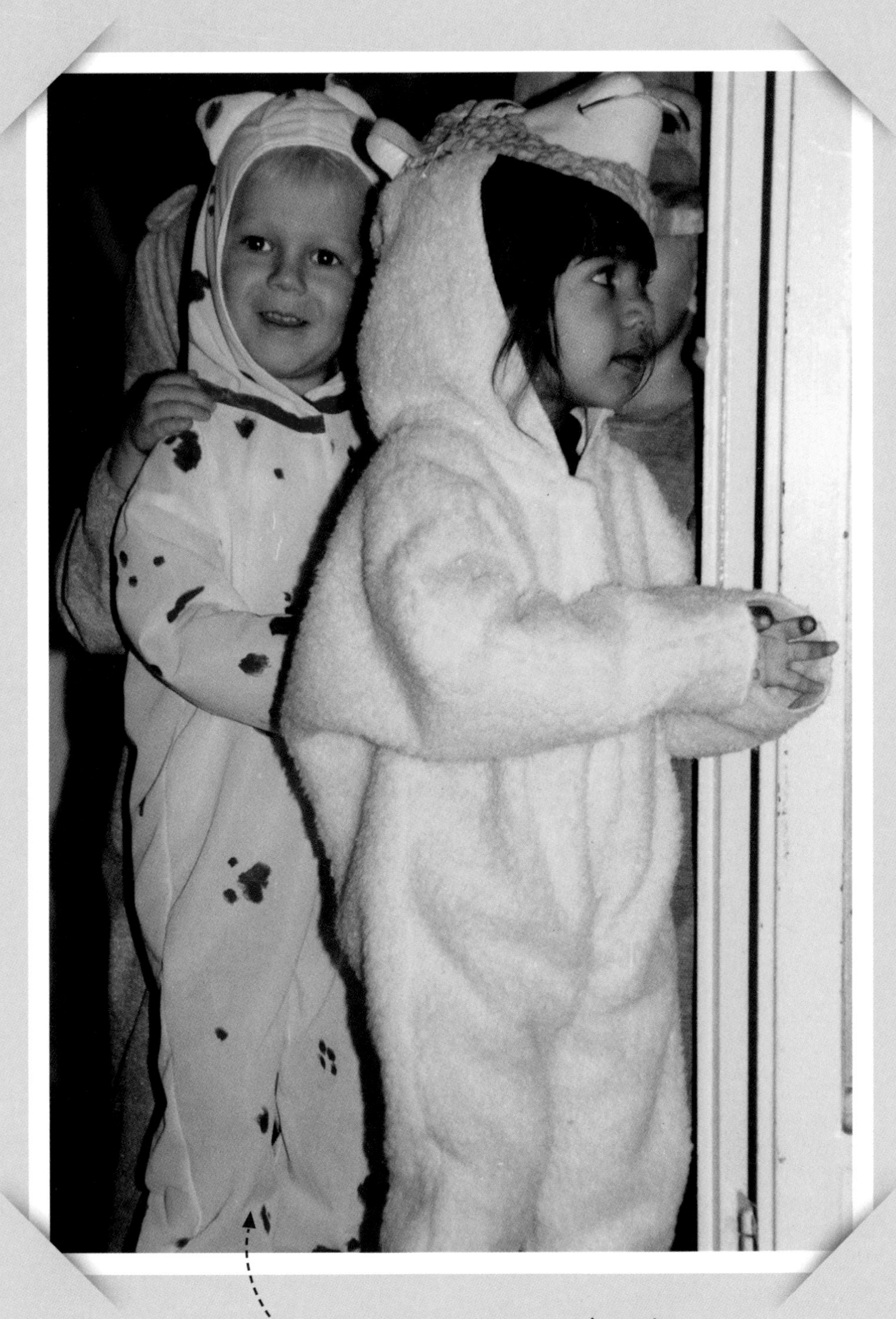

This outfit would make
Tyler Oakley jealous

The goggles did not keep the water out

When it came to swimming, both Theo and Caspar were considered "very promising".

Theo, Caspar and Florence the Border Collie in Durban.

Once we were safely locked inside numerous "slam lock" doors, we had our little piece of heaven and our magnificent pool, which Caspar, the little duck that he was, quickly learned to swim in. Once his water wings were off there was no stopping him. "Bombing" became the order of the day. Inside the house, our new Border Collie, Florence (dog number three), would run riot, barking madly and trying to keep up with Caspar. **Florence was my favourite dog ever. Whenever I cried she would come to me and rub her nose with mine to console me.**

Swimming became Caspar and Florence's thing. When Caspar turned three, he and Theo joined Seagulls, a swimming club renowned for producing Olympic swimmers, including Chad le Clos. Theo was taught to perfect her strokes by Graham Hill, head coach for the Olympic swimming team, while Caspar had the very kind Candice Crafford, who coaxed him gently into swimming his first twenty-five metres unaided. He was so proud of himself that day.

"Look, Mom, look at ME! LOOK!"

Oh my God, was he going to make it? What would happen if he went under, like he did when he jumped into the pool at the Johannesburg Country Club, and Jon had to jump in to save him?

"Go on, Caspar, go, you can do it!" I shouted, as I watched him spluttering and doggy-paddling his way down the length of the pool. At least he was surrounded by Olympic swimmers if he did go under, I thought.

He did finally make it. At the end he was rewarded with a lolly. *Is that all?* I was an immensely chuffed mum. My three-year-old - a big-headed blob of a baby - was swimming 25 metres all by himself. Maybe this was it? Maybe this was his calling?

When it came to swimming, both Theo and Caspar were considered "very promising". As long as they carried on training on a daily basis, sometimes twice a day (for the next 15 years), they too might make it to the Olympics. Wow, it felt good to be in South Africa. What sporting opportunities there were! As far as I was concerned, at that time, Caspar was definitely heading in that direction.

Above:

Caspar swimming for Clifton School at a Prize Giving.

Our neighbours, who ran a hairdressing salon from their home next door, became great friends of ours. Although all the neighbourhood's houses were surrounded by high walls for security reasons it didn't prevent their son, Caspar's friend, Filipe, who was a few years older, from clambering over the wall so he could join in with the swimming pool headstands and splashing competitions. Filipe was quite naughty and he secretly built a ladder for Caspar to climb over into his house, which resulted in a "Where's Caspar gone?" scenario. **I like to be mysterious.** We thought he had disappeared out the front door never to be seen again. Jon was furious when he discovered what was going on, and poor Filipe got a bit of a stern telling off. Filipe was great fun and became an older brother figure to Caspar. **Filipe was really fun to hang out with because he was older than me. He once dared me one rand - which is less than 50p - to jump in our pool with all my clothes on. I wanted to impress Filipe and I knew I could buy a sweet with that rand, so I did it. How funny.**

Back in Joyce Broadhead, Caspar became the noisiest boy in school, screaming and shouting his head off, always warrior-in-chief of the playground. And although the teachers weren't too concerned, I was.

Back in Joyce Broadhead, Caspar became the noisiest boy in school, screaming and shouting his head off, always warrior-in-chief of the playground. And although the teachers weren't too concerned, I was. He came home every day, his voice completely hoarse. This carried on for years. The hoarseness even lasted well into the holidays, and I became so worried I took him to a doctor who agreed that there must be a serious problem, and decided to operate. Nothing was found other than inflamed vocal chords, due to too much enthusiastic screaming and shouting. **Looking back I can't believe I actually made myself ill just from being loud. It's crazy! I don't remember ever being in pain though. I must have just got used to it. I guess screaming and shouting were more important to me than having a working voice.**

Caspar did (luckily) discover more gentle pursuits at Joyce Broadhead. His best friend, Cara, a beautiful little girl with red hair, loved ballet. We would go to her house and they would both dress up as ballerinas and dance around the room with glittery wands with a big star on top. **THIS NEVER HAPPENED. OK, it may have done. Alright, it did.** He was a little bit plumper than Cara, and it was a tight fit getting into her dresses.

But it was so sweet watching the two of them. He was like an angel with his long blond hair, despite being most un-angelic like in his movements, and Cara had near perfect grace and poise. *I think you'll find it was the other way round.* This love of dance carried on until well into his teens, and Caspar tells me it was so that he could get to "hang out" with the girls. *It was, Mom, but you appear to have ruined all the hard work I put in back then. And my love life generally.*

Cara and Caspar did so much together. When I was busy cooking and catering for film shoots (mostly nature documentaries about lions and the local wildlife, we were in Africa after all) and I was unable to be there to take him to school, he'd go and stay at Cara's and get spoilt rotten. They used to go to a show just before Christmas, where a winter wonderland was set up for the kids and a play was performed that involved a lot of elves. But one year Caspar decided he didn't like the hullabaloo of it all anymore because Santa wasn't giving him presents as good as Cara and Theo's! Theo got a Barbie who could do freestyle and his pile of Lego just wouldn't suffice. And then, of course, Theo told him Father Christmas didn't exist, and that was the end of our annual trip to Santa.

As their pre-school years continued, Caspar and Theo used to bring friends to stay in Fort Nottingham, along with their parents. We had closed the restaurant by the time Caspar was five, and so we used the place for holidays and fun weekends away. Cara and her parents came often, as did the Blanckenbergs and the Basckins. Theo was friends with Clarissa Blanckenberg and Sophie Basckin, and Caspar would befriend them and their siblings intermittently. Daniel, Sophie's brother, was the same age as Caspar, but they were often at loggerheads. When Sophie and Daniel came to play Daniel frequently wanted to go home early. Sometimes their fights became physical and Caspar vividly remembers one time when he threw a rock at Daniel. I thought that'd be the end of our friendship, but Daniel survived and so did their friendship. All the kids still keep in touch, even if it's just the odd "like" on Facebook. But I know Sophie and Theo are still the best of friends.

Theo was Mary, Clarissa was Joseph and Caspar got to dress up in Cara's ballet outfit (again) for his part as the angel Gabriel.

I still feel guilty about that to this day. That's the only (sort of) "fight" I've ever had, and I think it's fair to say they're not my thing.

When Caspar was five we celebrated the millennium in Fort Nottingham with the Blanckenburgs. The kids decided they would put on a nativity play in honour of the occasion. Theo was Mary, Clarissa was Joseph and Caspar got to dress up in Cara's ballet outfit (again) for his part as the angel Gabriel. *I looked fabulous, of course.* They knew all the words because they'd been drummed into them for the school nativity plays, and they loved singing Christmas carols.

Mom, were you not a little concerned about me waving the knife around my face and slamming it into the cake like a crazy psycho killer?

Caspar and Cara.

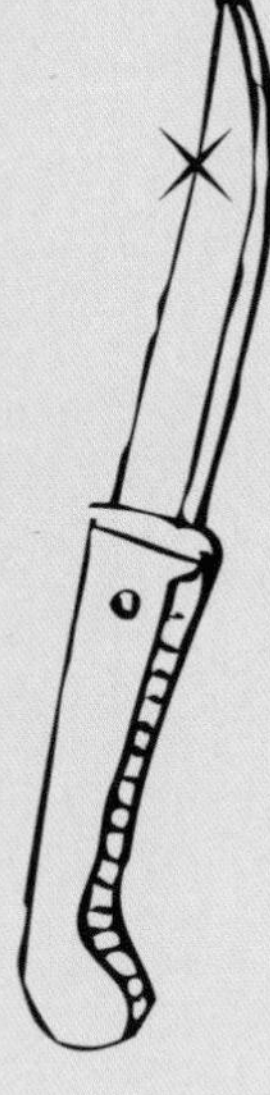

I put some beautiful duck and a creamy potato roast in the oven and decorated the table with all sorts of wondrous New Year treats. We had a few drinks while the kids had a bit of a rest before celebrating the Big One – the year 2000! The veg was ready but when I went to take out the duck I found, to my horror, I'd forgotten to turn the oven on. Outside the thunder and lightning had started, the rain was bucketing down and to top it all we had a power cut. This meant I had absolutely no chance of cooking the duck. We woke the kids and told them what had happened and they refused to get out of bed. There we were celebrating what was supposedly the biggest night of the 21st century away from all the wonderful parties and firework displays on offer in Durban, without power, without TV, and without the wonderful gourmet meal that had been meticulously planned. We could have been on another planet, and Caspar and Theo were definitely not impressed. I actually remember really enjoying this. We had a radio and we listened to all the celebrations and that made me feel like we were really a part of it.

The veg was ready but when I went to take out the duck I found, to my horror, I'd forgotten to turn the oven on.

We eventually hauled all the kids out of bed and had a candle-lit party containing cold veg, juice and champagne, with banoffee pie to follow. At least Caspar was happy!

Thankfully, the nativity play was a howling success on our veranda in the midst of thunder claps and lashing rain, with a very wet, soggy and terrified Florence making several guest appearances dashing through the show, looking for cover. Caspar was an exceptionally good Gabriel and gave us a great, if desperately out of tune, rendition of "Silent Night".

This was my first ever acting experience. It was also when I found out that one of the Three Kings is called Caspar. I thought that was really cool and it made me feel very proud of my name.
I will admit that my singing wasn't great. I couldn't keep in time and I had no rhythm, so all in all I don't think it was my finest performance. I'm still not the world's best singer, but I did sing on a charity single ("It's All About You" by McFly) for Sport Relief as part of the YouTube Boy Band alongside Joe Sugg, Marcus Butler, Jim Chapman and Alfie Deyes. I don't think I'll be signing a record deal anytime soon, but it was probably better than my "Silent Night".

Am I the only one who finds Father Christmas guys at malls creepy?

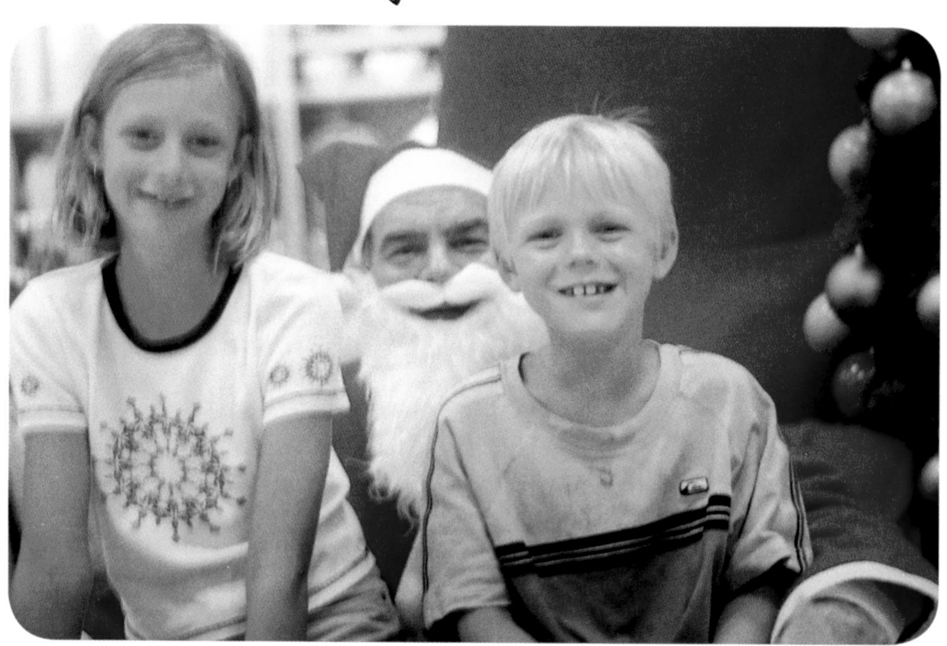

Caspar always wanted to do what Theo did, only bigger and better.

Caspar at Joyce Broadhead School.

Always surrounded by girls

CHAPTER ELEVEN

A pizza THE ACTION

We decided to send Caspar to a private school, Clifton Preparatory, a year earlier than normal, because:

1. He was ruining his vocal chords shouting in the pre-school playground.
2. He was quite a clever chappie.
3. He could make early use of the incredible sports facilities.
4. I couldn't wait another year to see him in the school's cute uniform.
5. He was raring to go.

So he stepped across the threshold into Clifton Prep at the precocious age of five and three quarters. As with all first days at school it was filled with anticipation and excitement. I couldn't believe the sight of our little boy dressed head to toe in khakis, and the floppy hat he had to wear was just the cutest thing ever. Maybe for you!

His teacher was delightful, and a lollipop was laid out on his desk. All went according to plan and he came home happy and with a big smile on his face and happy to talk about it... sort of.

ME: "How was school?"

CASPAR: "Fine."

ME: "Was it really lovely?"

CASPAR: "Yes."

ME: "How was your teacher?"

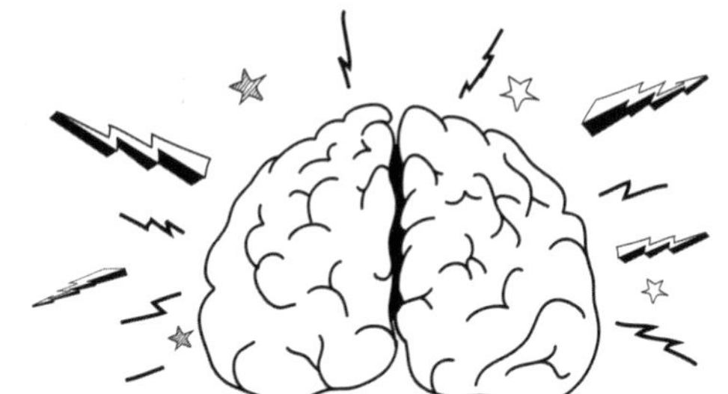

'Cute' apparently...

Minus the "cute floppy" hat...

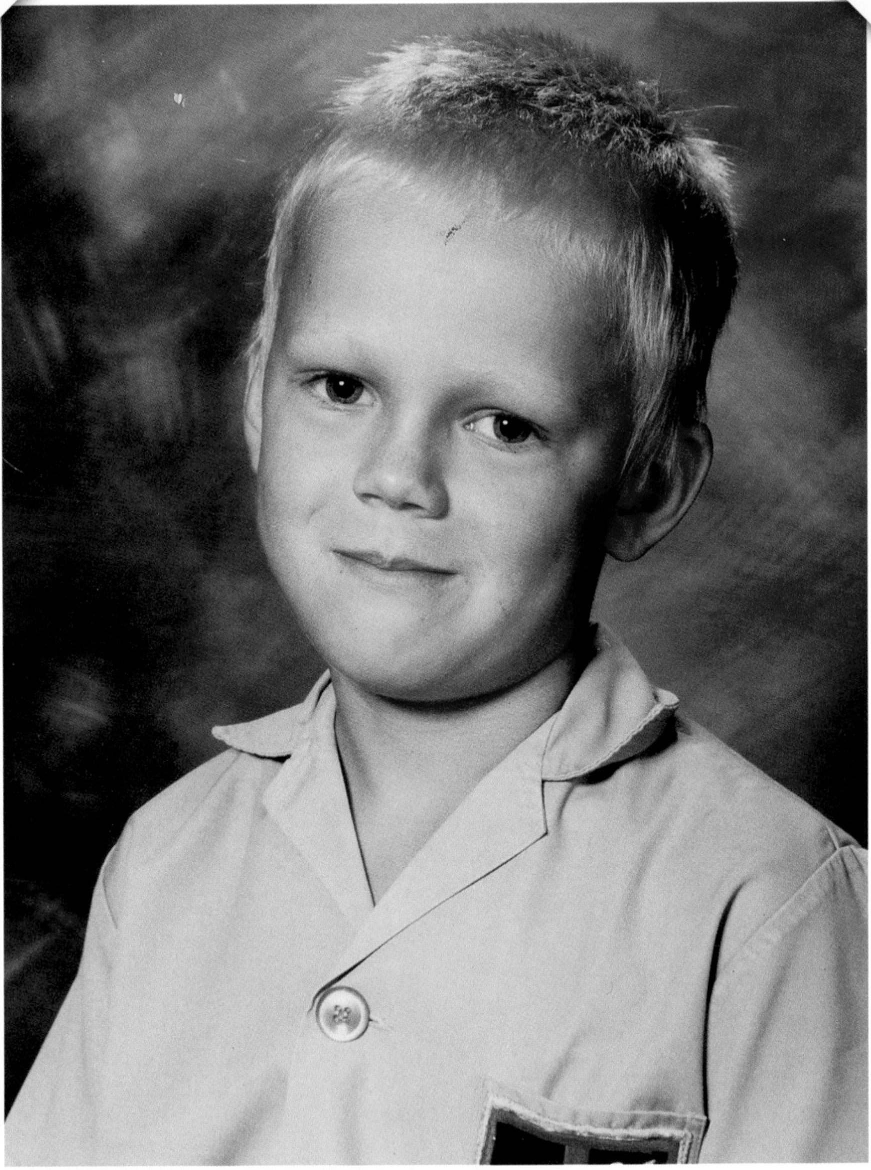

Jon and Caspar on his first day at school.

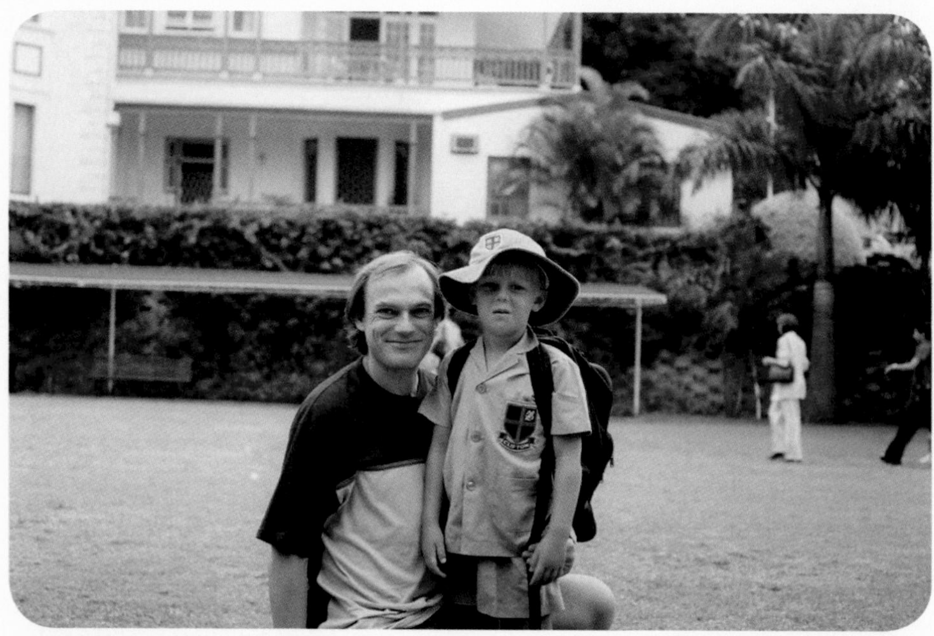

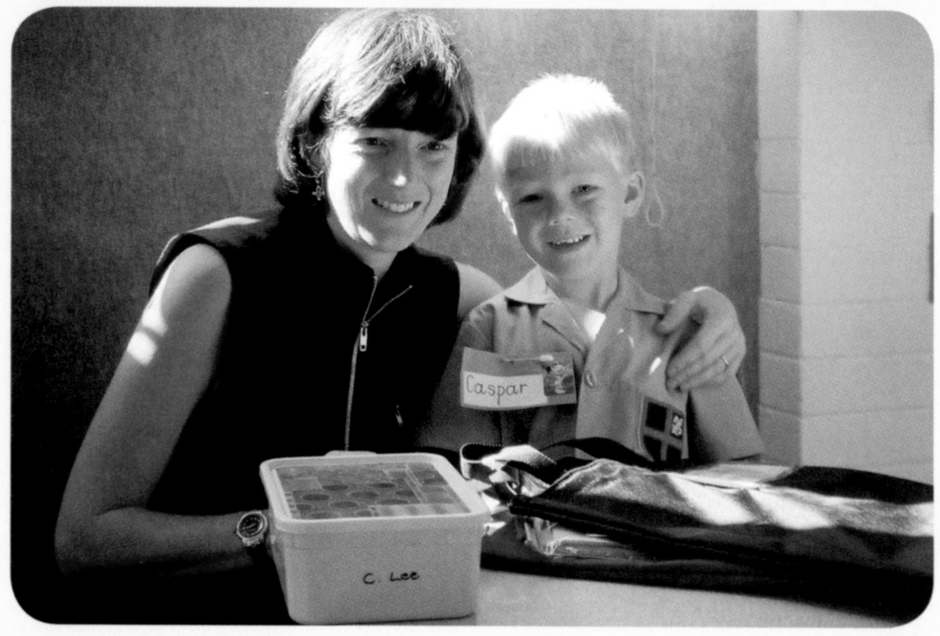

CASPAR: "Fine."

ME: "Did you make lots of lovely new friends?"

CASPAR: "Yes."

I was nice and chatty then! I did proudly tell Mom Id learnt two new words that day. But it turned out Id learnt the same word - look - with and without a capital L. My mom found it hilarious and I got all embarrassed.

The après-school discussions between mother and son would continue to be engaging, and this method of conversing continued throughout his days at school. Including the inevitable:

CASPAR: "I'm hungry, can we get a pizza?"

ME: "But I just gave you peanut butter sandwiches."

CASPAR: "I'm still hungry, Mom."

ME: "Did you eat your PBS's?"

CASPAR: "They got wet. Please, Mom, can I have pizza?"

And off we'd go down to Debonairs Pizza for a Hawaiian, but without the pineapple. For some reason he didn't like tinned pineapple on his pizza. Or avocados for that matter. **I've grown to like both now, weirdly. Any, and all, pizza is good.**

Caspar always had to have some treat when he was picked up from school, but a trip to Debonairs was always his favourite.

We all thought Grade One passed along quite nicely. Caspar took up tennis and cricket, and after school he carried on swimming with Theo. By then we had a new swimming coach called Ron.

Ron was quite strict, and wasn't too keen on the presence of us mums at all. We were never allowed to ask how our little darlings were progressing. That would have been considered far too pushy! We'd have to wait patiently and do as we were told. Ron was a serious coach, and Caspar and Theo both respected and liked him. Theo was becoming quite a star in the breaststroke division, and she broke the South African Under 9s record. Caspar wasn't far behind with his breaststroke either, and his butterfly was showing great potential, according to Ron.

A lot of Caspar's time was spent in the water. If he wasn't training with Ron, he would be in our pool at home, or at the beach with his body-board. The waves are quite big and strong in Durban but that didn't bother him. He was such a daredevil. The stronger the waves the better opportunities for him to shout:

"Look at me, Mom! Look what I can DO!"

I'm still the same now. Unless I actually hurt myself doing something I'm pretty fearless and I don't think of the consequences. I tend to rush into things and then think about it afterwards. I'm the same with the way I talk. I don't really think a lot before I speak, as I'm sure you've realized! It comes in handy when I'm doing my videos because I can say things off the cuff, which usually ends up being funnier. **Then again, I can edit out my mistakes in videos... but I can't do that in real life.**

At times Caspar's antics used to scare the living daylights out of me.

At times Caspar's antics used to scare the living daylights out of me. The problem was he always wanted to do what Theo did, only bigger and better. Even though there was three years between the two of them, there was always fierce competition. No matter how much approval I gave him, he still had to get one up on his sister.

Both kids were absolutely water mad and when we moved to a nicer house (with a larger pool), we were only ten minutes away from the beach, and only two minutes walk from Debonairs Pizza. Don't get me wrong, I wasn't one for feeding kids junk food. They had their fill of fruit smoothies, broccoli and green beans, but Caspar was always a fussy eater. He never liked "bits". Yoghurt had to be of the smooth variety, and tomatoes were definitely out. Even pizzas had to have certain things removed before they were palatable. Hot dogs were often produced at swimming events and, much to my annoyance, Caspar could devour two or three of these in one go. It's a talent.

With the "cute floppy" hat...

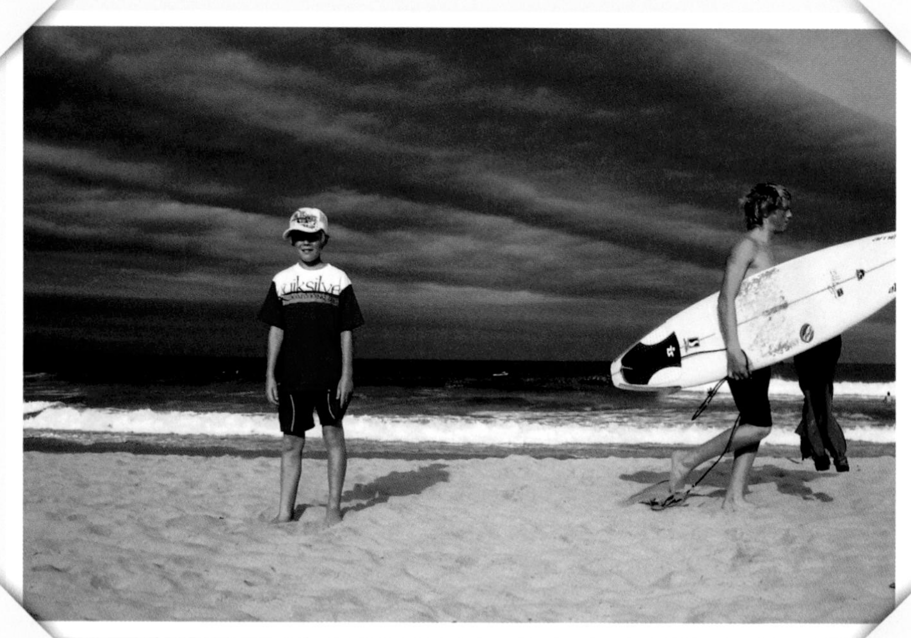

Surf's up:
Caspar loved being by the sea.

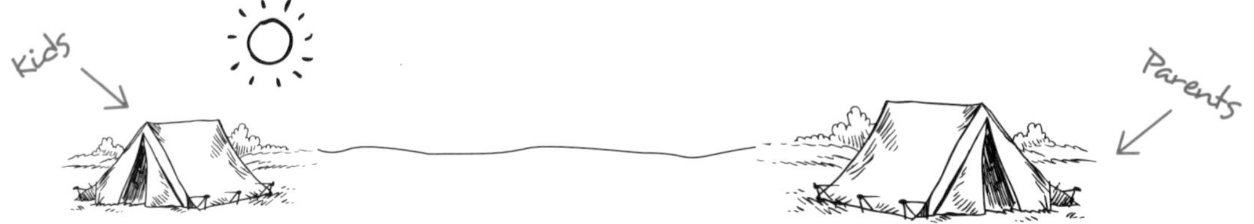

Our move to the new house came about after we finally sold Fort Nottingham. It was a great relief not to have to travel there every weekend, and Jon, on returning from his weekly stints in Jo'burg, had more time to spend with the kids.

At weekends we'd often partake in what is a bit of a South African obsession: camping. We'd drive up the coast to a wonderful place called Salt Rock, right on the coast facing the Indian Ocean and pitch two tents – one for the kids, one for us. We would cook up a lovely "braai" (barbecue) of "borewors" (delicious South African sausage) and vegetable kebabs, and sit around a campfire. Caspar and Theo always managed to bring friends, or make friends at the campsite. The ones they met in the camp were usually Afrikaans whose mums were always particularly welcoming to children. Caspar would often disappear into someone's caravan for a lot of the day (much nicer, he thought, than a tent). There he would also be plied with sweet treats of "koeksisters" (a sickly sweet kind of sticky doughnut) and the dads would produce "biltong", succulent strips of dried meat. *Along with pizza, decent biltong is one of my favourite foods.*

I remember the kids having so much fun diving into the huge rock pool, burying themselves in the sand and running into the very warm ocean. *I love the feeling of warm sand all over my body.*

Sometimes during the school holidays when Jon was away I'd go camping on my own with the kids, and we'd all be in one tent. One night there was a bit of shuffling around in the campsite due to some rather raucous drunken behaviour. The kids were asleep when I heard my tent being unzipped, and in came this horrible boozy-breathed so and so. I didn't really know what was going on. I thought it was just some drunken fellow who'd found himself in the wrong tent. But no, he had other intentions. I lay there terrified pretending to be asleep and saw him grappling around looking for my handbag and car keys and who knows what else. I sat up and screamed as loud as I could and woke the kids up, as well as the rest of the campsite. Luckily he fled, but not without ransacking the car, which I had rather stupidly left unlocked. That was almost the last time I took the kids camping on their own. Caspar and Theo were scared but I told them a naughty man had entered our tent by mistake, and they were soon lulled by the sound of the roaring surf.

At weekends we'd often partake in what is a bit of a South African obsession: camping.

Mom, this is terrifying. I wish I'd been big enough to protect you back then.

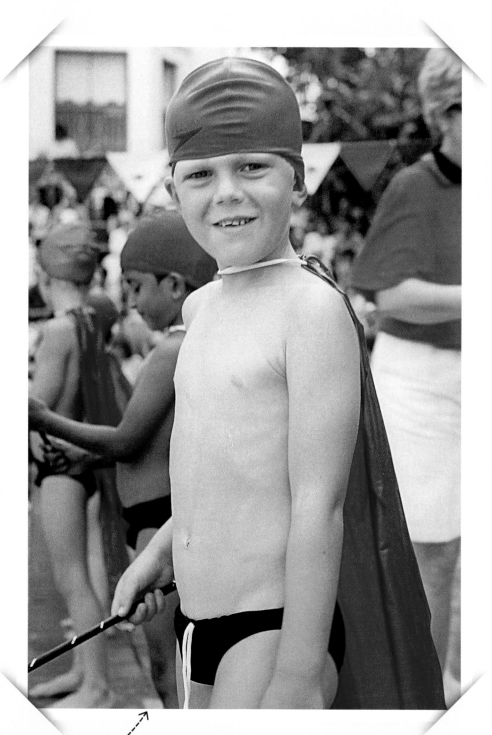

Caspar at Clifton School swimming gala.

I look like an R-Rated wizard

That's me,
Tarzan... again

CHAPTER TWELVE

Animal Antics

Our new house was enormous compared with the cottage in the Indian Quarter. It was so big that the kids would get lost and Caspar's screaming and shouting could often only be heard in the distance. **A blessing for all involved, I'm sure.** We created a beautiful bedroom for him there. Jablan painted a jungle scene all over his walls, complete with lions, giraffes, stick men and rondavels. We moved in all his toys and the Batman duvet cover in the vain hope that he might decide to sleep there.

Caspar was not one for sleeping on his own. He preferred his parents' bed, and no amount of coaxing would change his attitude. He simply wouldn't go to sleep at night without being held, and I'd lie there wide awake while he tossed and turned. It would often take up to an hour before I could sneak out and have dinner. If we tried to move him in the night he would wake up and it'd take another hour to get him back to sleep. I had read a book called *Three in a Bed*, which said bed sharing was a good thing, but often it was four in the bed because Theo wanted to get in as well.

Jablan painted a jungle scene all over his walls, complete with lions, giraffes, stick men and rondavels. We moved in all his toys and the Batman duvet cover in the vain hope that he might decide to sleep there.

Looking back I think Caspar was anxious at night and needed much reassurance when it came to bedtime. He had strange obsessions about things. He'd have to touch the bed head in the same place three or four times. Then he'd stop, before the process started all over again. I put it down to just being a "Caspar thing" and took no notice. He also jerked his legs continually and cried out in pain about his sore knees. I took him to the doctor about his knees but they couldn't find anything wrong, so it was all quite confusing.

I think I had growing pains. It was so sore and horrible and it made me cry a lot. I can't recall the pain now, thankfully, but I do know that it killed at the time.

My bedtime friends

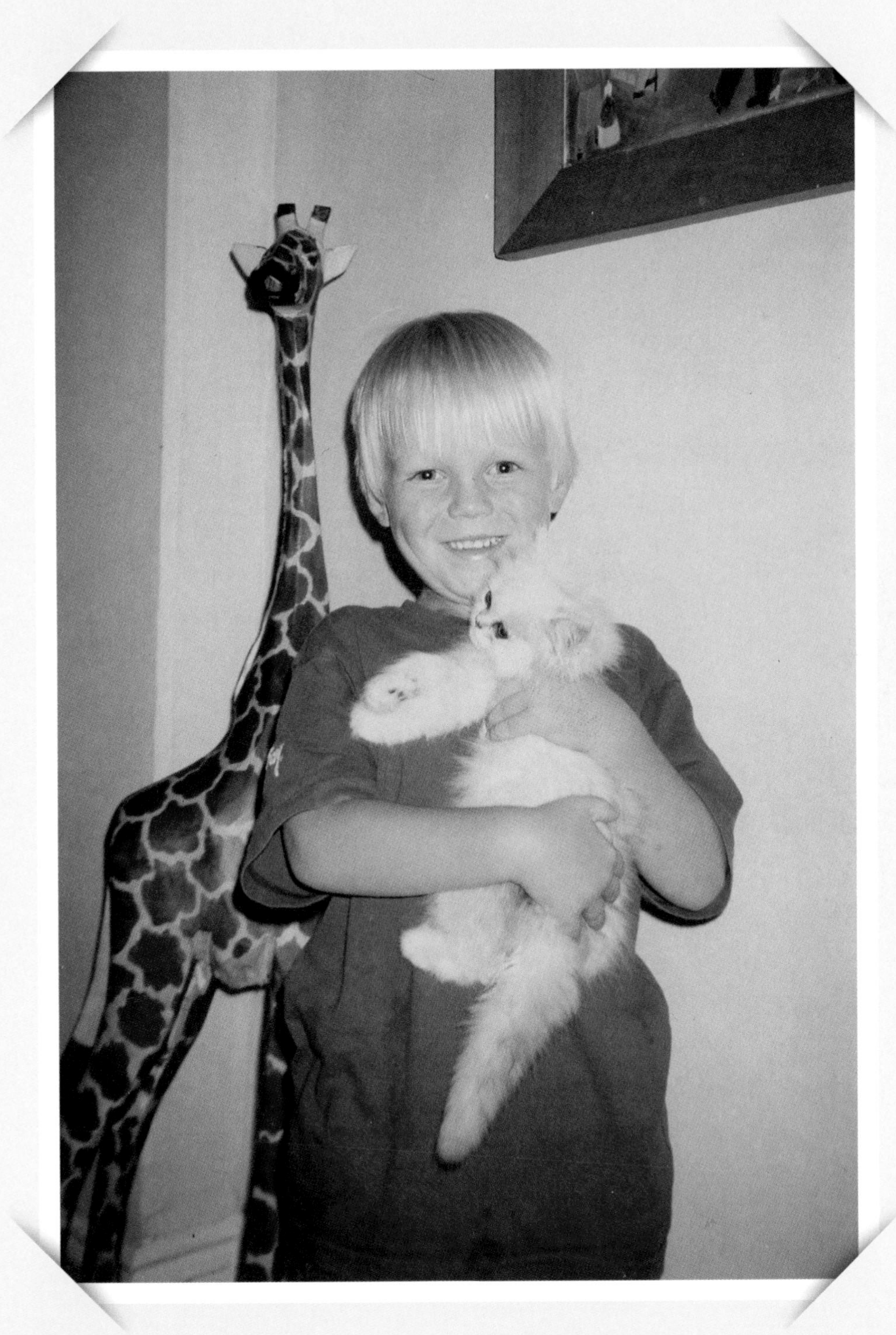

Caspar would often stand in dog poo, and because ever since he realized that he had the capacity to wash his own hands he hated anything to do with dirt, it caused him a fair amount of distress.

Caspar would often wake in the morning – far too early for my liking – bright as a button, ready for Hula Hoops (the breakfast cereal) and apple juice. He also woke up the dogs. By this stage Florence had been joined by several more rescue dogs. Theo and I are crazy about dogs and we loved going to the RSPCA and coming home with a new dog. There was a very moody cocker spaniel, called Marmalade, and a weird white pooch by the name of Scott, who used to stand rock steady on a bodyboard and get pushed by Theo and Caspar across the pool before leaping off the other side. **We loved doing this. Every time we had friends round we'd show off Scott's bodyboarding skills.**

Scott

Strangely enough he'd spend the rest of the day hiding under the bed, growling. There was also a huge black cross Border Collie/Labrador we called Debonairs. Caspar wasn't too fond of any of the dogs, but we hoped that calling a dog after his favourite pizza parlour might encourage him to like them. But no! He put up with them because he had no choice in the matter. The dogs weren't at all well behaved, and because there were so many house training became a big issue. Caspar would often stand in dog poo, and because ever since he realized that he had the capacity to wash his own hands he hated anything to do with dirt, it caused him a fair amount of distress. **I don't think I'm alone in this to be fair, Mom. I'm yet to meet anyone who enjoys standing in dog poo. And I'm not sure I want to meet anyone who does!**

Then along came Venice, the Siamese cat, who was more like a dog than a cat. Caspar adored this fine creature. He was clean, intelligent and used to walk up and down Caspar's back while he lay on his tummy, and then settle down to sleep just above his bum. He'd come when he was called, follow Caspar around all the time and had all the dogs (and us) under his control. That was until the arrival of Mini-Me...

Mini-Me, our best loved and still living chihuahua, came as a surprise to Jon and Theo. They went off to England to celebrate Caspar's grandfather's eightieth birthday, while Caspar and I stayed behind. For a treat, I took Caspar and myself camping in the Drakensberg Mountains. Unlike Salt Rock, it was a very secure campsite and I knew we would be safe there. It was midwinter and though it was freezing at night outside, I managed to plug in a heater so we were toasty warm. I'd brought our local newspaper *The Herald* with me, and as usual I looked at the dog section of the Classified Ads. I told Caspar about chihuahuas; these tiny little dogs that are smaller than a teacup when they are puppies. He liked the idea of them, and we found one for sale in Pretoria.

I'm actually pretending I'm riding this

Theo, Caspar, Jenny Basckin and me.

Hazel (Caspar's grandma), Caspar, Jon, me, Theo and George (Caspar's grandad).

The next day, on impulse, with the ground covered in snow, **Yes, we even went camping in the snow** we packed up camp and jumped into the car and drove a very, very long way to Pretoria to inspect this tiny creature.

We arrived at the home of what seemed like hundreds of chihuahuas. They were everywhere and we couldn't believe our eyes. The breeder was an eccentric Afrikaans lady who hardly spoke a word of English. She said the advertised puppy was already sold, but there was another one we could have at a big discount because he had an overbite. We immediately fell for this little lump of fur and I didn't hear a squeak out of Caspar for the full eight-hour drive home. He was entranced with this tiny rat-like creature. **I think his overbite made him even cuter. He looked more like a cuddly toy than a puppy.**

Jon and Theo arrived back from England a day later, and we smuggled him into the airport in my handbag. Theo was so excited with our surprise, but Jon wasn't sure what we were doing with yet another dog. But of course he took it upon himself to come up with a genius name for our new family member. Inspired by the evil dwarf in Austin Powers we named our fellow Mini-Me.

Swimmy

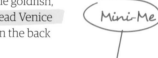

Mini-Me and Venice became the best of friends, charging up and down the long corridor at home chasing one another. It was a pretty wild household with four dogs, Venice the cat, Theo's parakeet Paw Paw, Caspar's hamsters Toffee and Gorgonzola and the goldfish, Swimmy. We were all terribly saddened when Jablan arrived one day with a dead Venice in his arms. He had been bitten by a snake, and we all cried as we buried him in the back garden. This was the start of our animal burial ground. Sadly Mini-Mo, chihuahua number two, fell into the pool as a puppy and drowned, and the goldfish didn't last long either. Caspar's hamster became too smelly for his own good and so it was given back to the pet shop and replaced by rabbits who lived outside. **Sorry, Toffee.** Marmalade unfortunately took a liking to the rabbits so they too were buried, along with Old Socks, another Siamese who died of old age. Our house was like a zoo.

Jon and Theo arrived back from England a day later, and we smuggled him into the airport in my handbag.

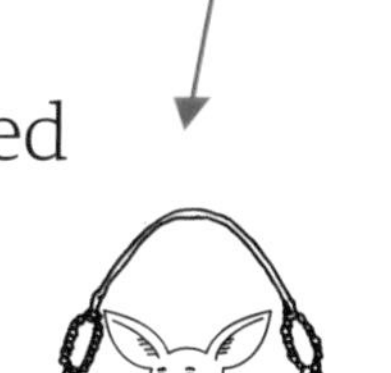

The dogs were incontinent and we (Jon and I) were constantly mopping up after them. They were never properly trained because we could never quite work out who was the culprit. One would be very well behaved and then the other would go ahead and mess on the carpet and we'd often smack the wrong dog, causing a lot of confusion amongst the pack. And Caspar, with his liking for cleanliness, was definitely not amused. Nobody is amused by dog wee and poo, are they?

RIP Venice...

CHAPTER THIRTEEN

A Diagnosis

Caspar's grandfather, Rick, believed Caspar was highly musical. He never forgot about Caspar being entranced by Schubert aged two, *Don't forget my amazing New Year's Eve rendition of "Silent Night"* and when Caspar was seven Rick decided it was high time he began learning to play the violin. We found a wonderful Russian violinist who played lead violin in the Durban Philharmonic Orchestra, and after much persuasion he agreed to take Caspar on as his pupil.

The first lesson began with being taught how to play just one note. I suppose so that Caspar could learn how to use a bow? Caspar found playing only one note far too boring and proceeded to deafen us all with the scrunch of horsehair against wire. It went on for days as he tried to master this terribly difficult instrument.

Rick was disappointed that his grandson would not be the musical prodigy he was hoping for...

When notes two and three were introduced Caspar thought he was made, and would have us listening to his scratchy rendering of "Baa, Baa Black Sheep". He couldn't hear how completely out of tune he was. Even the dogs ran for cover. *Very harsh, but also true.*

On about the fourth lesson, Mr Demitrov decided that maybe Caspar was a little too young to start - a polite way of letting us know that perhaps the violin was not for him. *He was basically calling me s**t.* Rick was disappointed that his grandson would not be the musical prodigy he was hoping for, and suggested that he should concentrate on the piano instead.

I found the violin really difficult to play so I wasn't very good at it. I didn't like it very much, if I'm being honest. It made me feel frustrated because I knew I had such a lack of skill. I never think about the fact that it takes a long time to get good at something; I just want to be good straight away. Obviously that's not how musical instruments work, it's all about practice, so I got bored very quickly and because I didn't master it immediately I gave up. I've always been much more enthusiastic about things I'm good at naturally. I guess everyone is?

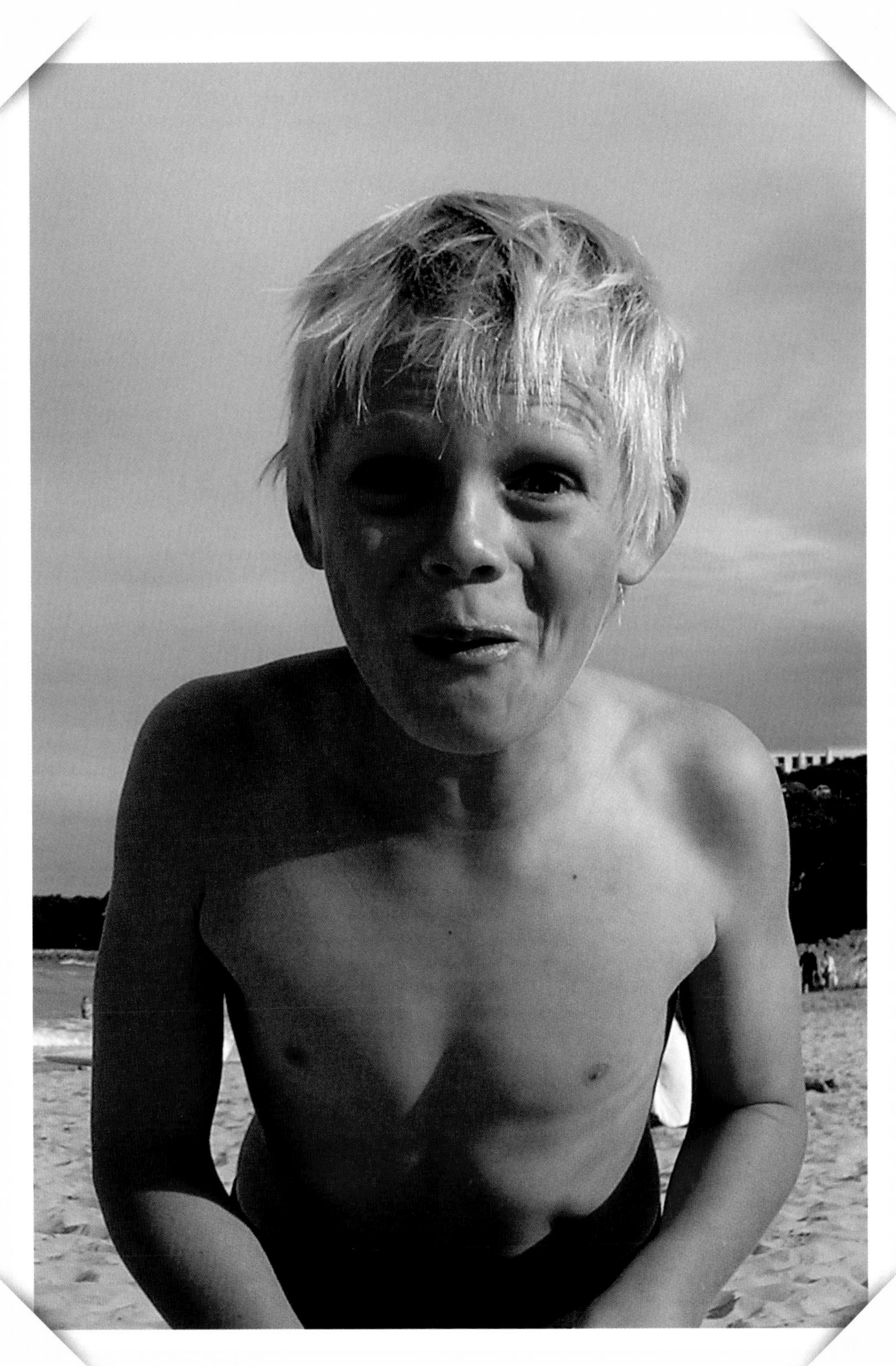

In reality, Caspar was far more interested in sport. He was a real South African in that respect. Many South Africans take pride in sport and start at a very young age. During his second year at school his favourite sports were, in order of best to worst:

1. Surfing
2. Tennis
3. Swimming
4. Cross country running
5. Hockey
6. Soccer
7. Cricket

Caspar never really took to cricket because he wasn't good at it, so what was the point? I think it was a bit slow for him. There was too much hanging around waiting for something to happen.

When it came to his school studies, Caspar took a keen interest too. He loved reading his first books, especially those that taught the alphabet. He was very keen on the letter "K" (we still can't work out why) and all appeared to be proceeding nicely. He made odd noises sometimes and we thought nothing of it until his teacher, Mrs Wieberswick, pulled me aside one day and said he had been snorting like a pig a lot of the time at school and was I aware of it at home? I realized that yes, he did make strange noises, but what of it? Surely that wasn't anything to worry about? It was just Caspar messing around. Then he started to shake his head a lot too. Maybe he was just a bit anxious and doing too much? I couldn't, and didn't want to, believe there was anything wrong with my son.

On advice from his lovely teacher, we took him to a paediatrician, who thought he might possibly have Tourette's Syndrome (TS). How could this be? Where did this come from? Was he going to go through life handicapped, shouting out uncontrollable, unthinkable obscenities? Mrs Wieberswick was calm and reassuring and said it could be just a very mild case, but we were still incredibly worried.

How could this be? Where did this come from? Was he going to go through life handicapped, shouting out uncontrollable, unthinkable obscenities?

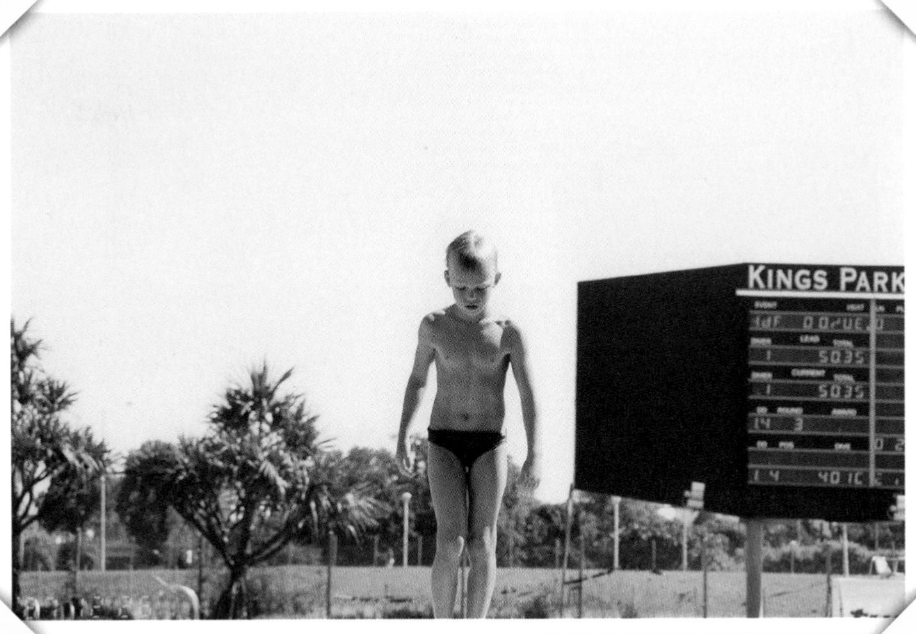

Caspar at a diving competition in Durban.

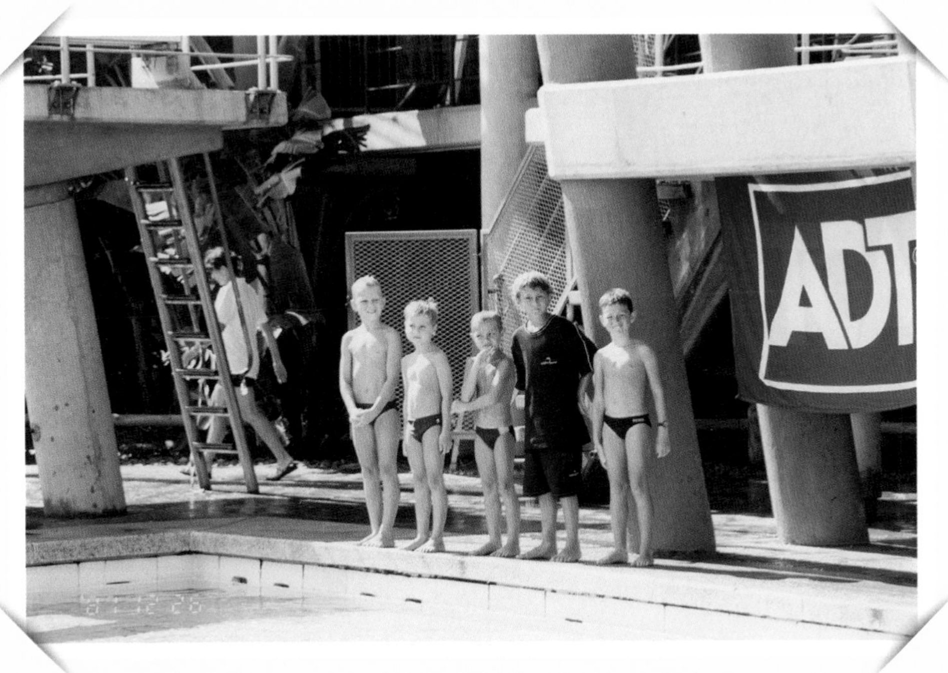

I truly was the king of the pool

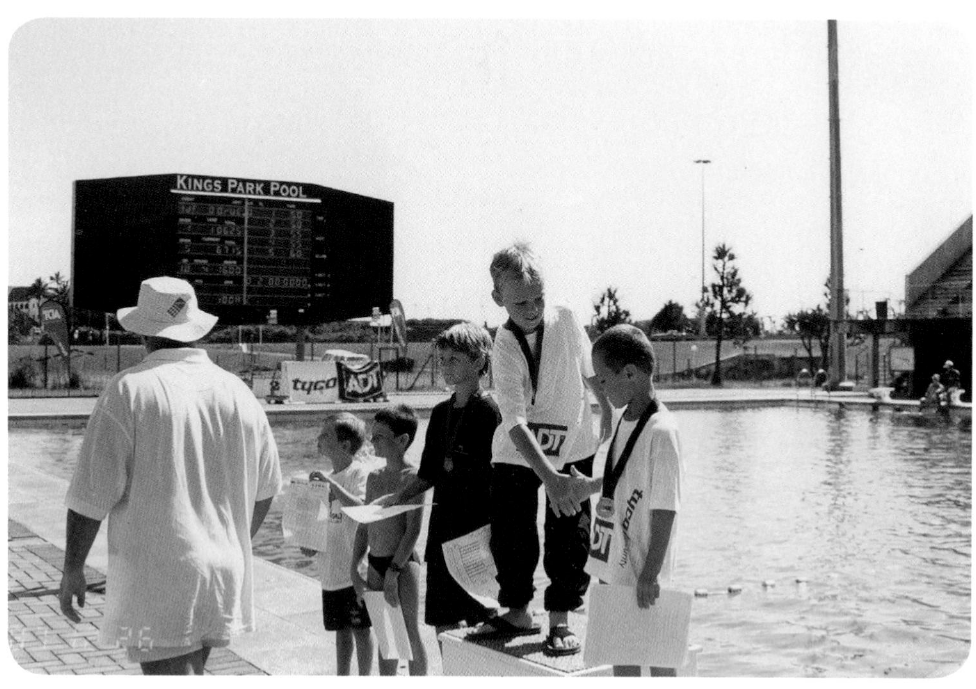

Visits to many doctors followed. Psychiatrists, neurologists, paediatric psychiatric neurologists, psychologists, audiologists, occupational therapists, and our wonderful GP and family friend John Blanckenburg were all hauled in. But the news wasn't good. Caspar did indeed have TS, and we were all going to have to learn how Caspar would live with it both now and in the future.

Initially Caspar wasn't too aware of it. He complained of a sore neck from having to shake his head all the time but it didn't stop him from enjoying his life to the full. He was medicated with antidepressants for his obsessive-compulsive disorder (OCD), which was just one of the myriad of problems associated with TS. He also had Attention Deficit Hyperactivity Disorder (ADD), and trouble with fine motor skills, and handwriting in particular. He was put on Risperdal, a strong anti-psychotic, which was supposed to ease the "tics". Tics are involuntary movements like head shaking, kicking and blinking repeatedly. The head shaking would often last for a couple of months, and then be replaced by knee jerking. Then the continual blinking would start. Often two or more physical tics would happen at the same time.

There were also the verbal tics to contend with. These started with snorting, and would then change to whistling, throat clearing, and high-pitched "eeks". After a while it began to frustrate him and he'd come to me crying saying, "Mom, why can't it just go away? I HATE it."

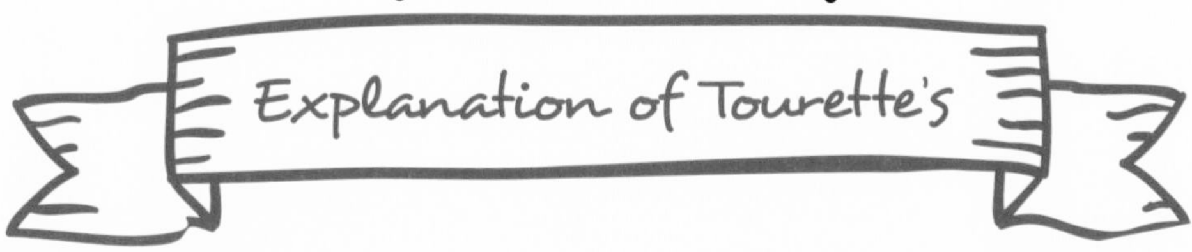

CASPAR'S

Explanation of Tourette's

It's difficult to understand how someone with TS feels. I can't describe the experience that everyone goes through because there are people who have it a lot worse than I did. For me the most difficult part was worrying about what other people thought. Teachers would send me out of class for whistling during exams, and other kids would bob their heads at me while mimicking my eye movements.

Dealing with that, along with the frustration of not being able to relax, was really difficult. It's like having the itchiest itch you've ever had that won't go away unless you scratch it.

I remember an adult telling my Mom to give me money if I could go 20 minutes without doing it. That was the most stupid suggestion I've ever heard. Yes, you can control it for a while, but eventually you just have to give in. Anyway, I have since become a lot better with age. Every now and then I have mild movements, but only in highly stressful situations or when I think about it.

While writing this, in fact, I've had a few more jerks than usual, because I'm thinking about it, but it's not something most people notice unless they spend a serious amount of time with me.

All I can ask is that if you know anyone suffering from anything like I've explained above, please never, ever, use it against them.

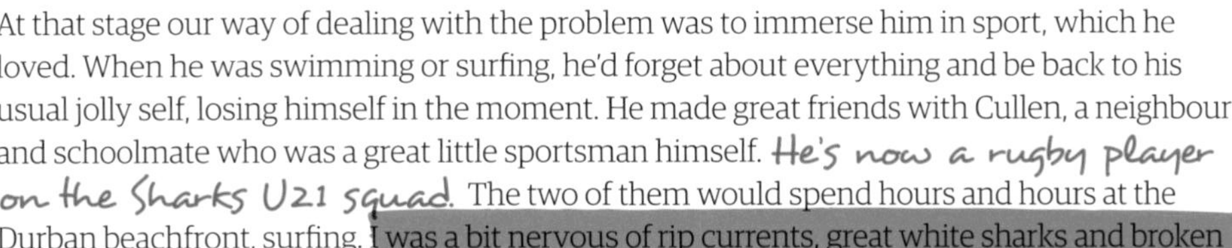

At that stage our way of dealing with the problem was to immerse him in sport, which he loved. When he was swimming or surfing, he'd forget about everything and be back to his usual jolly self, losing himself in the moment. He made great friends with Cullen, a neighbour and schoolmate who was a great little sportsman himself. *He's now a rugby player on the Sharks U21 squad.* The two of them would spend hours and hours at the Durban beachfront, surfing. I was a bit nervous of rip currents, great white sharks and broken bones, but in the end the benefits of surfing outweighed the risks. Cullen's Dad, Don, and Kenny, the surf coach, were always on the lookout. Theo and I whiled away many afternoons at the Durban Ski-Boat Club watching him riding waves, waiting for him to catch a "big one". Surfing was so good for him. It enabled him just to "be" without the worries of twitching and the obsessive touching of things.

So Caspar's next big obsession became diving. He was always into one big thing at any given time, and would give it all he had. He was full on.

Theo's swimming and the endless galas and training she did became a bit of a bore to Caspar, especially when he noticed how much more fun the divers were having at the other end of the pool. I let him have a go, and there was no looking back. There was a one-metre board, plus a five metre, plus the dreaded ten metres. An Olympic coach arrived from England to start a proper diving club, and best of all, lots of their training happened on a large trampoline, where Caspar quickly mastered the art of double somersaults forwards and backwards. He couldn't wait to get out of school and onto the boards. His swimming coach, Ron, rolled his eyes in disdain, from the other end of the pool, disappointed at losing his little breaststroker to such a mundane activity. He was desperately hoping his star swimmer, Theo, wouldn't be seduced by it as well!

So Caspar's next big obsession became diving. He was always into one big thing at any given time, and would give it all he had. He was full on. If he wasn't going to be an Olympic swimmer, then he would be an Olympic diver. TS may have been a bit of a handicap, but it also gave him amazing power to succeed and to be the best at anything he took up.

The higher boards used to terrify me and I spent much of Caspar's youth being in a state of high anxiety. The more fearless he became, the worse I got. Half the time, I couldn't even look at him. The ten-metre board was the height of a three storey building after all, and what if he did a belly flop? But these things didn't occur to Caspar. He had a mind of his own; he was a concentrated bundle of energy, and danger didn't play a part in it. He became so good at diving that he went on to win the Under 9s South African Championships and came home with a massive trophy. We were ever so proud of him. Unfortunately, the diving coach had to leave so Caspar's diving programme fell apart. But, of course, Caspar being Caspar, there were lots of other things for him to conquer.

CHAPTER FOURTEEN

Jumbo Problem

Two or three times a year we used to travel a very long way to Mpumalanga to stay in our family-owned private game reserve called Olifants. It was here that we had some of our greatest adventures. It wasn't actually owned by the Lees, but we got to go there by owning the tiniest share in a trust fund started by Caspar's great grandfather.

Caspar's great grandfather, Meiert Avis, was Dutch, and fought the British in the Boer War. He was a rather domineering and terrifying figure and built up a big family shipping business in Johannesburg. Word has it he used to time how long his employees spent in the bathroom and deduct money from their wages. *Surely this can't be true?* He became immensely rich *Ahhh, now it's making sense* and drove around in a Packard. He started a trust fund for all his descendants, but because I was a woman my share was tiny. I was expected to be "looked after" by whoever I married. But although we had little money at the time, Olifants was the one great luxury that we had access to. It cost us nothing, except for getting there and back.

With Caspar on board, getting there was a mission and a half. It was a good 14 hours drive if we didn't sleep over en route. First, there'd be the usual "How much further?" after only having travelled an hour out of Durban. Then:

CASPAR: "Mom, I need the loo."

ME: "But you've only just been."

CASPAR: "But I need to go again."
(Stop. Start. Leg kicking)

CASPAR: "Mom, there's a Debonairs, we have to stop! PLEASE, Mom. You said!"
(Stop. Start. Peace for a bit with much munching of pizza)

CASPAR: "Teedora spilt my juice and I'm all wet."

ME: "Caspar, we really can't stop again, we'll never get there."

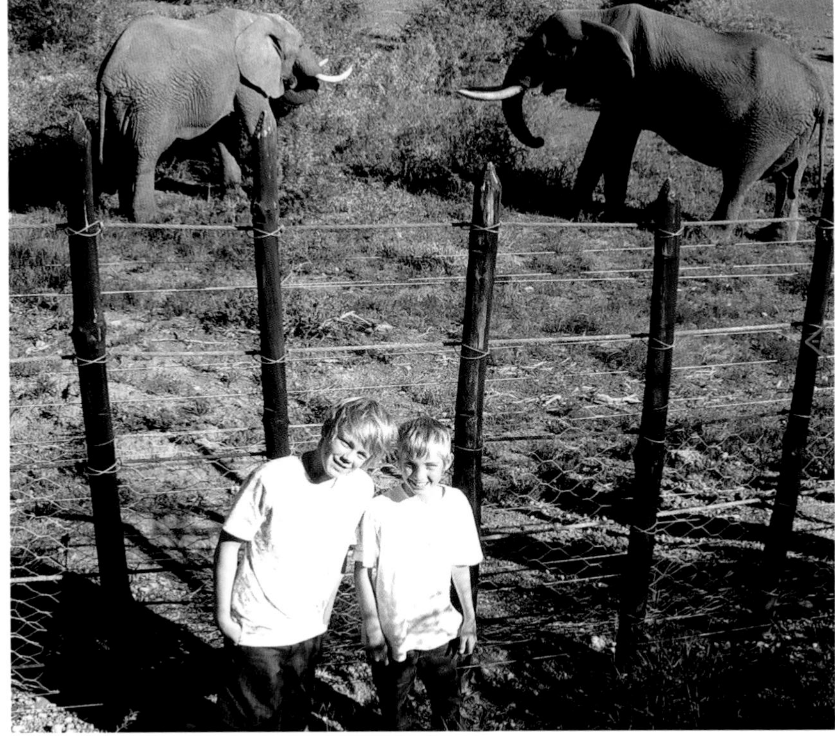

Thinking about it now, that fence doesn't actually look like it would stop a wild elephant

CASPAR: "But I'm thirsty, Mom. I'm so thirsty. I want Cream Soda."

ME: "No, Caspar, I said NO."

CASPAR: "I promise I'll be quiet if you get me a Cream Soda!"

Caspar's sugar-high would be interrupted by the most monumental smelling farts. When it came to body expulsions and explosions, he was king.

I stupidly gave in, as usual, because having a fight with Caspar was not fun. It was a completely exhausting, draining and horrible experience. He would never give up and always had to win. He had a way of grinding us down to blithering oblivion. *Even I'm finding myself annoying. I really can't have been that bad? I blame my love of pizza and Cream Soda. And Theo. I don't know why, I just do. Because I can.*

Caspar's sugar-high would be interrupted by the most monumental smelling farts. When it came to body expulsions and explosions, he was king. We'd open the windows as much as possible and hold our breaths until the smell was gone. They were deadly. *You've really mastered the art of oversharing there, Mom.*

The only time we ever made it to Olifants without wanting to kill Caspar was when we bought him the Harry Potter audio books. He was as silent as a lamb while we listened to the dulcet tones of Stephen Fry reciting the young wizard's exploits.

Caspar's Tourette's was certainly responsible for his difficulty with car journeys. I think he felt trapped in his body with little or no means of escape. The tics and obsessions would build up until he exploded, and my God did we all suffer.

Sometimes we'd stop over halfway in Dullstroom for the night to ease the pressure. Harry's Pancakes was the perfect panacea. Crepes with cheese and bacon, followed by banana split crepes with extra melted chocolate on the side. Caspar the Pudding Boy was happy at last. Across the road was a quaint old-fashioned sweet shop where Caspar would stock up on homemade vanilla fudge, and gooey pink coconut ice for the rest of the journey. *No wonder I was "lively".*

The house at Olifants was a place of dreams. It had a thatched roof, which was inhabited by a huge monitor lizard that was almost the size of a crocodile. Olifants had no electricity so at night we had candles and gas lamps. Wild animals roamed freely, and as there was no fence around the house, we'd have to be ultra careful to make sure no animals were around when we wanted to take our bags from the car into the house. At night you could hear lions roaring and hippos thundering past. We were virtually on our own in the middle of the bush. *Perhaps this is where I got my love of Bear Grylls from.*

Do you read me, over?

During the day we'd drive around in the very battered old Land Rover looking for game. We had a set of walkie-talkies so we could communicate with other residents as to the whereabouts of the elephants, lions, leopards, cheetahs, or whatever else we thought was out there. Caspar loved getting his hands on the walkie-talkies and travelling to the animals that had been spotted as fast as possible. *Maybe I was more like David Attenborough?*

"Go, Dad, go! We've got to get there fast! They might be GONE!"

The Land Rover was so old it had to be coerced into changing gear. There would be a lot of double declutching and scrunching going on – enough to frighten away any sensible animal. The best sightings of animals always happened when we turned the engine off and just waited for something to appear.

On one such occasion a rogue elephant came upon us. Now, a rogue elephant is a chap who has been expelled from his troop and is particularly dangerous and violent. We had a guide with us who was sitting on the bonnet of the Land Rover and Jon was in the driving seat. The kids and I were in the back, sat high up on the viewing seats. The elephant was a mere six feet from us and he was flapping his ears and blowing his trumpet. Clearly not a good sign!

The elephant was a mere six feet from us and he was flapping his ears and blowing his trumpet. Clearly not a good sign!

We all froze, except for Caspar. He was wriggling around next to me whistling his head off. I whispered gently to him to shut up, but he couldn't and the elephant was getting angrier by the second. I pulled Caspar across my lap, covered him in a blanket and straightjacketed him in my grasp, and Theo hid under a blanket as well. She was stiff with fear. We were in extreme danger. This elephant could turn the vehicle upside down with one flick of his tusk and we'd all be trampled to death. It was one of the most terrifying moments of my life. I held on to the two of them praying we'd get out of this dire situation.

Jon had to turn on the engine so that we could reverse out because the elephant clearly wasn't going anywhere. The problem was it would be very noisy to start it, and would he be able to get it into reverse? Not at all easy, but our only option...

Frightened by the Land Rover's full throttle, the elephant turned his back to us and trundled back a good few yards, only to turn around so that he could get a good charge at us. Luckily, the Land Rover started up immediately (for once!) and Jon managed to get us to reverse down the hill at a high speed to safety. We were all so relieved. I love elephants but I never want to get that close to one ever again! *I seem to remember I was also making monkey noises. I'm really sorry to everyone involved, but I couldn't help it.*

I took the kids to an amazing pool that was situated right in the middle of the game reserve to try and forget what had happened. We played underwater handstands, and held a mini competition of who could do the best one. There were a couple of rhinos eyeing us up *This was normal to us!* but we were safe because the pool was fenced in. Hippos could get through, and often broke down the fence in the middle of the night, but not rhinos. Then we went for Magnum ice creams, as we always did every day while staying at Olifants, bought from the little shop next to the pool. **My favourite part of the day, obviously.**

Caspar took a fancy to the Land Rover and would often sit on Jon's lap and pretend to steer. At about the age of nine he decided he wanted to learn to drive properly. *You know, after my massive success with the Porsche.* He was hardly tall enough to reach the pedals but he was determined to give it a go, and as Jon had grown up on a farm in Sussex driving tractors from an early age, he agreed. We found an open area near the pool and Caspar began his very first driving lessons. I couldn't bear to watch and refused to have anything to do with it.

Caspar did well and managed to drive all the way from the pool to our house, which is a good ten minutes, without crashing into anything or anyone. Not bad for a nine-year-old.

A few days later as he was practising again he couldn't quite reach the brakes and managed to crash through the fence and nearly took the car for a swim in the pool. We were worried about reporting the incident to the manager of the Reserve, for fear of being charged a fortune to fix the fence, so it got blamed on the hippos, **They're bad drivers too** and it was a long while before Caspar was allowed (or indeed wanted) to drive again. Caspar and cars were never a good mix, as we were to discover again in later years...

> A few days later as [9-year-old Caspar] was practising again he couldn't quite reach the brakes and managed to crash through the fence and nearly took the car for a swim in the pool.

Not guilty!

— KING OF FARTS —

L'Insolite

CHAPTER FIFTEEN

On the ROAD AGAIN

In Grade Three Caspar moved schools. We wanted him to be in the same educational establishment as Theo. It was a brand new school called Crawford, with a 50-metre swimming pool and playgrounds that extended for miles and miles. It was more liberal in approach than Clifton and khakis were replaced by denim shorts and t-shirts.

Although it had fewer regulations, it was definitely smart. A security guard at the school's entrance used to doff his cap at every single car that passed through the gates each morning. Because it was a large school Caspar reckoned the poor man must have had to do this nearly a thousand times a day! **I genuinely felt bad for him. It must have been exhausting.**

Academics weren't considered all that important and he wasn't too well behaved in school. He was noisy and had a habit of interrupting his teachers.

Caspar carried on with his usual enthusiasm for sport. Perhaps he was inspired by Theo's achievements in swimming and cross-country, where she often came first. He always wanted to follow in her footsteps, perhaps to stay close to her. They were incredibly close at this time. Academics weren't considered all that important and he wasn't too well behaved in school. He was noisy and had a habit of interrupting his teachers. Caspar had a sharp mind and queried everything. He also liked to play around with his mates, throwing paper aeroplanes and setting up whoopee cushions for his teacher, that sort of thing. He was charming though, in a cheeky way. He seemed to get away with it most of the time, and was rarely in detention.

It feels weird that you're being so nice about me, Mom.

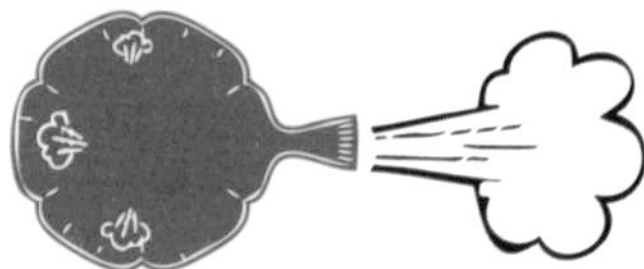

How could you inflict that
haircut on a defenceless child?

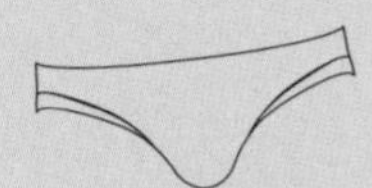

Finally a sport that doesn't require Speedos – so much less embarrassing

He took up dance and was the only boy in his class to do so. He was a big hit with the girls *See? My plan totally worked* but not very co-ordinated, to say the least. *You can't have everything.* He used to get teased a bit, but stood up for himself. He liked being friends with girls (and still does) and didn't give a damn what anyone thought. I'm sure he probably had his first kiss around then too!

My first kiss was actually when we went on holiday to England when I was 11. I snuck into the woods with a girl called Sophie and I picked a strawberry to make my breath taste good. She refused to talk to me the next day even though I went to her school to see her because I really liked her. Creepy, I know. I wonder where she is now?

He made great friends with another young chap from England called Carlo. He had a kid's motorbike. His sister also became friends with Theo and they used to hang out together at the mall. The girls were all made-up and dressed up to the nines, while Caspar and Carlo snooped on the older boy-gangs and used to run away and hide from security when the lads got into trouble. *I was quite well behaved but some of my friends were quite naughty and they weren't scared of fighting. I was always the first to run away and hide when something kicked off. It was a lot of fun running around that mall.*

Caspar was a big hit with the girls but not very co-ordinated, to say the least.

I didn't like Counter-Strike. *Mom, it was the best game in the whole entire world!* It was full of guns and blood and people killing each other. I far preferred The Sims, and wished Caspar had stuck to creating fancy houses with polite little families, and having one or two babies, which needed to be fed in the middle of the night. But no, Counter-Strike it was, and guns and guts and gore played a big part in Caspar's life for many years. The "pow, pow, pows" and the screams of "F**k it" coming from his bedroom used to drive the whole family nuts!

Thank God he carried on with his physical games as well. At Crawford he started running cross-country, and like his sister he outshone his fellow athletes with his long gazelle-like strides. He ran barefoot with his feet wrapped in bandages. And boy, was he fast! He made it on to the Provincial Cross Country Team. He was thrilled. We drove him way up into the wilds of KwaZulu-Natal to compete. We bandaged up his feet (a common procedure for all long-distance runners) and off he went.

It didn't go well. The course was covered in bits of broken glass, and he arrived at the finish with his feet bleeding heavily and suffering an asthma attack at the back of the pack. After that he lost interest in cross-country, which upset me a bit because I was addicted to running myself. **I'll be honest, up until that point I was doing really well at cross-country and I was second in my district. But the glass really messed me up and I came flat out last. That was the end of my love for running.**

> Thank God he carried on with his physical games as well. At Crawford he started running cross-country, and like his sister he outshone his fellow athletes with his long gazelle-like strides.

When Caspar turned ten I took up a full-time job selling houses, and for a while things went exceptionally well. The family had money and we opened a shopping account at the local Spar. The kids were allowed to go there and buy "healthy snacks". They loved the freedom. They also discovered how to order Pizza from Debonairs. Caspar and Theo used to be treated to pizza and a movie once a week – but once a week only. But this rule got severely abused. Caspar began to call Debonairs himself, without asking us, and have pizza delivered to our door.

"Hi. Can I have a Four Seasons, please, but without the olives and no avocado? Repeat, no avocado. And my sister will have... hang on a moment... THEEE-OOO! Theo, quick, what do you want, before Dad finds out! HURRY UP!"

Theo took charge of the situation. "OK, we will have a Four Seasons without the olives and without avocado. I will have a Hawaiian without the ham. Oh, and two Cream Sodas... and make the pizzas extra large!"

Caspar went, "Are you sure they know about the no avocado?"

NO AVOCADO!!

She put the phone to her chest. "I will eat it if they forget." She picked the phone back up. "What? Yes we can pay for it. Our dad is buying it. Have a nice day!"

She hung up and they put on the television to watch *The Wild Thornberrys* and await their favourite pizzas in the whole world.

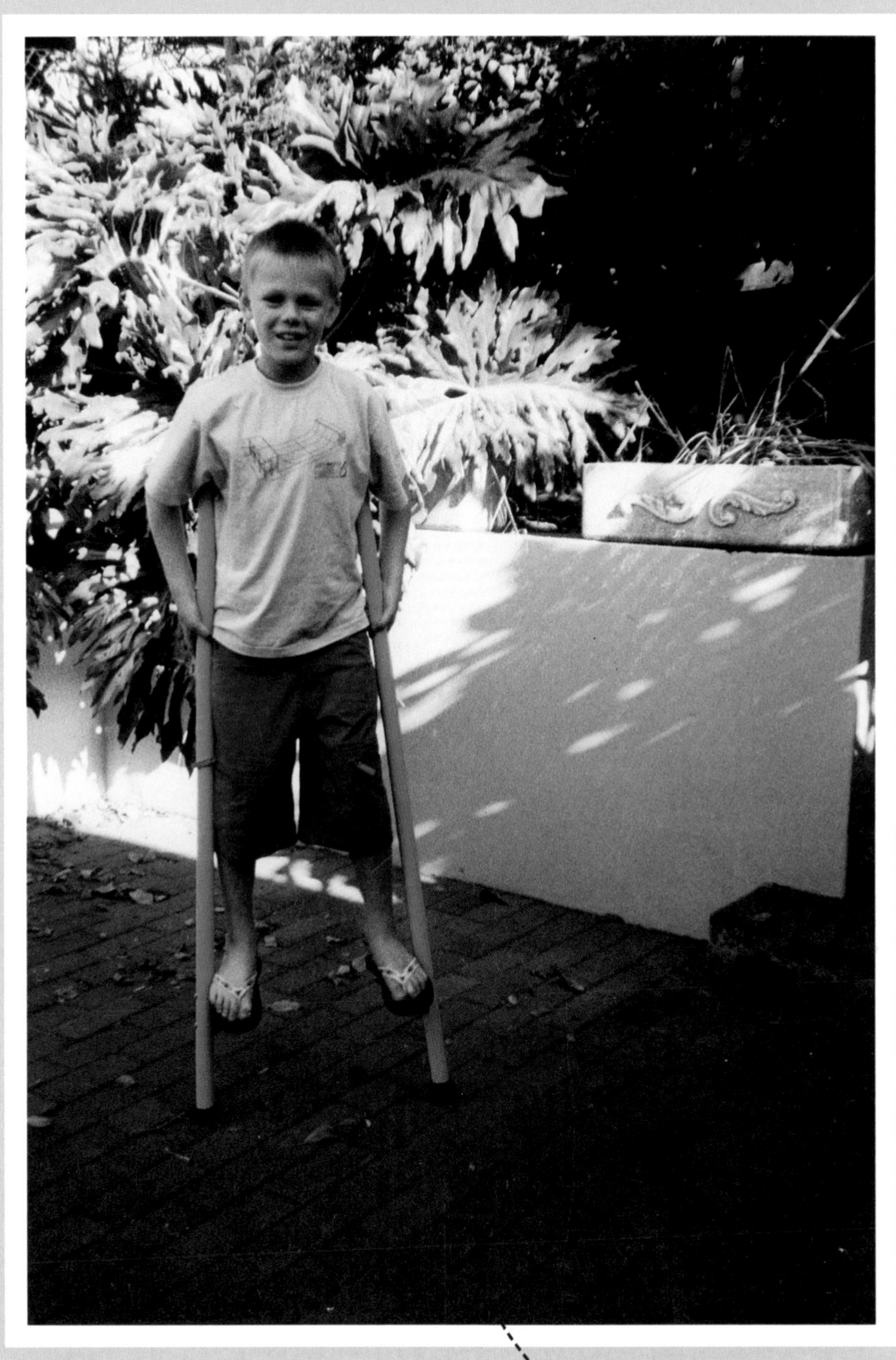

Joe needs a
pair of these

Half an hour later the doorbell rang. Theo and Caspar raced to answer it but Jon got there first. After a lot of shouting he told the delivery man to go away. The kids were mortified.

"How could you do that to the poor pizza man, Dad? That's his job. They are going to hate us!" Theo shouted. Caspar was already bawling in his eyes out in the background.

"I'm so hungry!" he wailed.

"You're starving us, Dad!" Theo added.

At this point, I arrived home and got the sob story from my very distraught kids. I tried my best to be cross with them, because their dad was right, but their wailing was not my idea of a quiet evening, so I took them out for pizza and Jon was furious. He didn't mind eating the leftovers, however!

People were hungry and had to get money by whatever means it took. Hijackings were a regular event, and most criminals thought nothing of shooting you for your mobile phone.

To this day, whenever one of my kids orders a pizza from that branch of Debonairs, the order needs to be pre-authorized by us, the parents. Perhaps this whole ordeal strengthened Caspar's life-long love of pizza, still without the avocado!

Amidst all these happy events, there was always an undercurrent of danger. We were living in a city where rampant crime was on the increase. The gap between rich and poor was enormous. There was no social welfare. People were hungry and had to get money by whatever means it took. Hijackings were a regular event, and most criminals thought nothing of shooting you for your mobile phone. You had to get used to it or try to put it to the back of your mind. And then something happened to Theo...

At the time, we had an au pair who used to look after the kids when they were done with school, so that Jon and I could carry on working. Her name was Christine and she had long blonde hair and was studying for her Masters in Mathematics. She was strict on the kids, but in a good way. They both absolutely loved her. One afternoon Christine was driving Theo back from swimming. They stopped at a traffic light and a homeless man came up to Theo's window.

"Theo, move closer to me, that guy is going to do something," Christine warned. Theo edged in her seat, unsure of what Christine meant. Homeless men, and women, are very common in South Africa and are usually harmless. But something wasn't right about this young guy.

Within seconds, Theo's window was smashed with a brick that appeared out of nowhere, and this man clambered into the car on top of her.

Christine started yelling in Zulu, "Get out! Get out!" Theo's head was turned towards the back seat and she kept completely quiet. The guy grabbed whatever belongings were in the car while Christine continued to shout, hoot her horn and clobber him with her handbag. When he produced a knife she let him take everything, but as he ran away down the highway, she stuck her head out the window and shouted, "There's no money in my purse and my phone has terrible battery life! I wanted to get rid of it anyway, you scumbag!"

They drove home with a smashed window while Christine kept going on about how dangerous South Africa is. There was nobody home apart from our nanny, Ntombi, who took Theo in her arms and suggested that they spend the afternoon baking cupcakes. Theo felt better after some much-needed sugar, but was very scared of getting in a car after that, so we decided to send her to therapy.

My poor little (big) sister. This must have been a truly horrible thing for you to go through at such a young age. You've always bounced back from things pretty well though. It's one of the things I admire about you the most.

On top of this incident, our house also got burgled while we were sleeping, and Cara's dad got shot in the leg. Our house was surrounded by razor wire atop high walls and electric fences but it still wasn't safe.

Around the time of these incidents, I went to run a marathon near the Western Cape, in a beautiful seaside town called Knysna. I noticed there were no high walls there, let alone electric fences. I completely fell in love with the place and decided there and then that we would sell up in Durban and move the family to Knysna. We could sell property just as well there, after all. We had developed good sales techniques so moving to a new town shouldn't be a problem. We'd all be safe, and most importantly, the schools were good. Durban was fast becoming a dangerous place to live with hijackings on the increase, and we both were happy to consider living in a safer environment.

So, once again, the Lees hit the road. The remaining dogs, Mini-Me, Florence and Bruiser (a naughty pug, who was a new addition to the zoo), the cats Rusty (whom we inherited from someone leaving South Africa) and Whitey (an albino cat we got from an animal welfare charity) and the rabbits, all piled into the car. Another long car journey ensued, which needs not be discussed. Suffice it to say we nearly lost the cats out the window and the dogs peed all over the show.

The smell was even worse than my farts!

Woof

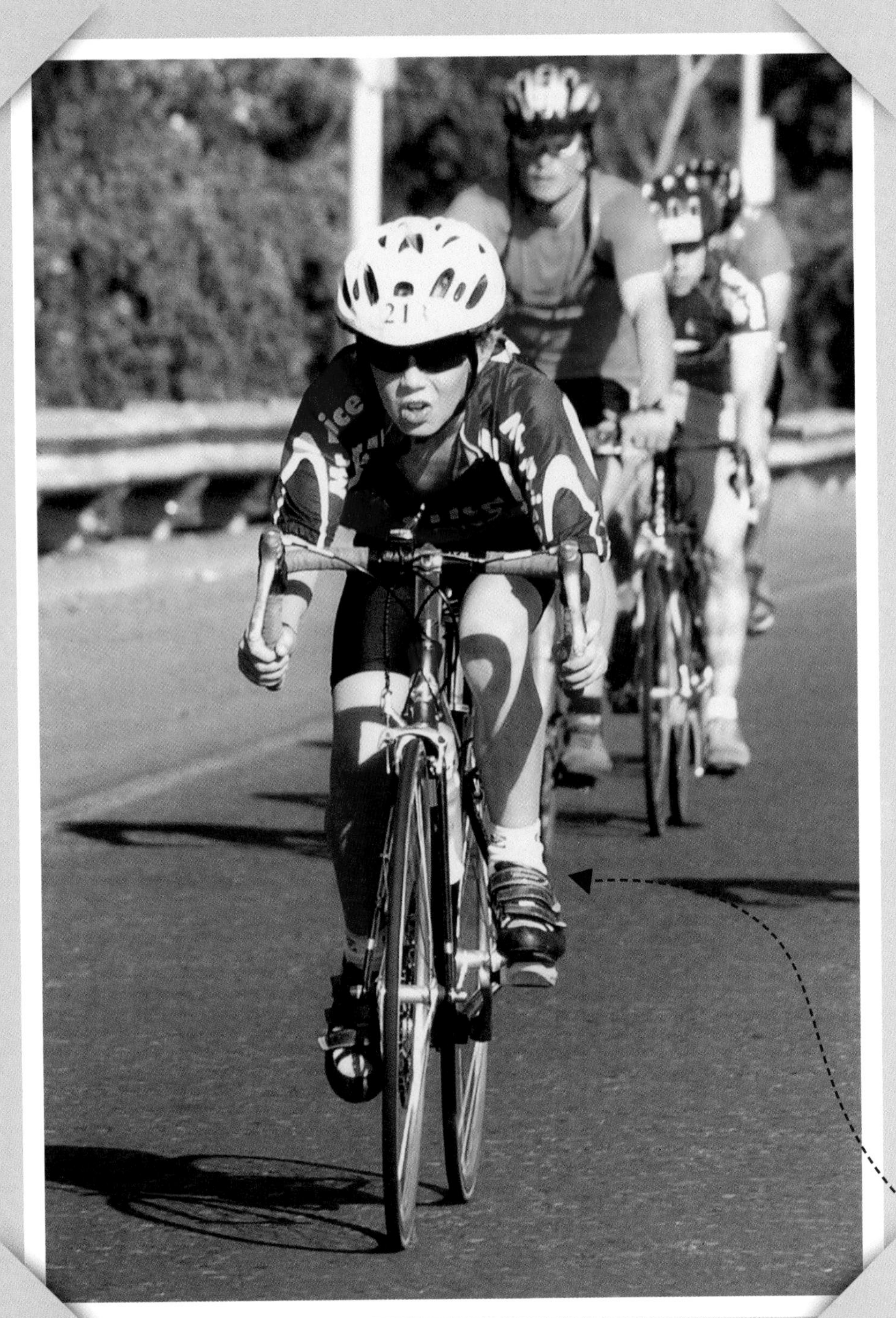

He made great friends with another young chap from England called Carlo.

Carlo's awesome kid's motorbike

Sports mad:

Caspar had always been an adrenaline junkie.

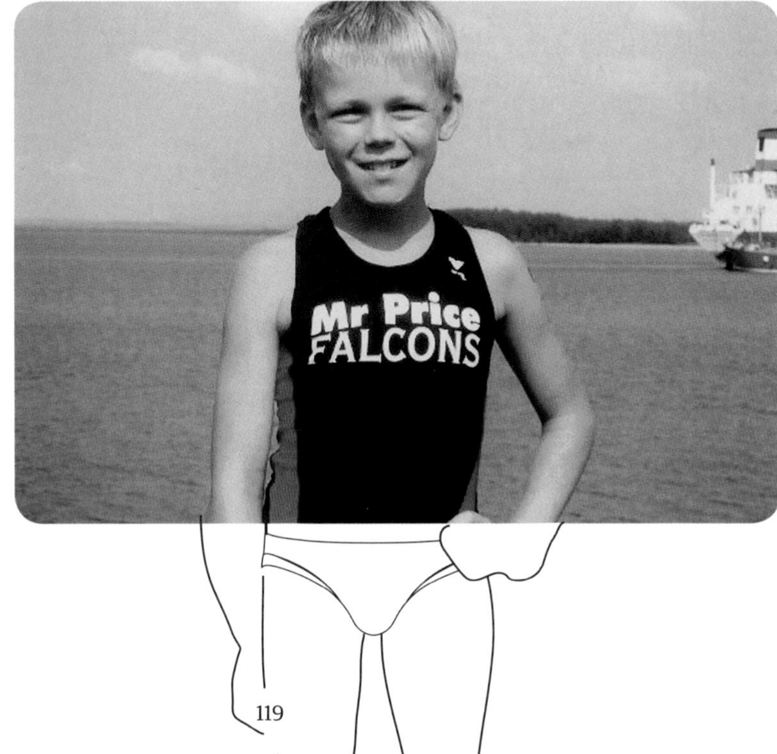

I've never seen someone look more of a wanker riding a bicycle in my life

CHAPTER SIXTEEN

Monkey Business

We arrived in Knysna in a state of high excitement. Back-to-school shopping was seriously getting underway. We were about to buy our eighth set of new school uniforms! We could open up a museum for all the uniforms we'd accumulated in the cupboard. Theo had changed schools six times, and Caspar three. I loved looking at schools and always thought the one around the corner might have something better to offer the children, and they agreed. **I don't remember this.**

Knysna was known for being a bit of a hippy town, so Montessori seemed ideal for both Theo and Caspar. Here, several age groups were taught together, and the general idea was to encourage self-learning. They had to muck out the school pigs, *My least favourite job for very obvious reasons!* look after the chickens **Quite good fun** and feed themselves by learning how to cook and wash up. **Which I'm still terrible at.** My kids were going to become fully rounded, self-sufficient human beings. There would be no more PlayStation or hanging around in shopping malls. From now on Caspar and Theo would be "nature kids", and their creative juices would start flowing in abundance. Finally, the kids would grow up in a way that I wanted, and I hoped they would be happy. We had found a school that I believed in, and although it was "alternative" I liked its philosophy.

Theo had to board (sleep on school grounds), even though we lived only half a mile away, because she was of an age where she could be negatively influenced by external factors. All Montessori kids had to board from aged 13. Caspar enjoyed being at home on his own with all the extra attention. **With Theo gone, it was all about me... finally!** and he loved Montessori because it was less formal than what he was used to. No one took a blind notice of his Tourette's, and there was loads of time to play.

We were about to buy our eighth set of new school uniforms! We could open up a museum for all the uniforms we'd accumulated in the cupboard.

I remember thinking I'd grow a proper beard by 16. I'm now 22 and still no luck

Caspar reading Harry Potter on the beach in France.

Caspar in London as a 9 year old.

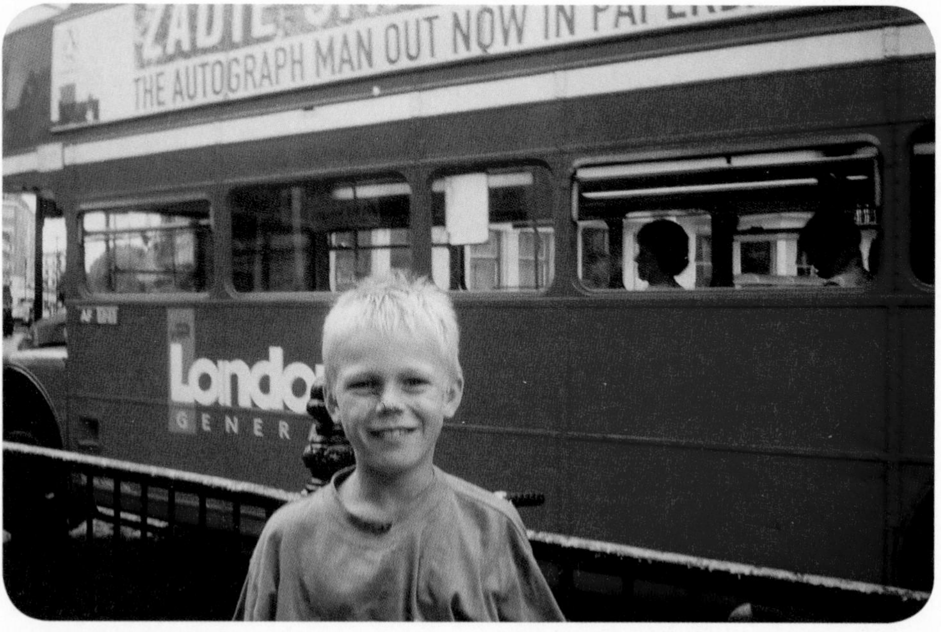

Caspar at a fish shop in Walberswick, Suffolk, on one of our annual holidays in England.

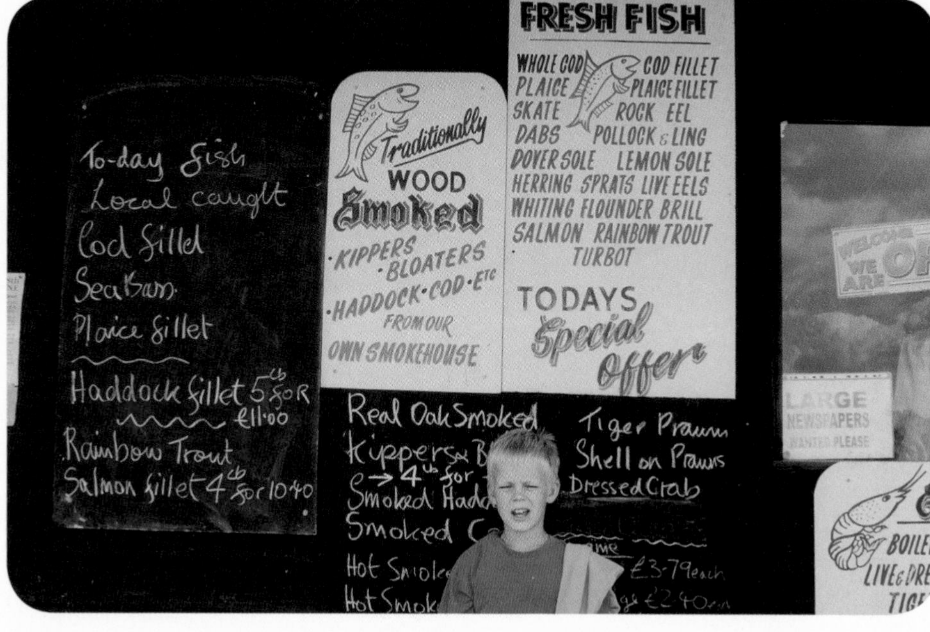

We were able to buy a house in the middle of a forest filled with baboons and monkeys and there was a lot of barking from the dogs when the baboons threatened to steal the fruit from our table. **Mom, this is possibly one of the most ridiculous sentences I've ever read.** They managed to steal a mobile phone once, but flung it to the ground when it didn't taste nice. Caspar used to scream at the monkeys to go away, but they took no notice of him. We were always worried that Mini-Me would be taken prisoner and dropped from a high branch. In reality, Mini-Me had other, more serious, problems to contend with. Firstly, he was nearly killed by a pellet gun. I suspect one of the neighbours was so fed up with him barking all day at the monkeys that they shot him. *That was so horrible. I still can't get my head around how anyone could do that to a tiny, defenceless dog. What is wrong with people?* It narrowly missed his heart, according to the vet. Then on another occasion he managed to escape out the front door and went missing. We went searching for him for hours, calling out for him in the dense forest. Eventually Bruiser, the pug, sniffed him out and we found a corpse-like chihuahua covered in blood and barely breathing in the undergrowth. **Again, this was so upsetting. I remember being hoarse from calling his name.** It was heart wrenching. He had been mauled and then tossed around like a plaything by our neighbour's boxer. We rushed him to the vet, and yet again he survived, after many days in hospital. **He may have been small, but he was a strong little bugger.**

We were able to buy a house in the middle of a forest filled with baboons and monkeys and there was a lot of barking from the dogs when the baboons threatened to steal the fruit from our table.

Knysna was not a normal South African town. It was more like a beautiful Mediterranean resort, situated on a large lagoon. Tourists from all over the world flocked into the expensive hotels and resorts, and there were loads of fine restaurants. Rich South Africans had holiday homes there, and during the Christmas season it was as busy as St Tropez in August. The rest of the year it was quiet enough though, so for us it was a mini paradise. While we hated the enormous divide between rich and poor, and the fact that the only people who had money there were white, we felt incredibly blessed to live there. It was beautiful, and, best of all, it was safe. I couldn't have lived there forever, but we loved our time there.

Caspar continued to play a lot of tennis outside of school and Peter, his coach, was ever so patient and encouraging. There wasn't much in the way of competitive sport on offer at Montessori. They didn't believe in competition as such. It didn't fit in with their ethos. So what were we doing sending these sports-mad kids to such a school? Theo hated boarding. She used to cry when we took her back every Sunday evening, and super-brainy Caspar **SUPER-BRAINY. Thanks, Mom. I'll pay you later!** wasn't progressing as we would have liked. He wasn't ever challenged, really, and started to fall behind his peers academically.

> He was worried about us as a family being agnostics, and was told by his teacher that we would never get to heaven unless we changed our ways... It really did worry Caspar that we were sure to go to hell.

So we took Theo out of Montessori and sent her to the state high school where she lasted two weeks, before buying yet another uniform and finally landing on her feet at Oakhill School. We couldn't really afford Oakhill for either of them. It was a wonderful school, with a liberal attitude, but it was expensive and all the other schools considered it snobby and only for spoilt rich kids. Rick very generously paid for Theo, and Caspar expressed a wish to go to Knysna Primary. It had a lot of sports on offer, and we liked the fact that it was completely multicultural. And there was no way he'd want to become a boarder at Montessori. **That would have been my idea of hell.** Caspar could never have coped with boarding and all its rules and regulations. He would have hated washing up and cooking, and being away from his mobile phone, which was banned at Montessori.

So off he went into a class of 30 kids from all different races and backgrounds. It was strongly Christian as most government schools are in South Africa. Caspar began each day singing hymns in assembly and he took to reading the Bible in bed at night. He was worried about us as a family being agnostics, and was told by his teacher that we would never get to heaven unless we changed our ways. Jon and I were quite amused by it all and considered it a passing phase, and thought it rather sweet. He attended special church services for children at the local evangelical hall, where there was much hymn singing and guitar strumming. It really did worry Caspar that we were sure to go to hell. He was quite secretive about his new beliefs because he knew we were agnostic. He also probably felt we'd take the piss out of him, which he wasn't far wrong about.

CASPAR: "Mom, can I go to a concert tonight?"

ME: "Where darling?"

CASPAR: "Oh, just somewhere in Old Place, I have the address."

We hopped in the car and, much to my amusement, the address in Old Place lead us to a church. I laughed my head off at Caspar trying to disguise the fact he was going to a church service.

I remember pulling the priest aside and asking him what's going to happen to my dad when he dies if he doesn't believe in God. He told me he'd go to hell. That's the moment I realized the whole religion thing wasn't for me.

An absolute masterpiece

CHAPTER SEVENTEEN

Just Joshing

Knysna Primary School was very traditional. As well as the heavy leaning towards Christianity, it also had prefects, head boys and girls, and traffic marshals. Exceptionally well-behaved kids would be rewarded with the opportunity to wear luminous waistcoats and hold up STOP signs to allow the children to cross over the road to the sports fields. Caspar desperately wanted to be both a traffic marshal and a prefect, and certainly considered himself to be head boy material. He liked the idea of wearing a blazer festooned with award badges, and he gave it his best shot. He always arrived at school on time and dressed in the correct fashion. He called his teachers "sir" and "ma'am" and tried terribly hard to be the model pupil.

I'm trying to work out how I could sound any lamer?

His Tourette's, which had been kept under control by medication, suddenly took a dive for the worse. The headshakes became continuous, he kicked his desk, and his whistling and grunting noises became distracting for his teacher. He pinched and punched himself until he bruised; things became really bad. Though I had tried to explain to her about the Tourette's, she didn't really understand that telling him to stop only made it worse. She suggested that, for his own good, he might prefer to sit outside in the hallway. It meant she couldn't handle him any longer. Instead of helping, it made him isolated from the rest of the class, and only worsened his anxieties.

His Tourette's, which had been kept under control by medication, suddenly took a dive for the worse. The headshakes became continuous, he kicked his desk, and his whistling and grunting noises became distracting for his teacher.

We changed medication and he had a terrifying reaction almost immediately. His eyeballs rolled back and all you could see were the whites of his eyes. He trembled and shook. He was in extreme fear; his legs went stiff. He couldn't walk, he couldn't see and he was screaming out,

"Do something, Mom, do something!"

OAKHILL

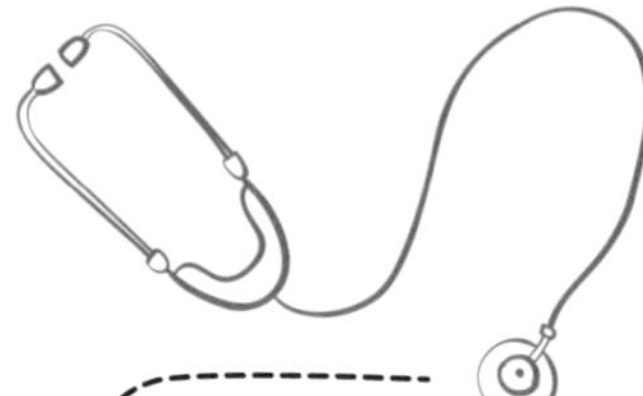

I was in a state of panic; it was so awful I honestly thought he might die as I rushed him to our wonderful doctor, Dr Deidre Richman. She was amazing and kept telling him he'd be alright as she drove us both to the hospital, where she administered an ultra strong dose of Valium, whereupon he gradually loosened up and came to his senses. I think he had probably suffered some kind of epileptic shock from the new drugs. **I remember having absolutely no control over this and feeling absolute panic. It was the worst feeling in the world.**

Back at Knysna Primary School, at the end of year assembly, Caspar was bitterly disappointed to find that he was made neither prefect or head boy. He always wanted to be the best, but the school had other ideas. As far as he was concerned the boys who were chosen weren't nearly as suitable as he was, and there and then he wanted to leave and join his sister at Oakhill. Caspar always had strong opinions and considered himself a leader. Again, it was his competitive feeling that he wanted to give everything his best. There was no way we could afford it but we desperately hoped he might win a scholarship. His academic grades were OK, but not enough to secure a place. He could probably have won a sports scholarship had they offered them but they only gave out academic scholarships, and we didn't think he'd stand much of a chance of getting one.

He sat the exam, which also involved performing a medieval poem about a ticking clock, after much coaching from his sister. They loved his acting ability, and the academic exam turned out to be more about IQ than revised subject knowledge. We were truly astonished when, a few weeks later a letter arrived from Oakhill School.

THE JOY OF LEARNING

Dear Mr and Mrs Lee,

We would like to thank you very much for entering your son into the Oakhill Scholarship Exam. It has been a difficult decision as there were so many applicants.

We would like you to come and meet the headmaster at your earliest convenience.

Kind regards,
Headmaster's Secretary

Headmaster's Secretary

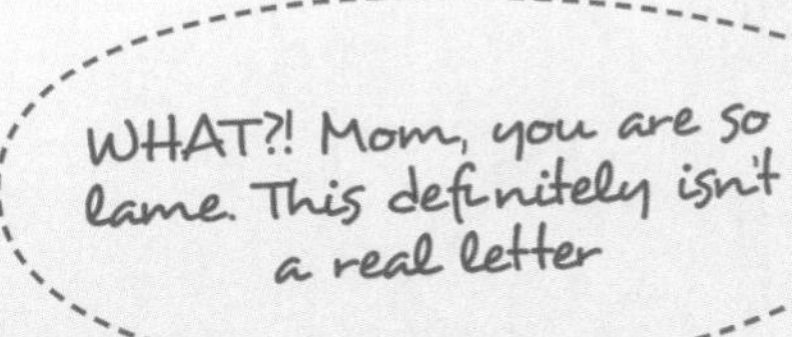

WHAT?! Mom, you are so lame. This definitely isn't a real letter

Uitsig Street Heuwelkruin Knysna 6571 South Africa

info@oakhillschool.co.za | Tel: +27 44 382-6506 | Fax: +27 44 382-5753 | www.oakhill.co.za

Holy Moly, what was that supposed to mean? Had he got it, or hadn't he? And what were they offering or not offering? We thought it might just have been a "thanks, but no thanks" scenario, and there was no one to fill us in on more details. We just had to wait patiently until the headmaster was ready to see us. And the Lees don't do patience at all.

A gruelling week later we entered the headmaster's office, who said, "Thank you for coming. The reason we have asked you in is that we have so many deserving applicants this year it's been very hard to chose who to offer the scholarships to and as you know our scholarship budget is limited by the restraints of..." He didn't finish the sentence.

And then, "What we'd like to know is... would you be in a position to keep Caspar at school here without a scholarship?"

So it was down to personal finances. Of course, we couldn't afford it so we said, "No, it would be a severe financial hardship. He wouldn't be able to be a pupil in this wonderful school without the scholarship you have on offer."

We left the headmaster's office a little disappointed. Again we had to endure another nail-biting week, and then the letter arrived.

WHOA. It read:

Dear Mr and Mrs Lee,

We are pleased to announce that we would like to offer your son Caspar Lee a 50 per cent scholarship for the rest of his term at Oakhill School.

He must abide by the school's regulations at all times and be an example to others.

We reserve the right to remove his scholarship on an annual basis if he does not fulfil his role and comply with the above conditions.

Kind regards,

Headmaster's Secretary

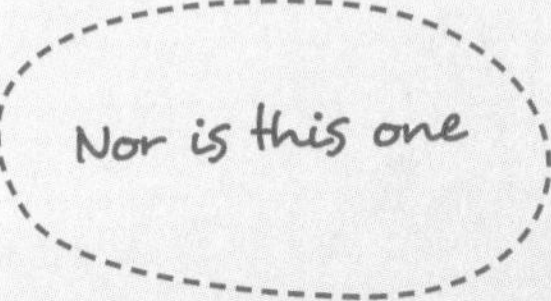

Uitsig Street Heuwelkruin Knysna 6571 South Africa
info@oakhillschool.co.za | Tel: +27 44 382-6506 | Fax: +27 44 382-5753 | www.oakhill.co.za

We were over the moon. He had done it! And what's more Caspar had won the largest academic scholarship on offer at the time. (And we thought he was just good at drama and sport.) We danced on the table, the dogs barked their heads off, and we went for pizza and tiramisu (double portion for Caspar) at Mario's, our wonderful local Italian restaurant, to celebrate. Rick came along too, he was so incredibly proud of his grandson.

Caspar explained his tics to his fellow classmates. From then on he never had a problem at school.

On Caspar's first day there, all the teachers were accommodating about his Tourette's. Mrs Lifson the Life Skills teacher (a common South African subject on the Matric curriculum; the South African equivalent of GCSEs) went out of her way to help. In his class they discussed how all children are different and how they should be proud of their differences. Anyone who wanted to discuss their own personal issues was invited to stand up and talk to the other kids about it. There was a lot of discussion. Several kids had a lot to say about their ADD and Caspar explained his tics to his fellow classmates. From then on he never had a problem at school. He could whistle away to his heart's content, and no one blinked an eye. I can honestly say Oakhill was the best place for him. It encouraged free thinking above all and kids who would often not fit in in a traditional sense thrived there. Many schools in South Africa are very old fashioned and traditional. They have a strict uniform policy, and a lot of things are based on the traditional British public school system.

Drama, Art and Music were taken as seriously as sport and academics. **This was definitely the school for me. There was a great balance between academics, culture and sports.** There was always something there to be good at. And once a week the pupils were allowed to wear "civvies" (home clothes).

Caspar became quite an eccentric when it came to civvies, often turning up in pyjama bottoms, slippers and a peaked cap. And because it was hot he would often arrive at school topless! I always hated those peaked caps of his, and still do, but they kind of became his trademark. And as for his pyjama bottoms, I think he may have started a fashion trend. A lot of kids at that time seemed to enjoy walking around in pyjama bottoms.

I was ahead of my time and loads of people wear them now. I always thought they were very stylish but I can't remember many people copying me back then sadly. I still wear them all the time – I don't know why anyone wouldn't? I'm never happier or more comfortable than when I'm lazing around in pyjama bottoms! I'm wearing some now, in fact!

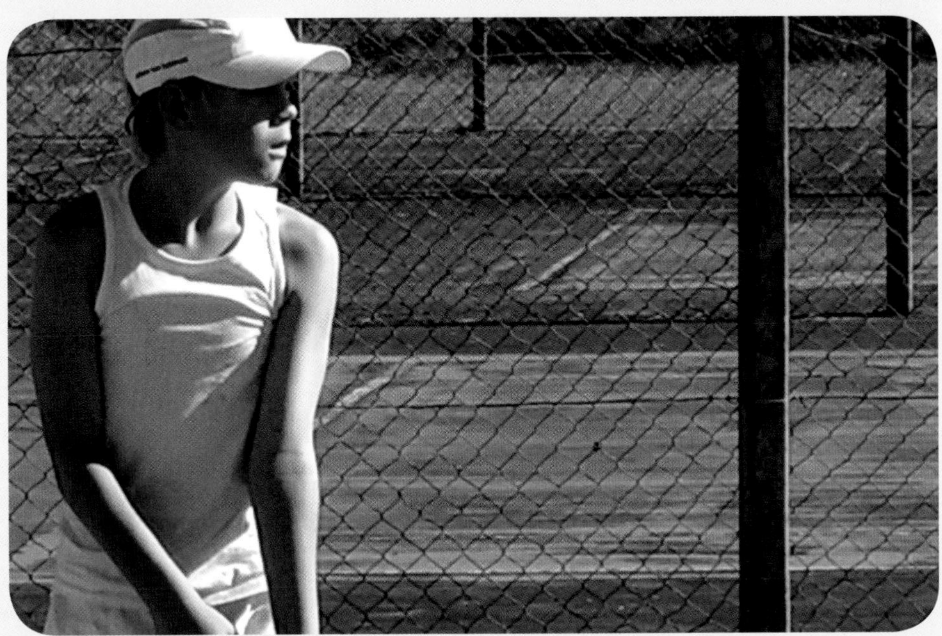

I on the other hand
LOVED those peaked caps!

It's Caspar with an "a", Dave Pryke

COLLEGE EXTRA-MURAL REPORT

NAME: CASPER LEE GRADE: 7

HOCKEY

Attendance	5	Attitude	5+	Enthusiasm	5++
Potential	4	Performance	4		

Strengths: Casper has the most amazing enthusiasm and is an incredibly passionate hockey player.

Focus: Casper has played goalie and impressed me tremendously. Many hours of goalie practice will make you "quality".

Comment: Casper has a huge role to play as a goal keeper and I strongly advise he focused on this discipline of the game.

Coach: Dave Pryke **Date:** 20/09/07

KEY: 1 - Poor 2 – Acceptable 3 - Average 4 - Good 5 - Excellent

This is how you spell it

COLLEGE EXTRA-MURAL REPORT

NAME: CASPAR LEE **GRADE:** 7

TENNIS

Attendance	4	Attitude	4	Enthusiasm	5
Potential	5	Performance	4		

Strengths: He is strong physical player and highly competitive

Focus: He is encouraged not to over-play his shots and use his strength strategically.

Comment: I am looking forward to see him perform during competition next term

Coach: [signature] **Date:** 19/09/07

KEY: 1 - Poor 2 – Acceptable 3 - Average 4 - Good 5 - Excellent

He quickly made friends, and caused quite a stir on the tennis court, where he had his first encounter with Josh.

Josh was in his grade at school and was quite the sports star. And, in the beginning, he didn't take much of a liking to Caspar or his tennis. In their first match Caspar beat him.

This tall young man was highly competitive and Caspar would constantly come home and moan about him. We told him not to worry about it, and to just get on with life and make other friends. I used to tell him that there was always going to be the odd person you don't get along with at school, it's no big deal. Josh was a strong character and so was Caspar, and neither of them liked being beaten on the tennis court.

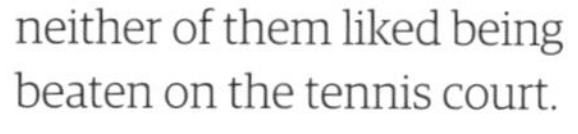

After a while they both settled down. One day, Josh arrived on our doorstep.

"Is Caspar in?" he asked, rather shyly.

Why on earth is Josh looking for Caspar? I thought.

"Sure, he's upstairs, go on up!" I said, all jollily.

From then on, for the next several hours all I heard was loud noises, laughter, and a lot of guns going off on Counter-Strike. By bonding over Counter-Strike, Josh and Caspar were able to work out their differences on and off the tennis court.

Josh and I totally bonded over Counter-Strike. We were in a clan called S3 - I can't remember what it stood for - with three other guys who lived nearby. Every weekend we'd bring our computers together at someone's house and play battles together. It was so much fun and that's when Josh and I started hanging out loads.

As soon as Caspar walked through the doors of that school on his first day wonderful friends and teachers surrounded him. I genuinely don't know what would have become of him if he hadn't gone to Oakhill.

Above:

Gaby, Caspar and Sasha.

Thirteen **and** ***Thriving***

"Smack his bottom!" shouted doctor.
"Waaa!" screamed the baby boy.
"Look honey it's the newest recruit to the Lee household." said his father to his mother. This was a fat red baby that was born on the 24 April 1994. He later grew up to be a teenager…. me. Hello my name is Caspar George Richard Lee. I am 13 years old and it is the year 2007. My life all started when I was 0. In a little town called London… I'm joking it is actually an amazing, huge, full of snotty people sort of town. Lucky, ily today is different.

After living in that huge city for about 1 year, my parents started to hear rumours, (true ones), about the bad behaved youth of our city. So my mother had an idea. When she was younger her mother, Patricia, (my deceased grand mother), lived in Africa, actually South Africa. ~~It was at that point,~~ My mother had made up her mind, in the same impulsive way I ~~am~~, that we would leave for Southern Africa. On the plane I made a bit of a mistake. I used to love my blanket and as soon as the poor old lady next to us through up, I was down there as quick as a hare. Sadly I later found out that it was in fact not my blanket but blue coloured puke. Ok enough of bad talk. When we landed in this certain airport called JHB National Airport, we had just started our new and improved lives.

At the tender age of 3, I had all ready got my SA accent and had learned to ride a bicycle. In London, I think it would have taken a lot longer. My sister and I would already

Right:

Caspar's story at Oakhill.

always watch Marry Poppins and sing the two children's parts as a duet.
I used to always sing "A spoon full of sugar helps the medicine go down, the medicine go down, the medicine go down." And I was always fascinated by the cartoons and the people on the same screen. I had long blonde hair down to my shoulders. I loved the Tele Tubbys and wore my costume with pride, luckily we have no photos. All while this was happening I was living on a lovely KZN midlins farm/restaurant.

Being five and flying was great. I had left pre-school to start my path to excellence or just finish. I had moved to Durban when I was 3 and a half and at this point in my life I was at Clifton Pre-Primary. I was a kid with enthusiasm and full of fun. Every brake I would play soccer. That's when I found my love for sport. I used to love to follow my sister's footsteps by swimming and running I also tried cricket but it wasn't for me. Later in grade to 2 I would start a bit of a liking for tennis.

To be 10 and a treasure. I had left Clifton at the end of grade 2 to start at my new school, Crawford. I was already in the senior primary when my mother moved us to a town called Knysna. At first I was a bit upset but then I started to settle in and make new friends. It was not long before I would become quite a well known boy in Knysna.

I am now 13. I go to Oakhill College. I had school hopped from Montersorri to Knysna Primary to Oakhill. I am really happy at my new school and have 3 great friends, Gabriel, Paul and James. I hope I will spend the rest of my schooling career at Oakhill. I play tennis and love it. I am already booked up for the day. This is Caspar Lee saying, "I hope you enjoyed my life because I sure did."

CHAPTER EIGHTEEN

The Sweet Smell OF SUCCESS

Caspar, aged 13, continued to play Counter-Strike and when our internet ran out of steam (i.e. Caspar had used our monthly data allowance in one day) he used to go to an internet café above the local cinema, known as a "movie house" in Knysna. The movie house was where the young teenagers used to hang out, and it was also next to Debonairs pizza parlour. It was small and only sat around 30 people, and the movie projector used to continually stop working during movies. There was more talking and pranks than actual movie watching.

Caspar used to take dates there. I have some of my best memories from around this time. I used to like holding hands with my dates because I took that as a sign that they liked me and that felt cool.

First there was Claudia, aged 12, a no-nonsense kid, who gave Caspar a run for his money. She was as strong-willed as he was and I liked her coming to the house very much. She loved dogs as well, particularly Mini-Me, which was a good thing. If you didn't like dogs, you wouldn't last long in our house. Caspar and Claudia used to play around, build dens in the forest and, what's more, she was about the only girl who managed to lure Caspar away from his computer.

Mom, you're confused, she was never my girlfriend and we've never been on a date. She was just a friend.

> Caspar had used our monthly internet data allowance in one day.

I considered the internet café a rather seedy place, filled with dubious characters, but we were told by management it was perfectly safe to leave your kids there and that they would keep an eye on them with a security camera at all times. On one occasion a suspicious character asked Caspar for help with a computer problem. While trying to assist the man, he had his Blackberry phone and wallet stolen.

Caspar's bedroom.

This is how I lived before Joe whipped me into shape

Ever the sportsman!

Let me explain a little better... The guy actually sent me instant messages through Counter-Strike while I was in the café and told me I had to give him my phone and that if I didn't he would come and get my family. I asked if I could keep my SIM card and he said yes, but then I was shaking too hard to take it out, so he took the whole thing. Maybe I should have told the guy sitting next to me what was going on, but I was too worried he'd have a gun. I heard the same man later robbed loads of people at gun point so I guess I got off lightly. And I had phone insurance, thankfully.

Hey, isn't that my phone?

Caspar was in a terrible state, more from the shock of it all than anything else. Here we were in ever-so-safe Knysna and *this* happened. They caught the man eventually and I had to take Caspar to the prison for an identity line-up. I think that was even scarier than the mugging. Although we were told the prisoners couldn't actually see us and that there was a two-way mirror separating us, the way that this perpetrator stared at Caspar gave us the heebie-jeebies. Caspar was sure this guy could see us, and would come and get us. However, Caspar kept his cool and identified him. It was like what you see in action movies, but as frightening as it was, I think Caspar found it rather thrilling! We discovered later that the thief was a serial mobile phone stealer and kids were his prey. Needless to say there were no more trips to the internet café, and from then on Caspar had to find friends with decent internet to carry on with his addiction to Counter-Strike.

He particularly liked going to Thesen Island, which was a gated estate that you had to drive on a bridge to get to because it was surrounded by the Knysna Estuary, a place everybody dubbed "The Lagoon". It consisted of islands interconnected by bridges and walkways. Most of his friends lived there, including Josh, and all the children were free to roam from house to house. Lots of people owned boats; it was a bit like spending time in the posh Hamptons in New York, or the Florida Quays. Caspar wanted us to move there too, and he'd spend much of his time with his friend Sasha (whose parents owned a local estate agency) perusing the brochures of houses for sale there.

I loved going there and hanging out with Josh and Sasha. We used to ring people's doorbells and run away and then watch them come outside, where we'd be hiding like spies.

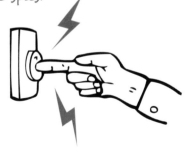

They caught the man eventually and I had to take Caspar to the prison for an identity line-up.

In the meantime, Jon and I struggled again financially to keep the family afloat. There was certainly no thought of houses on Thesen Island. We were lucky to have food on the table. We needed a new business idea, so on impulse (a familial trait) I decided to go to France to learn how to make chocolate!

One of my favourite films is *Chocolat* starring Juliet Binoche and Johnny Depp. I always had dreams of being Juliet Binoche in that role and becoming a chocolatier in France. I've always been a devout chocoholic. I love nothing better than snuggling up in bed with a bar of Cote D'Or with hazelnuts, and polishing the whole thing off in one go. It was only after discovering a very good chocolatier in South Africa who made sensational chocolate, and learning that making chocolate wasn't that difficult a thing to do, that I became inspired to try it for myself.

Can you imagine the kids' excitement with all the different chocolate tastings, dipping their fingers into the large vats of melted chocolate and having to sample all my latest concoctions?

I enrolled in an online chocolate making course, and passed with flying colours. My next step was a post-graduate degree in Chocolate, *Ha-ha, I loved telling all my friends at school that my mom was a student of chocolate!* in Paris, of course. Doing it for real, and in the chocolate-making capital of the world? My family thought I'd gone half-crazy, but I was in my element. The kids were very happy with the idea, of course. Lots of yummy chocolate for them! It also fulfilled my creative desires, and I hoped it would earn money as well.

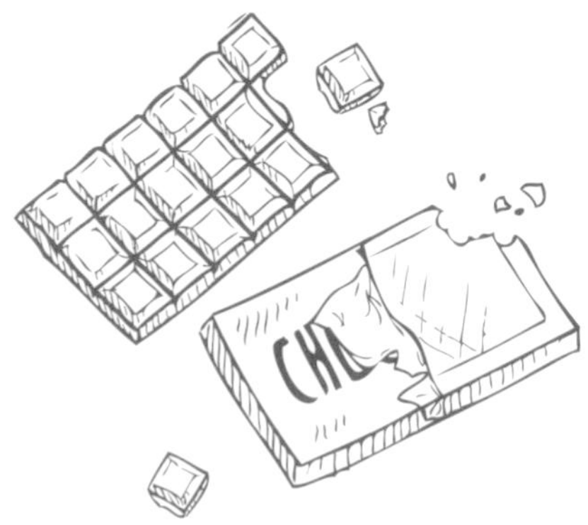

I came home and within a month we'd opened up our very own chocolate factory, which we called Chocolats Marionnettes. Can you imagine the kids' excitement with all the different chocolate tastings, dipping their fingers into the large vats of melted chocolate and having to sample all my latest concoctions? Caspar was in his element with an endless supply of white chocolate infused with saffron and cardamom, and Theo loved our Chocolate Mice.

This was like every kid's dream come true. I would seriously love to go back and do that all again now. It was so exciting that we could eat chocolate non-stop.

Caspar selling chocolates at the Artisan Market near Sedgefield.

What the children didn't like was the fact that Jon and I were never at home, and always working. Caspar complained bitterly when Jon was always late picking him up from school, and there was a fair amount of friction between them as a result. For a while we were so busy growing the business that I'd be working 12 hours a day and sometimes I even worked throughout the night to fulfil our massive orders.

On Saturdays Caspar would often be forced out of bed at 5am to come to the Artisan Market in nearby Sedgefield to sell the chocolate. Claudia was also there, helping her grandmother sell olive oil, so we thought it would be fun to set up shop and join the trade. It was also about time we thought Caspar should start some odd-jobbing at the market. Fair enough, he thought, until he had a bad day and he came back with only a few rand in his pocket. After that, he refused point blank to do the market ever again. He didn't see the point of working if you didn't make lots of money. **Like the true entrepreneur I was. To be honest, it wasn't as much the lack of money as the 5am wake-up time on a Saturday.** He'd come to visit our stall occasionally to hang out with Claudia, and eat Bar-One cake, a chocolate cake made with an ungodly amount of Bar-One (a South African version of a Mars bar) chocolate bars, and home-made vanilla fudge until he felt sick, but no more 5am starts for him. He considered his sleep far more important, and still does. Caspar likes his sleep, and he made it quite clear from then on that nothing would ever interfere with his weekend lie-ins!

CHAPTER NINETEEN

Big Changes

When Caspar was 14, Jon and I separated. It wasn't an easy time for any of us, though the kids may have half expected it as there was constant friction between us while the marriage fell apart.

When I told the kids, they were initially shocked but not entirely surprised.

I didn't think divorce was possible with my parents. But then, I guess no one does. It was such a big shock. I remember going to school that day and feeling really out of it and not focusing properly at all. I knew my mom and dad had fought a bit around that time but I never thought they would actually break up.

You always hear stories about other people's parents getting divorced but I never imagined for a moment mine wouldn't be together forever. Everything happened quite quickly and it made me realize that my parents were real people and their lives weren't perfect like all children probably imagine. They went through stuff just like everyone else, and just because they were my parents it didn't mean they knew everything. They had their own stuff going on behind the scenes Theo and I didn't know about.

I think I really started to understand things more later on down the line when both of my parents met new partners. It all made more sense to me and I could see that it was the right thing in the long term because they were both so much happier.

I spoke to Theo about the divorce a lot at the time and it brought us much closer together. It was great to have my big sister there throughout it all.

I love you mom

you make my heart boom and you make me cry when you cry.

I love you so much

you are the best mom there is.

love
caspar
atherwys
your son.

P.S
I HOPE YOU GET BETTER.XXXXXXXXXXXXXXXXXXX

Theo was old enough to really understand because family life hadn't been good for quite a while. She was sad but she saw the positive side of it as well. There would be less friction in the house, and if we were both happier apart then it was a good thing for all of us. It's never nice for kids to see parents arguing and not getting along like you expect them to do.

At 14, Caspar was still quite young and he was worried about how it might impact his life. Where was he going to live? What was Dad going to do? Would he still be able to go to Oakhill?

I answered all his questions as openly as I could, and assured him that his life wouldn't change that much, and that if there were changes it would be for the better. I was in a more fortunate position than Jon because I had met someone who I'd fallen in love with, and that's always hard for the other partner, being left without the support of a loved one. It was a very hard time for him and he suffered a lot. A few months later, Jon met his future wife Lindsey, who was in fact a childhood friend of his and was born on the same day in the same hospital in Horsham, West Sussex.

I met Sham, the kids' future stepdad when, on another crazy impulse, I went to run a half-marathon on a remote island off the west coast of Ireland, and we fell in love. That was it. There was no turning back.

Sham came to Knysna shortly afterwards and we rented a house on Thesen Island, where Caspar and Theo came to stay. Caspar was in his element in this beautifully decorated holiday home, with its high speed internet and carpets smelling no more of dog pee.

Sham and I got on well straight away. He had a great sense of humour and he really impressed me because he was into sports.

I assured [Caspar] that his life wouldn't change that much, and if there were changes it would be for the better.

After only a couple of days there Caspar excitedly dragged Sham to Vanita's estate agency to look at houses, for real. Within a week we had bought our very own house on Thesen, situated right on a canal, and one that Caspar had been eyeing up for quite some time. Two weeks later we moved in lock, stock and barrel, and Mini-Me joined us. And of course yet another dog soon arrived. Sham bought a lovely Labrador puppy and we named her Summer. Sham was a fast mover and he wanted his new family settled as quickly as possible. We decided to get married.

He took on the role of stepdad to the best of his ability, and having been a fine sportsman himself, he was keenly interested in Caspar's hockey and tennis. As Sham was retired, he was free to take the kids to school, pick them up on time, and attend every single match.

Caspar, me and Theo at my wedding to Sham.

Caspar with his new family

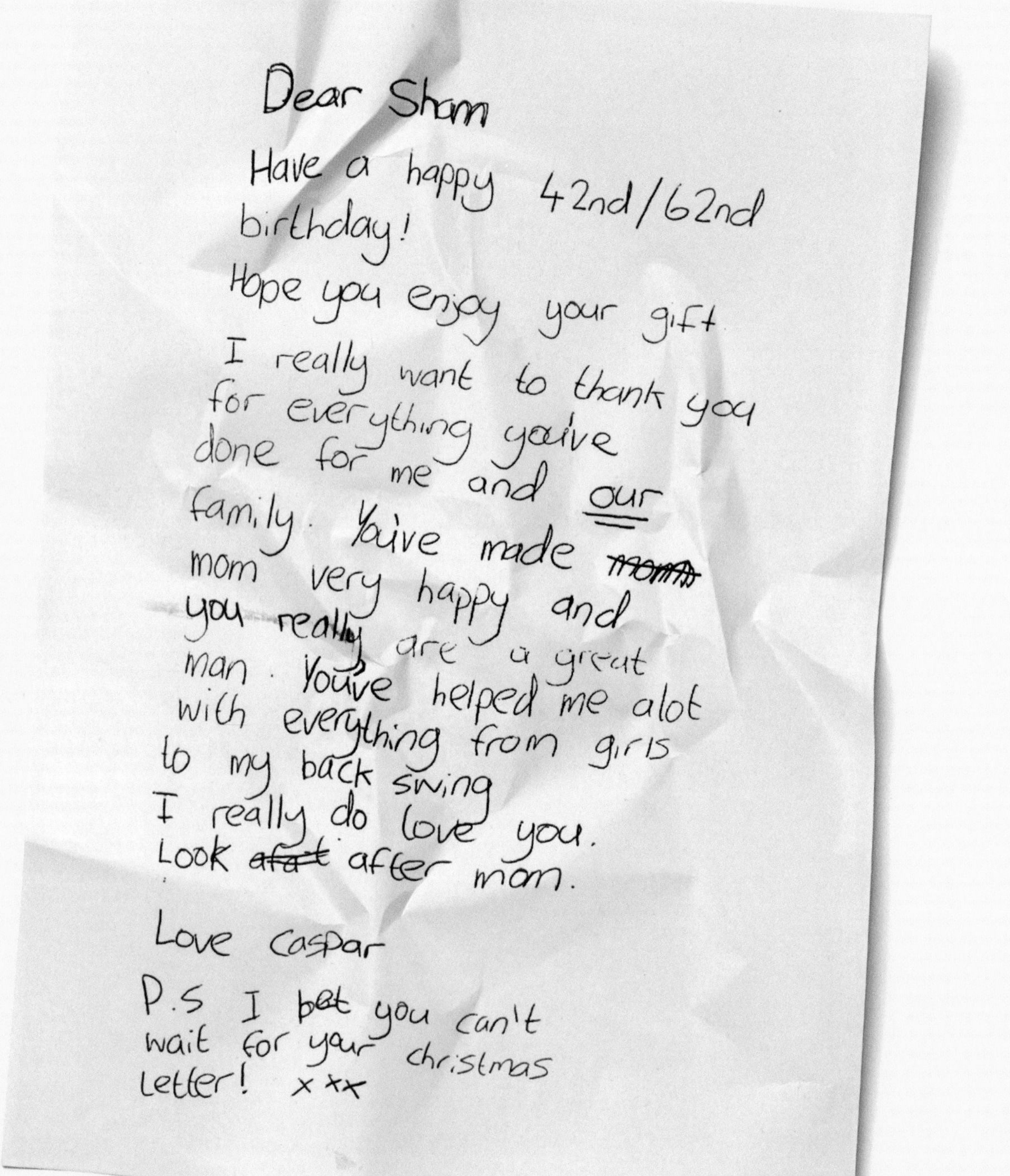

Dear Sham

Have a happy 42nd/62nd birthday!

Hope you enjoy your gift

I really want to thank you for everything you've done for me and our family. You've made ~~mom~~ mom very happy and you really are a great man. You've helped me alot with everything from girls to my back swing

I really do love you.

Look ~~afat~~ after mom.

Love Caspar

P.S I ~~bet~~ you can't wait for your christmas letter! x x x

Caspar and Sham had a close bond.

One day, when they were stopped at traffic lights on the way home from school, Caspar had a bit of an identity crisis that had to be aired.

CASPAR: "If you and Mom get married will I still be Caspar Lee or will I be Caspar Riordan?"

SHAM: "You'll still be Caspar Lee, of course."

CASPAR: "Oh, phew, that's OK."

No way did Caspar want a name change. That was the only worry he had about the new family arrangement. He liked being Caspar Lee. They continued to see their dad, who worked not far away, in the chocolate factory.

So, Caspar's dream of living on Thesen Island came to fruition. He had a lovely big room and Wi-Fi was installed. Result! His computers got bigger and bigger and if he wasn't on the hockey pitch, or playing tennis, he was in front of the screen. He'd stay up until all hours playing FIFA on the PlayStation, effing and blinding; getting him up in the morning remained, as always, a constant nightmare! Our neighbours were often shocked at his bad language and came to complain. I felt guilty about being a bad parent by allowing him to stay up late, particularly in the mornings when he didn't want to get up. All teenagers are like that, Mom.

He'd stay up until all hours playing FIFA on the PlayStation, effing and blinding... Our neighbours were often shocked at his bad language and came to complain.

CASPAR: "I feel sick, Mom. I can't go to school!"

He buries his head in the pillow and tosses away from me.

ME: "Come on, Caspar, I know you were up half the night."

Squirm, squirm, as he bundles himself into a tight ball.

CASPAR: "I can't go, I haven't finished my history project."

I decide I have to be strong for once and in a loud voice I boom:

"Get up, now, Caspar, you have to go to school"

But in spite of that I get the usual response:

"But, Mom, you don't understand, I need to sleep, and then I can get my history project done at home. And I feel sick." Blah blah blah.

> I wanted him to be more creative like his sister, who was busy making videos all the time. I'd catch her filming bits of her favourite show *The OC* from the television and then edit the clips into her own trailer.

So I resort to my fail-safe back up.

"OK, I'll have to talk to Sham."

In walks Sham, who says rather firmly:

"Up now, Caspar, we're leaving in five minutes."

And up he gets with no more nonsense.
Sham had a way with Caspar that no one else ever had. Caspar respected him, and a few boundaries were put in place. There was no more skiving school and there were no more giving into demands to buy the latest tennis racquet. Caspar always thought that a new tennis racquet would improve his game and he was ever so persuasive when it came to acquiring new ones. He started with Wilson and then progressed to Babolat, each racquet becoming slightly more expensive each time. You could hardly move in our store room without tripping over tennis racquets! Sham taught Caspar that "more" is not the answer to all your problems.

"Use what you have, boy!" Sham would say in his strong Irish (Cork) accent.

"A new tennis racquet/hockey stick/computer/X-Box won't make a blind bit of difference!"

This is very true, and now I completely understand where they were coming from.

So Caspar began to learn a few life skills that up until now he had been sorely lacking. This was partly my responsibility. I tended to spoil him and always gave in, mostly because I wanted peace, even if it was only temporarily.

The same thing applied when he was picked up from school. He always needed something desperately after school, whether it was a chicken pie from Ole Mama's Bakery, or an electric toothbrush, there was always something on his mind that he simply couldn't do without when he came out of school. It was kind of like an obsession and definitely had something to do with his Tourette's.

Sham decided to clamp down on it. Before Caspar got into the car after school, and had the time to even utter one word, he would say:

"No, Caspar. The answer is no!"

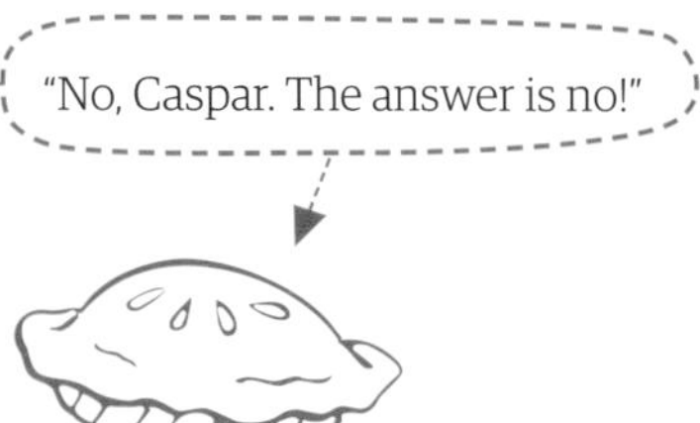

By golly, it seemed to work. I'd be there to meet him at home and he'd have forgotten all about what he "needed" and he'd scuttle off up to his bedroom to play on the computer. Computers were a kind of escape from all the turmoil going on in his head and he'd also get temporary relief from his tics. We allowed him to play computer games as much as he wanted, so long as he got his homework done, and went to school without complaining. I wasn't sure it was the right thing to do. All other sensible parents restricted computer games, but they didn't have a kid like Caspar. It could have gone terribly wrong, but so long as he was socializing and still playing sport, we let him continue.

I think it was while I was playing video games that I first learnt to make people laugh. When I played them I was in character and I had a microphone so I could speak to other people and put on voices and act silly. I was always trying to be funny and I felt like I could do it a lot more then than I could in real life. I guess it felt safer in a way because I was being someone else. It was definitely great practice for my later videos.

I wanted him to be more creative like his sister, who was busy making videos all the time. I'd catch her filming bits of her favourite show *The OC* from the television and then edit the clips into her own trailer. She had her own *The OC* Fan Page on Bebo (a social network before Facebook) and uploaded these types of videos regularly. I remember one of them becoming the most watched video on Bebo for a whole week! We were all very proud and I was sure Caspar took inspiration from all of this. In fact, I gave him his first little camera for Christmas that year, which he tossed in the drawer and never used.

I did appreciate it, but I didn't really have a passion for photography because this was before Instagram. Like any younger sibling I did like to copy what Theo did and her early interest in videos definitely influenced me, but it was a while longer before I became involved with YouTube.

Caspar wanted to be a lawyer, he said, or a business entrepreneur, anything that would enable him to be rich and travel First Class. Being creative and making arty films like Theo was a "girly" thing and definitely wasn't Caspar's cup of tea. There was also far too much work involved with all that editing and filming. Fourteen-year-old Caspar wasn't even vaguely interested in any of it. He'd much prefer to kick a ball with his classmates at break time than direct his friends in front of a camera. And when Theo tried to involve him, he'd often squirm away, saying he didn't like being in her videos. Maybe he just wasn't quite ready, but we can safely assume that something was beginning to spark inside of him, something which would soon ignite.

CHAPTER TWENTY

Poker Face

When Caspar was 15 he became goalie on the school first hockey team and it was a position he greatly enjoyed. He was good at team sports and it took away a lot of the pressure he put himself under when it came to individual sports, like tennis. His frustration on the tennis court drove him bananas. He'd scream and shout at himself and break many tennis racquets, flinging them to the ground in anger. But hockey was different. I liked being part of a team and I felt like we were all in it together. I'm a perfectionist so I always tried my hardest, but knowing I had the rest of the guys backing me up, and because the pressure wasn't all on me personally, I enjoyed it more.

The exasperations were still there but he didn't have to feel so individually responsible. And he was a mighty good goalkeeper. He was fearless and a fast mover and not many balls got past him. He gave up tennis and loved going on hockey tours with all his best mates. Josh was by then the number one hockey player in the school Josh must never read this and along with their mates they spent hours practicing. Although Oakhill was a very small school, their hockey team became a force to be reckoned with. A lot of it boiled down to PeeBee, their wonderful coach who was also a fantastic maths teacher.

PeeBee understood Caspar and was critical as well as super encouraging. PeeBee was a legend. He was tough when he needed to be but always supportive. I really looked up to him. He was a little older than most of the other teachers and definitely matched Caspar in his own eccentricity. He was a wine connoisseur as well. On one occasion, Caspar took his team on a wine tasting jaunt and came home with a case of hugely expensive Cabernet Sauvignon Reserve, which we were secretly hoping he might give us as a present. However, he said he was going to "lay it down" for several years so that it would come to full maturity when he was old enough to be allowed to drink it.

Although Oakhill was a very small school, their hockey team became a force to be reckoned with. A lot of it boiled down to PeeBee, their wonderful coach who was also a fantastic maths teacher.

Being a goalie is a lot harder than it looks, okay?

taboo

Josh (top left), Caspar (middle bottom), PeeBee (second from right).

We were surprised that he'd spent all his birthday money on wine, but obviously he had been so impressed with the wine tasting experience that he couldn't say no. And then the wine became a bargaining tool. If Caspar needed extra pocket money for poker, *This makes me sound like I was hanging out in seedy gambling dens. I wasn't!* he would sell us a bottle. And if he forgot a Christmas present, another bottle would be produced. I'll never forget that wine and its deliciousness... even though I had to buy it off my own son! *I told you I'd make a good business entrepreneur!*

At the end of the year, Caspar was presented with the PeeBee Trophy for someone who had excelled on the hockey pitch. PeeBee and Caspar had a close bond. I asked PeeBee to write down some of his memories of Caspar for this book and this is what he said:

"My first encounter with Caspar was at an indoor hockey arena in George where I met this perpetual motion fearless creature. I instantly decided he would be my goalkeeper in what was to become an excellent Under 16 team.

Caspar was a fearless goalkeeper but he was stubborn, he would stand in goal with his lily white legs and play one-handed, without fear of looking gawky.

Caspar would always sit next to his friend Luke Bell in Maths and Luke knew all the answers to every single question. He would sneak the answer to Caspar who would blurt out the correct answer and await teacher's approval with a beaming smile. I remember one time when I challenged Luke and Caspar to determine the nearest two palindromic dates before the year 2000. I sent them outside and within a minute they came in to claim the R100 reward. Later I found that the calculation was Luke's.

Caspar is not just a bag of fun. He is tough in his soul – and humble and determined."

Caspar was presented with the PeeBee xtrophy for someone who had excelled.

PeeBee was the most inspiring teacher Caspar ever had, and even to this day if PeeBee doesn't like a Facebook comment from Caspar he'll let him know. So Caspar, you'd better watch out!

Caspar's other great sport at the time – if you can call it a sport – was the aforementioned poker. Josh's dad, Leslie, was a poker aficionado and used to invite Caspar over to play. There wasn't much money involved, maybe 100 rand or so (around £4), but Caspar became quite good at playing.

Caspar persuaded me, and I don't quite know how, **It's still a total mystery to me too** to lend him my credit card so that he could play poker online. I had a strict 200 rand rule and said that he could only borrow that amount off my card and the rest was up to him. But it wasn't quite as simple as I thought it was. It never is with poker, is it?

While Caspar was building up quite a healthy online account balance, Josh who had wangled a similar deal from his father managed to lose his allowance. As every poker player knows hope springs eternal. So Caspar was loaning Josh a portion of his winnings. In order to pay Caspar back Josh told his Mom that prices in the school tuck shop had gone up, and that he needed more money for food. Eventually the real story bubbled out and Poor Josh's poker exploits came to an end. A warning to you all out there: gambling is not plain sailing. But Caspar was lucky and, thankfully, did well. I never lost a cent.

It was around this time that both the kids were assigned to make a short film for a school drama project. Caspar got together with his best mates at the time, Josh and Luke, and they made this incredibly silly film where Josh and Caspar played two detectives called Thompson and Thompson (taken from *The Adventures of Tintin*, Caspar's favourite books). Poor Luke is put on trial for murder and it all goes pear-shaped when Rosie, the new girl in their class and, awkwardly, the murder victim, turns out not to be dead at all. It had a very lame script and was terribly acted, but it was also somewhat cute in its terribleness. You can watch it on YouTube. *You'll soon realize how utterly brilliant it was.* They filmed it on Theo's camera, and I can't remember who did the edit, but I suspect it was Theo. *It was.* It certainly wasn't going to win any awards but they had a lot of fun doing it. This was Caspar's first shot at filming, and within a few weeks he would discover YouTube and decide he wanted to do more. A lot more.

AND SO IT ALL BEGINS

That's still my favourite camera I ever had

YouTube was in its infancy and had only been going for a couple of years – but you could sense that it was changing the way people watched and shared online content. Although Caspar loved his all-night-pyjama-party Counter-Strike sessions with Josh, Jake and Luke, he also thought that YouTube could offer him something more. He could act, he could be as crazy as he liked, and he might get a few followers as well. I knew little about YouTube, but I loved the fact that Caspar was finally thinking about doing something creative.

Caspar's first video was hilarious. He developed this character called Dick of Africa who had an Australian accent and spent much of his time sitting in the bath surrounded by floating rubber ducks and bubbles, commenting on various life experiences. Dick used to talk about the many interesting things to do in the bath, including reading Anatole Kaletsky's book *Capitalism 4.0* while playing with the ducks. Dick was a bit dim, but crazy and adorable. Kind of like me, apart from the dim part, obviously. We all so loved that video and when he uploaded it he got several likes very quickly, but I suspect most were from his mates. Actually, these were mainly from accounts I created myself.

I loved the fact that Caspar was finally thinking about doing something creative.

Dick didn't have many friends so "Andrew", a colonial wooden statue of an African man sporting a white hat and a blue shirt, became Dick's best friend. Dick always went to Andrew for advice because Andrew was a proper upstanding (if wooden) citizen. Andrew put up with a lot, but never complained. He was always there for Dick and all his foibles. No, Josh, he wasn't based on you.

And that was the beginning of it all. From then on, Caspar never looked back. His followers grew to more than a hundred and we thought that was serious success. My one concern was who might be watching my son sitting in a bath all day? The internet was a big world open to all and who knew who these followers might be. But Caspar was happy and excited about his new project, and I was so pleased to see him do something other than play Counter-Strike that I decided to encourage him. None of us could ever have expected quite how big Caspar's hobby was going to get.

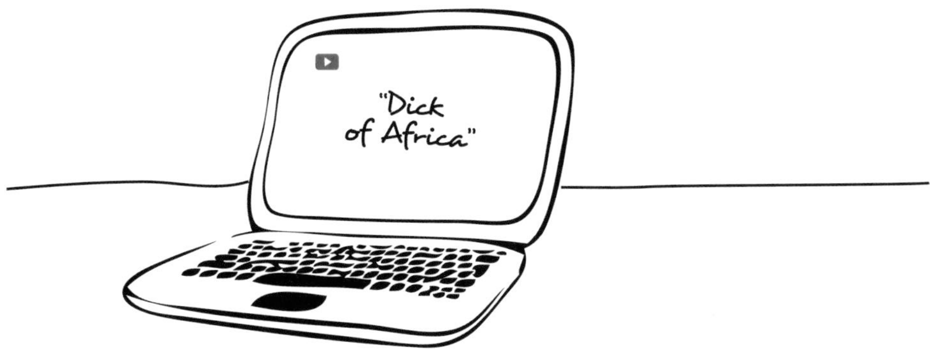

CHAPTER TWENTY ONE

500 Followers

Caspar spent quite a lot of his school holiday time in either England or Ireland. In July he would go to England to stay with his cousins, Christoph and Isabella, whose parents had a house near the Hurlingham Club in London. **I like the way my mom expects everyone to know where that is. For those who don't, it's a private members' club in West London.** He adored going there. It was so different from South Africa, with its manicured lawns, antique furniture and scrumptious afternoon teas. The Hurlingham Club became his stomping ground. There were tennis courts and a grand swimming pool where there were lots of opportunities to meet girls. He and Christoph had the freedom to wonder around unsupervised. I think Caspar had his first kiss there, but I may be wrong. He'll have to fill you in on that. *This is the one I talked about earlier, Mom. Keep up!*

The two of them came sailing with Sham and myself in Spain, but I'm not sure how much they actually enjoyed it. I think they suffered from seasickness a bit, or perhaps it was boredom? **It was both.** However, they entertained themselves by decorating the walls of their cabin with magazine pictures of beautiful girls and stayed below deck. **This sounds so wrong, Mom.** Christoph had a machine that translated English into Spanish and they had a blast one night, venturing out to dinner in Baiona, all on their own with this little machine. They were gone for hours and had a slap up meal of beef fillet and crab - God knows what else happened! We were happy to give them a little bit of independence, but we were even happier when they arrived back on the boat still in one piece.

SICK BAG

We used to spend Christmas in Ireland because most of Sham's five grown up children lived there. There were his step brothers and sisters to get to know: Sham Junior, Sally, David, Joanna and Mark. They got on really well but Caspar was never too overjoyed about the house, as beautiful as it is, it was old and rather dusty, which didn't help his asthma, and the weather was predictably terrible. Caspar preferred the sun and high season in Knysna, where Christmas was celebrated al-fresco and his friends would be just around the corner. The second Christmas we spent in Ireland was one of the coldest ever, and you could hardly leave the house because of all the ice on the roads. **I feel cold just thinking about it. As much as I love living in London now, I don't think I'll ever get used to the cold weather.**

Sham, me, Caspar and Theo outside Ile De Pain in Knysna.

So Caspar did his normal thing when things outside weren't so much fun. He took to going to bed with his laptop and never once got out of his pyjamas. He borrowed my credit card for online poker (again) and spent a good few days hiding out in his bedroom. Then he announced that he had won over one thousand euros, and we made him stop there and then so that he wouldn't lose it all. And you know what he did with his money? He went out and bought a brand new camera, a Canon D600, so that he could make better YouTube videos. There is no way I would have bought him a camera like that, however much he'd pleaded with me.

> I was so excited to show the kids the Eiffel Tower and to go to fabulous eating establishments, but it was so bitterly cold Caspar wasn't at all impressed.

We stopped off in Paris en route back to South Africa. It was supposed to be a treat. I was so excited to show the kids the Eiffel Tower and to go to fabulous eating establishments, but it was so bitterly cold Caspar wasn't at all impressed. We climbed to the top of the Eiffel Tower and nearly froze to death. He gave it two thumbs down, particularly with all the walking we made them do along the banks of the River Seine. Caspar couldn't wait to get back to sunny Knysna. He just didn't get what Paris was all about. Until, of course, he took his girlfriend Gaby, a few years later for Valentine's Day. *It's an amazing place. I was probably too young to appreciate it back then.*

Back in South Africa, "Dick" carried on with all his antics on a weekly basis, and Caspar somehow managed to get a few appearances on YouNow. At home he was rarely off the computer, and his followers were creeping up to the 500 mark.

For the Easter holidays we travelled to Sri Lanka to visit Caspar's grandfather, Rick, who had recently moved there from South Africa. We zigzagged around in tuk-tuks, and one day Theo and Caspar saved a man and his daughter from drowning in the hotel swimming pool, where we'd just eaten lunch. I was so proud of them.

Wow, yeah! I remember how I froze when I saw the man latching on to his baby's armbands to stay afloat. The baby's head kept being dunked under. It was Theo who dived in, losing her bikini top in the process. I retrieved it for her as she lifted the man to safety. It all happened so fast, but luckily Theo and I were watching and were able to do something. And I somehow also managed to hand Theo the rest of her bikini before anybody noticed.

Animal crazy:
Caspar was never short of furry friends in our house.

We stayed in a slightly run down beach resort where the three of us shared a room, and Caspar gallantly slept on the floor. During the day he refused to leave the hotel because he was so obsessed with building his YouTube channel. Theo and I gave up trying to get him to go to the beach with us, and when we came back one evening he was so overjoyed to tell us that he'd reached 1000 followers. What a milestone that was! We couldn't believe it, and we forced him to come to the beach with us to celebrate.

Needless to say, when we returned from Sri Lanka a new computer was required. He needed, he said, a MacBook Pro. He'd made yet more money from online poker and we agreed to help out with the rest. He was either going to become a professional poker player or a YouTuber – we weren't too sure which – but he definitely no longer wanted to be a lawyer. We kept him on top of his homework and hoped he'd be inspired to work harder at school after a brilliant job shadowing experience at Knysna Radio, the local FM station in our small town, where he spoke brilliantly on the airwaves – a natural entertainer we all thought. If only he'd try harder at his drama practical exams! We tried to the best of our ability to keep him motivated at school, endlessly nagging him, but after a while we gave up. As long as he wasn't getting behind at school it was OK by us, and Caspar was clever enough to keep up. He had an amazing ability to do very little at school, yet still do reasonably well. I also began to feel he was seriously on to something, as far as YouTube was concerned. He used to show us his videos, and I watched every single one of them before they went out.

Theo and I gave up trying to get him to go to the beach with us, and when we came back one evening he was so overjoyed to tell us that he'd reached 1000 followers.

"Mom, take a look, what do you think?"

Invariably the reply would be:

"Wow, Caspar, that's cool. Well done!"

"Are you sure, Mom, it's OK, really?

"Yes, really!"

"WOOHOO! Thanks, Mom!!" with big bulging eyes and a massive grin.

Caspar, like most kids at that age, often had a bit of self-doubt and looked for encouragement from friends and family. He didn't really need it – his videos were good enough to hold their own – but we all gave him a lot of encouragement along the way.

www.oakhillschool.co.za
"The answer's not always in the textbook."
Caspar Lee
Matriculated in 2012
Social Media
Celebrity

I really can't believe I'm on the bus.
I've never seen it in real life. Maybe someone just
Photoshopped this and it's all one big sick joke.

CHAPTER TWENTY TWO

A Spot of Bother

Caspar's acne came as quite a shock to us all. It began with a couple of pimples which oozed a bit *Gross, Mom,* but however much he squeezed them they wouldn't go away. I didn't take much notice and told him not to worry so much and eat less chocolate and they would surely clear up. But over a period of a few months the pimples spread, turning Caspar's beautiful face into a splattered maze of spots. He was not a happy chappy.

We tried all the usual remedies:

1. Dove soap, which is free of chemicals and fragrances.
2. Witch hazel, to dry out the puss.
3. Toothpaste, which had a nice stinging feeling, so it must be good. → *Didn't work...*
4. Tea tree oil, to kill the bacteria.
5. Luxurious face masks at Pezula Spa.
6. Zinc – apparently many acne sufferers are zinc deficient.
7. My anti-ageing moisturizer.
8. Diet, but Caspar's not the greatest at them. He could never give up Pringles, pizza or tiramisu!
9. Homeopathy.

Nothing seemed to work so he would have to go to school with his face covered in thick foundation. *You're making me sound like a Kardashian, Mom.* Luckily, he wasn't alone in his problem, as Josh and Luke were also afflicted by an onset of acne. But again, at Oakhill, nothing was a big deal and the boys just got on with it, pimples or no pimples.

> But over a period of a few months the pimples spread, turning Caspar's beautiful face into a splattered maze of spots.

After a year or so of trying everything we resorted to skin doctors and Caspar was put on heavy-duty antibiotics, which, after about eight months, did the trick nicely, and he was ever so pleased.

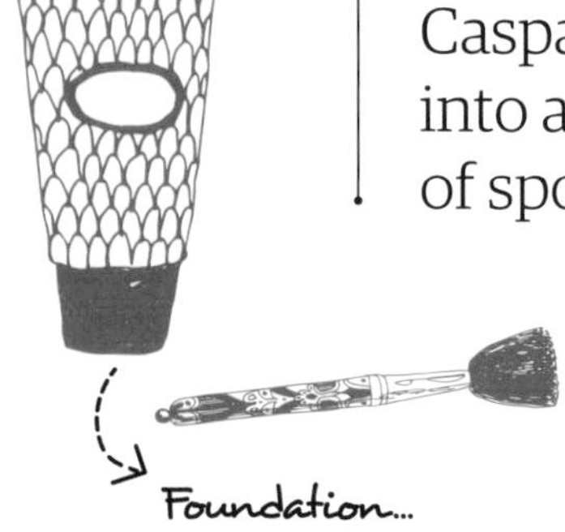

Caspar ice-skating at Hotel De Ville on our family trip to Paris.

His skin problem also kept Caspar indoors because he was warned to keep out of the sun during treatment, as the drugs would make him burn more easily. This wasn't much of a problem for Caspar as you can imagine. It became a great excuse for more YouTube time.

There was a positive side to getting spots after all!

> He appeared to have an innate ability to predict the trends that I didn't fully understand in the fast growing business of YouTube.

When Caspar reached about 5,000 subscribers with his "Dick of Africa" character, he decided the duo was becoming a bit tiresome. I was also very worried that Dick might be attracting the wrong kind of audience. I mean a young boy, broadcasting to the world from his bath? What kind of sane mother wouldn't worry? *Now that I think about it I probably should have been more concerned too.* But Caspar assured me this wasn't the case and he managed to find some kind of statistical graph to prove to me that his followers were mostly teenage girls. I relaxed then and was sad that Dick was getting the heave-ho. I loved that character and really lamented his departure. They were truly hilarious videos, but Caspar wanted to move on. He wanted his own voice now.

So he changed his channel name, first to Dickafrica and then to DiCasp, slowly weeding out Dick. *So many jokes, so little time.* He started producing videos with what he considered more substance. For me, they were more like the kind of things everybody else was doing on YouTube. They had a formula. What I loved about the Dick of Africa videos was the way Caspar's completely wacky humour came to the forefront. But Caspar knew what he was doing. If he was going to become a serious YouTuber he had to play the game and produce content that the medium demanded.

For someone so young he always seemed to make the right decisions in relation to his career, despite my misgivings. He appeared to have an innate ability to predict the trends that I didn't fully understand in the fast growing business of YouTube.

We had a close relationship, and I believed in him and his ability to crack it. So once again I let him get on with it, and Dick was gone but not forgotten.

You're killing me, Mom.

Caspar began to make more and more appearances on YouNow, and his slots got substantially longer with more thumbs up than down. He'd usually only get kicked off when our internet went down, which it did frequently, much to Caspar's annoyance.

For anyone who doesn't use YouNow, the object is for you to get your videos to stay up as long as you can by getting more thumbs up than thumbs down. So losing internet connection really sucked.

"Why is the internet so f**king terrible in South Africa?" he'd bellow from his room upstairs.

"Mom, Sham, you have to do something about it! There must be something we can do. It's so annoying. I could have made zillions of rand on YouNow and now I've lost it all 'cos of our stupid bloody internet."

You didn't get money as such, you got prizes. I could have won myself a decent hoodie. I could never understand why we didn't just get better internet. It wasn't 2002 anymore. I may as well have been still using dial up!

We dug up pavements, we called in all the experts and we bought new Wi-Fi routers, but whatever we tried the internet connection remained dodgy, and Caspar learnt to bury his frustrations and work his way around it.

His new weekly videos, with him mostly just sitting in front of the camera, were proving to be a success. His humour shone. His drama teacher at school, Jaci De Villiers, was hugely encouraging, and when Caspar turned 16 she wrote the following in his school report:

I always liked her.

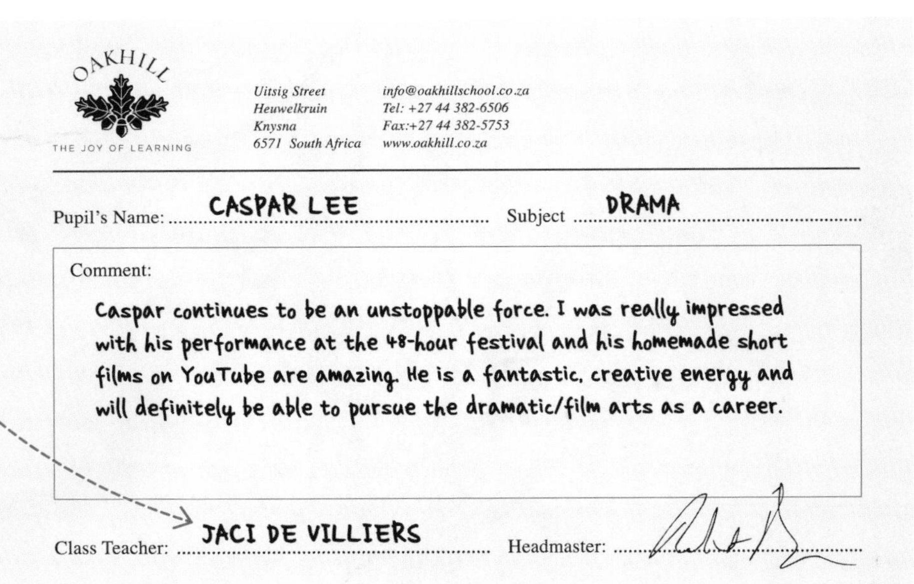

OAKHILL
THE JOY OF LEARNING

Uitsig Street
Heuwelkruin
Knysna
6571 South Africa

info@oakhillschool.co.za
Tel: +27 44 382-6506
Fax:+27 44 382-5753
www.oakhill.co.za

Pupil's Name: CASPAR LEE Subject DRAMA

Comment:
Caspar continues to be an unstoppable force. I was really impressed with his performance at the 48-hour festival and his homemade short films on YouTube are amazing. He is a fantastic, creative energy and will definitely be able to pursue the dramatic/film arts as a career.

Class Teacher: JACI DE VILLIERS Headmaster:

His Headmaster wrote in the same report

And him

OAKHILL

THE JOY OF LEARNING

Uitsig Street
Heuwelkruin
Knysna
6571 South Africa

info@oakhillschool.co.za
Tel: +27 44 382-6506
Fax:+27 44 382-5753
www.oakhill.co.za

Pupil's Name: Caspar Lee

Headmaster's Comment:

Caspar is a critical thinker who continues to challenge the status quo and I have no doubt that this skill will hold him in good stead in the future.

Headmaster:

His English teacher was not quite so impressed:

Her, not so much

OAKHILL

THE JOY OF LEARNING

Uitsig Street
Heuwelkruin
Knysna
6571 South Africa

info@oakhillschool.co.za
Tel: +27 44 382-6506
Fax: +27 44 382-5753
www.oakhill.co.za

Pupil's Name: Caspar Lee Subject English

Comment:

Erratic, dramatic, charismatic! Allow all these to work together to create the finished product. This result is disappointing as it only reflects an inability to do the work that needed to be done, not the excellence within you.

Class Teacher: Headmaster:

No wonder I'm the one writing this book! You're actually writing this book because I signed the rights away without realizing it.

"Challenging" and "unstoppable", "erratic" and "dramatic"! How right they were! In other words, there's no point in arguing with Caspar, he's always right. Yep. And if a job's too boring but it has to be finished, find someone else to do it. When it comes to working, delegation is the key to success after all. At last, Mom, you're finally starting to understand me.

> What I loved about the Dick of Africa videos was the way Caspar's completely wacky humour came to the forefront. But Caspar knew what he was doing.

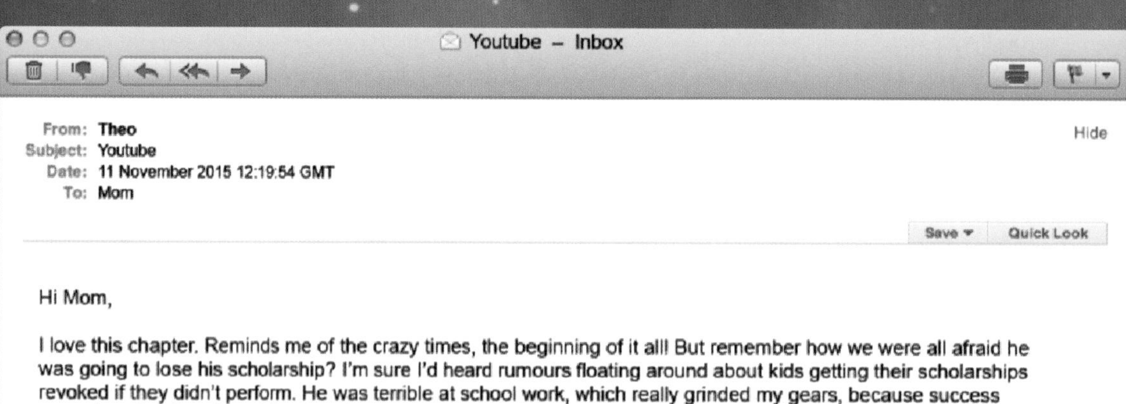

Youtube – Inbox

From: **Theo**
Subject: Youtube
Date: 11 November 2015 12:19:54 GMT
To: Mom

Hide

Save ▾ Quick Look

Hi Mom,

I love this chapter. Reminds me of the crazy times, the beginning of it all! But remember how we were all afraid he was going to lose his scholarship? I'm sure I'd heard rumours floating around about kids getting their scholarships revoked if they didn't perform. He was terrible at school work, which really grinded my gears, because success came from hard work, not floating about in your pyjama bottoms and talking to a camera all day!

At the time, I was rehearsing for a two-hour Anton Chekhov play at drama school and I was the lead role, which meant discipline and determination. Caspar had determination but no discipline. It wasn't fair! So I decided to have a serious chat with him. I sat him down and told him that even though he didn't care about his school work, he needed to jack up, because he had the brains – so why not use them? OK, so I may have white-lied and told him I'd heard from his headmaster that his scholarship was on the line. He went completely white and asked if I would help him to study. Of course, I took this on full-force, I was more than happy to slip back into my role as my little brother's teacher, but this time, it was serious. We managed to get in two hours of Afrikaans grammar. It was a feat beyond all feats!

Better go, Caspar's about to Skype about a girl he met the other night and Andrew has started barking like a baboon to get my attention.

Theo Xx

I will have my revenge!

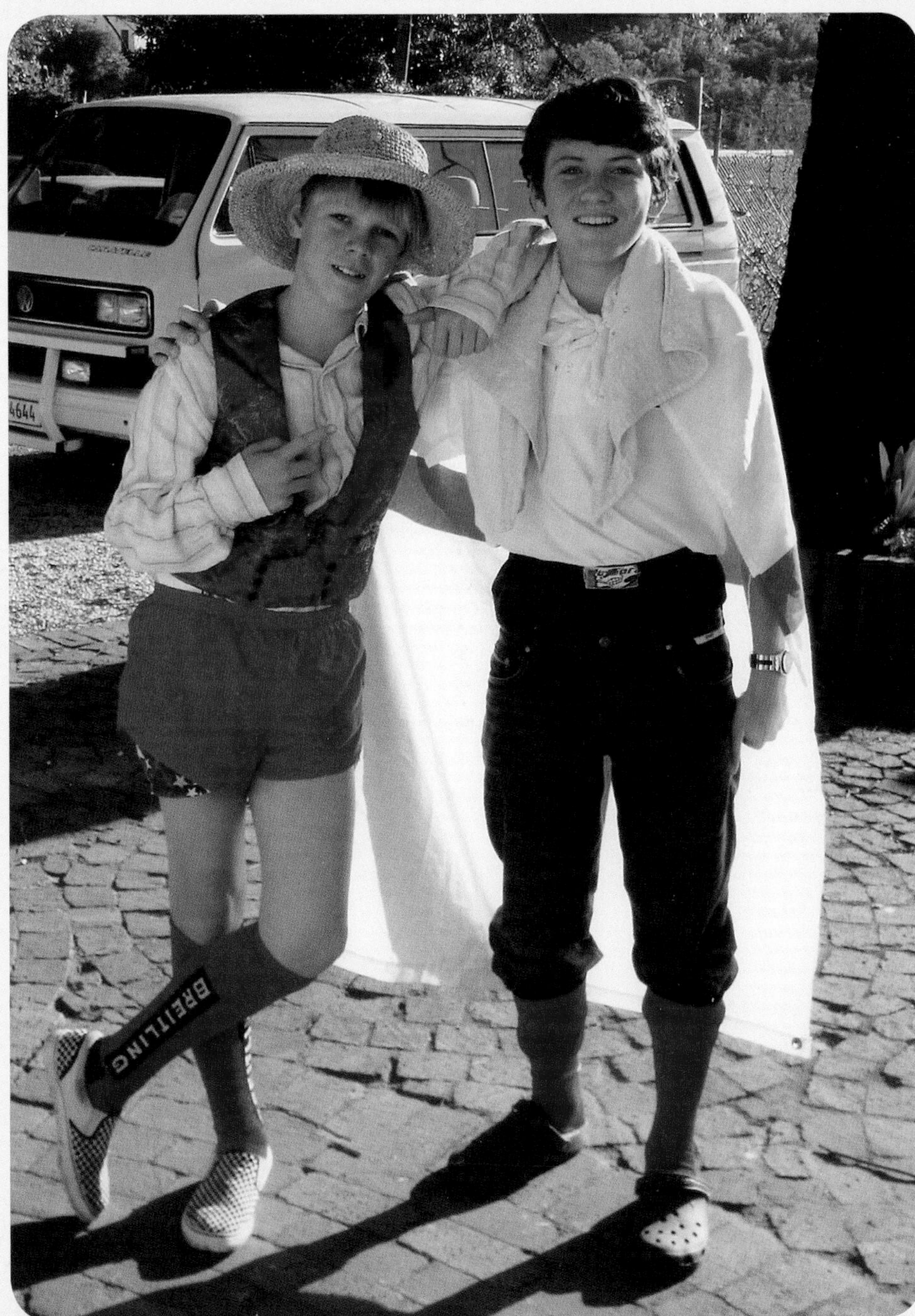

Caspar and his friend Nick looking their best..

WTF!

CHAPTER TWENTY THREE

Sweet 16

Caspar's 16th birthday was about the only big birthday party Caspar had ever had, up to then. We hired a large hall on Thesen Island and there must have been over a hundred teenagers there. People appeared from all over the place, and I remember freaking out at the amount of alcohol being consumed. Sixteen-year-old kids would arrive with bottles of vodka hidden under their jackets, and there was much vomiting in the bushes. Not from me, thankfully. The DJ failed to arrive, which didn't help matters, so Caspar and Josh had to quickly rig up a sound system, which kept breaking down. There were so many people arriving from God knows where and the empty bottles of vodka were piling up. You could tell by the look on Caspar's face that he wasn't quite enjoying his "rager" and would maybe have preferred to keep it low-key. But once everybody forgot about the on/off music, Caspar relaxed. It was a great relief to us all when the party was over, and ever since then Caspar likes to keep his parties small.

I can't recall too much about Caspar turning "sweet 16", perhaps because most of it was spent in his bedroom.

I can't recall too much about Caspar turning "sweet 16", perhaps because most of it was spent in his bedroom. If he wasn't there, he'd be over at Josh's house, playing poker and gaming. There was a fair amount of tubing and wakeboarding on the lagoon too. When Caspar ventured outside we all breathed a sigh of relief. Caspar's skill on water-skis was quite incredible, leaping over the waves on his wakeboard, he made it look so easy. We could never go fast enough for him. He was fearless.

Of course, he preferred going out in Josh's parents boat than ours. Josh had a skipper's licence you see, which meant that parents didn't have to be involved. Also, Josh's boat was a proper speedboat with a sound system on board, so it'd inevitably be filled with girls, and they certainly had far more fun than in our rubber duck-sized boat, which had a persistent leak, making it floppy and unglamorous. Caspar tried using our boat a few times, but he invariably broke the engine or crashed into something.

Caspar talking to school friend Rosie, with Paul, another school friend, in the background.

—

Caspar with Hannah and Max

—

Caspar was never very good at mooring the boat at our pier, so there was a lot of panic and bids for help. Not quite smooth sailing. Once, our Labrador jumped into the canal in an effort to save Caspar from deep s**t. The plan was that we would focus on her and her doggy paddling and forget about Caspar's terrible skills as a skipper. *This only happened a couple of times, and it was definitely more that rubbish boat's fault than mine. Have you ever tried to control something while it's sinking?*

Caspar is not very good when it comes to machines. I don't think he ever quite got over crashing the Land Rover when he was nine years old. He was learning to drive again in our little convertible Peugeot, just around Thesen Island, between our house and Josh's, but he continually managed to lose the keys. And then he managed to break the mechanism that opens and closes the roof, so we were left with a permanently open top that continually beeped. *Look on the bright side, at least you got a good tan while you were driving!*

Caspar's stepsister, Sally, was married to Brendan, a South African, and they lived in Plettenberg Bay, just down the road from Knysna. They have two children called Hannah and Max, whom we all adored, and Caspar had a particularly close relationship with them.

Caspar carried on surfing at our local beach, and never seemed too concerned about the great white sharks, of which there are many in that area. We never actually saw one, but every year someone would lose a limb or die in the vicinity. He never became a surfer dude as such, but really enjoyed being among the waves, and they all looked after one another. I really liked it when he went surfing. It meant he was out of his bedroom!

Caspar was keen on girls, obviously, but the spots had kept them at bay for a while. When they started to clear up, mysterious young ladies would appear on our doorstep and, after a quick introduction, would quickly disappear upstairs. There seemed to be a constant stream, and a few hours later they'd be gone. *Mom, I'm hardly Harry Styles.*

We spent that Christmas, and every Christmas since, in South Africa. The kids were delighted not to freeze their butts off in Ireland and there was plenty of family around. Caspar's stepsister, Sally, was married to Brendan, a South African, and they lived in Plettenberg Bay, just down the road from Knysna. They have two children called Hannah and Max, whom we all adored, and Caspar had a particularly close relationship with them. Caspar is extraordinarily good with small children, and the feeling was mutual. Max was five and Hannah was two when we had our first Christmas in Knysna, and from then on they were regular visitors to our house with many sleepovers.

Christmas is always a big thing, as you can imagine, in our family. Some of our many traditions include:

a. Stockings (no matter the age), filled mostly with sweets and the odd spiky pineapple.

b. Coins in the brandy pudding. Five rand coins are Caspar's favourites.

c. A glass of champagne, to make the present opening less tedious when it isn't your turn.

d. One person has to act as Santa. For seven consecutive Christmases Theo has managed to land that role by simply refusing to let anybody else do it.

e. Christmas swims are mandatory, even in Ireland.

There were lots of presents, and our whole garden deck was festooned with garish flashing reindeer, and a gigantic blow-up Santa saluted the passing boats. We would compete with our neighbours over who had the most Christmas lights. Present opening time was moved to 11am, so that we could all get a bit of a lie-in after our Christmas Eve celebrations, but Caspar hated that. It was about the only morning of the year that he woke up early.

I like presents

As a small boy, he got used to digging in to his presents at 6am, but that just had to stop. He wasn't very good at giving and Theo and I used to buy most of his gifts for him. However, I am now very happy to say he much prefers giving than getting!

What? Are you doing this on purpose, Mom?

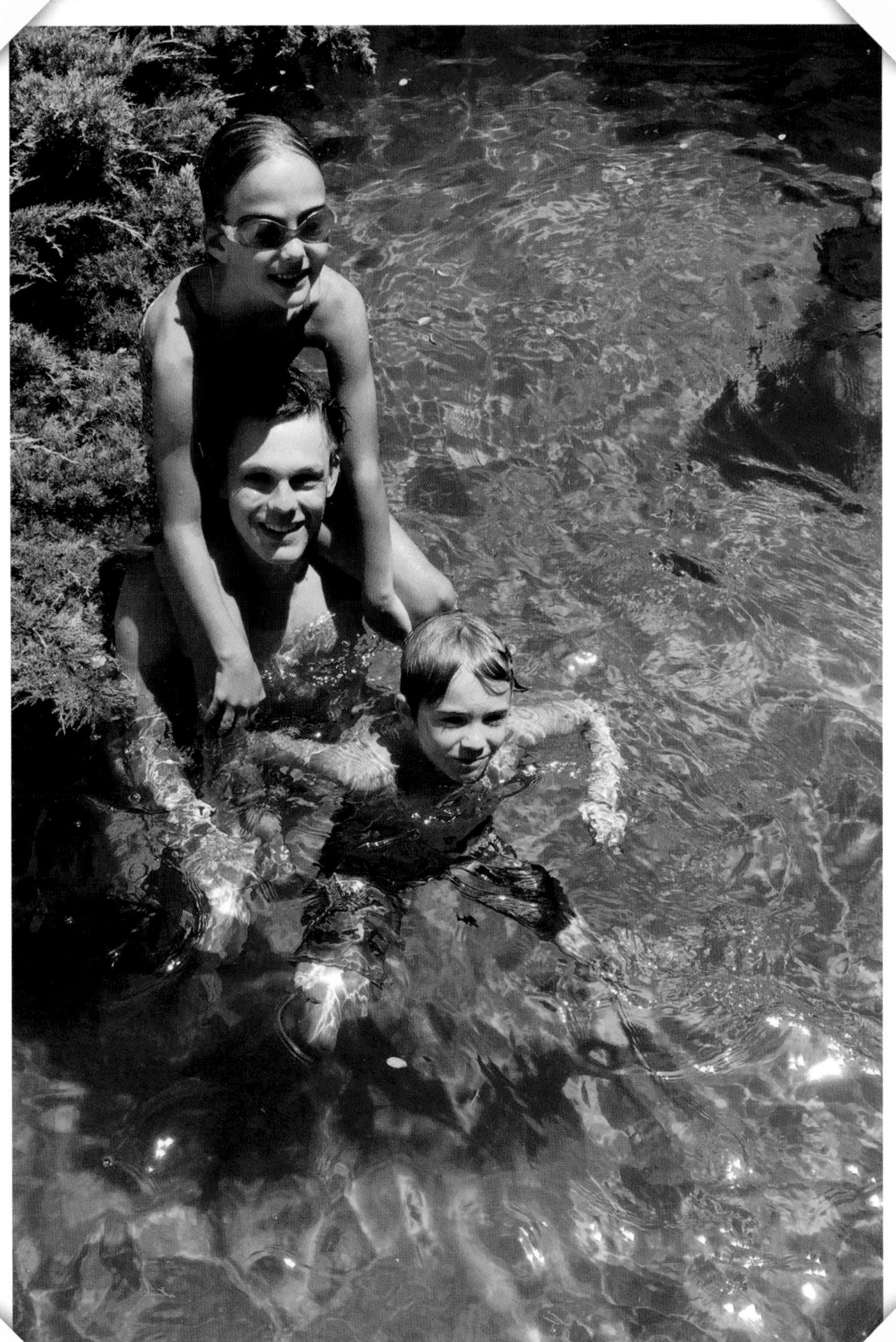

Hannah, Caspar and Max.

CHAPTER TWENTY FOUR

London Calling

In his penultimate year in school, Caspar began to make many new friends on YouNow, including Troye Sivan, who had played the lead part in a very successful South African movie called Spud. Caspar had begged me to let him audition for it, and I'd had to say no because we lived too far away at the time. He also became buddies with Jack Harries of JacksGap, who was already making quite a name for himself on YouNow, and was beginning to upload videos onto YouTube. Caspar knew that networking was the way to go, and if he wasn't on YouNow, he'd be Skype-calling his new online friends.

Jack invited Caspar to stay with his family in London during the July school holidays. It was something I had to think seriously about. I knew nothing about Jack, except that his parents lived in Wimbledon, his father was a well-known film producer, he had a twin brother called Finn, and was a year older than Caspar. Nothing to worry about, I thought. I knew Caspar was on a mission and that saying no this time was not an option. *No, Mom, it was not.*

All of a sudden my 17-year-old son was heading off to London on his own to stay with people he had never met, except online, and yet he seemed to know exactly what he wanted to do. It was Caspar's life calling. He had his Dad nearby, who was spending more and more time back in the UK and his London cousins to fall back on, in case of emergencies. And, of course, Vic and Trevor were ever so generous and assured me he'd have a place to stay if need be. But, he ended up spending his whole time with Jack and Finn developing his YouTube channel. They were truly inspirational and it was a turning point in Caspar's career. *After I collaborated with Jack and Finn, it really opened me up to collaborating with the rest of the YouTube community, and I travelled around London meeting and making videos with as many of them as I could.*

All of a sudden my 17-year-old son was heading off to London on his own to stay with people he had never met, except online, and yet he seemed to know exactly what he wanted to do.

C.P.
KEEP
CLEAR

That summer, he had his first meet-up in London in Soho Square, right outside the offices where Jon and I used to work. Jon went along to the meet-up and it was quite astonishing how many fans turned up. In the end Jon took as many photos as the fans, and it was a very jolly occasion.

As people who watch YouTube will know, a meet-up is where I get to go along to events and meet a lot of my viewers. They're organized by people who put together conventions and they're so fun. I get to hang out with so many people, but I do wish I had more time to get to know the viewers properly. That's the only downside to being so busy - often I only get to chat to people briefly. It's such a surreal experience but I always come away having absolutely loved it.

Caspar came home beaming from ear to ear, the trip was a success. He'd even collected a lot more fans. He was well and truly "launched".

> We were all pretty delighted with the way things were panning out. Caspar started making money, and Oakhill gave him one of his first jobs.

At this stage Caspar's channel contained lots of videos with Theo and myself, Hannah and Max, and Summer the Labrador and Mini-Me the chihuahua. It was fun for us all to be larking around together, making fun and being made fun of. They were very much the modern equivalent of making home movies, and pretty crazy and silly. Our house was filled with tripods, and furniture was constantly being moved around. Sham and I never knew what experiment was going to happen next, and there was a definite increase in the volume of the high-pitched voices emanating from his bedroom. Caspar was in his element.

We were all pretty delighted with the way things were panning out. Caspar started making money, and Oakhill gave him one of his first jobs. The school commissioned him to make a promotional video about the school, and he was paid a whopping 2000 rand (around £80).

Some of his teachers expressed concern about his under-performance as far as his school work was concerned, but we told them not to worry and that his Matric results didn't really matter. He clearly wasn't going to university to study law anymore – he was planning on making YouTube his career. His teachers didn't really understand, but they let him be. So Caspar did no studying. I did worry at times, but I knew he would be OK, even if his results weren't going to be the greatest. I also figured that studying in the future was never going to be his thing. With his ADD, concentrating on what he considered boring was virtually impossible, no matter how much Ritalin he took. *I hated that stuff.* There were a few other kids in his class who also had ADD, but the school was always accommodating, and rather than being hard on the children the teachers concentrated on individuality and bringing out the best in each pupil.

When you spend most of your life preparing your kids for the best university, it can be a hard thing for parents to come to terms with the fact that perhaps that life doesn't suit them. Luckily, Caspar had found something else that he loved doing, and fitted in perfectly with his personality and lifestyle. And, better still, it was something that could earn him money. I was happy with his decision. He was following his dream, and it was working, so I gave him my full support. I never thought about "What if?" or "Where's it going to lead?" like his teachers were probably thinking. I knew that for once in his life this was something Caspar wasn't going to get bored with, and I had never seen him so determined to achieve his goal.

Thanks for believing in me, Mom. I really mean that. You supported me from day one. A lot of other parents would have thought what I was doing was ridiculous, but you were always there for me and helped me to believe I was on the right path.

When he was eighteen, just before his final Matric test, Caspar was becoming quite the celebrity in South Africa. He went on a hockey tour to Cape Town and was mobbed by fans on the hockey pitch. His first newspaper article, written by a friend of ours, Jo Thesen, appeared in the *South African Mail & Guardian* and started a flurry of further journalistic reports in the South African press. He was flown up to Johannesburg to be interviewed on 5FM, a cool music radio station, and he appeared alongside gaming guru Grant Hinds on *Breakfast TV*. He was earning serious money for a school kid and none of us could really believe what was happening. ***I couldn't believe it either!***

Between all the rising success, I went to go and visit Theo at Stellenbosch University. She had a fairly good idea of what was happening, so I thought it would be nice to talk about it one on one. It's hard to know how to deal with something so unexpected.

Caspar with gaming guru Grant Hinds.

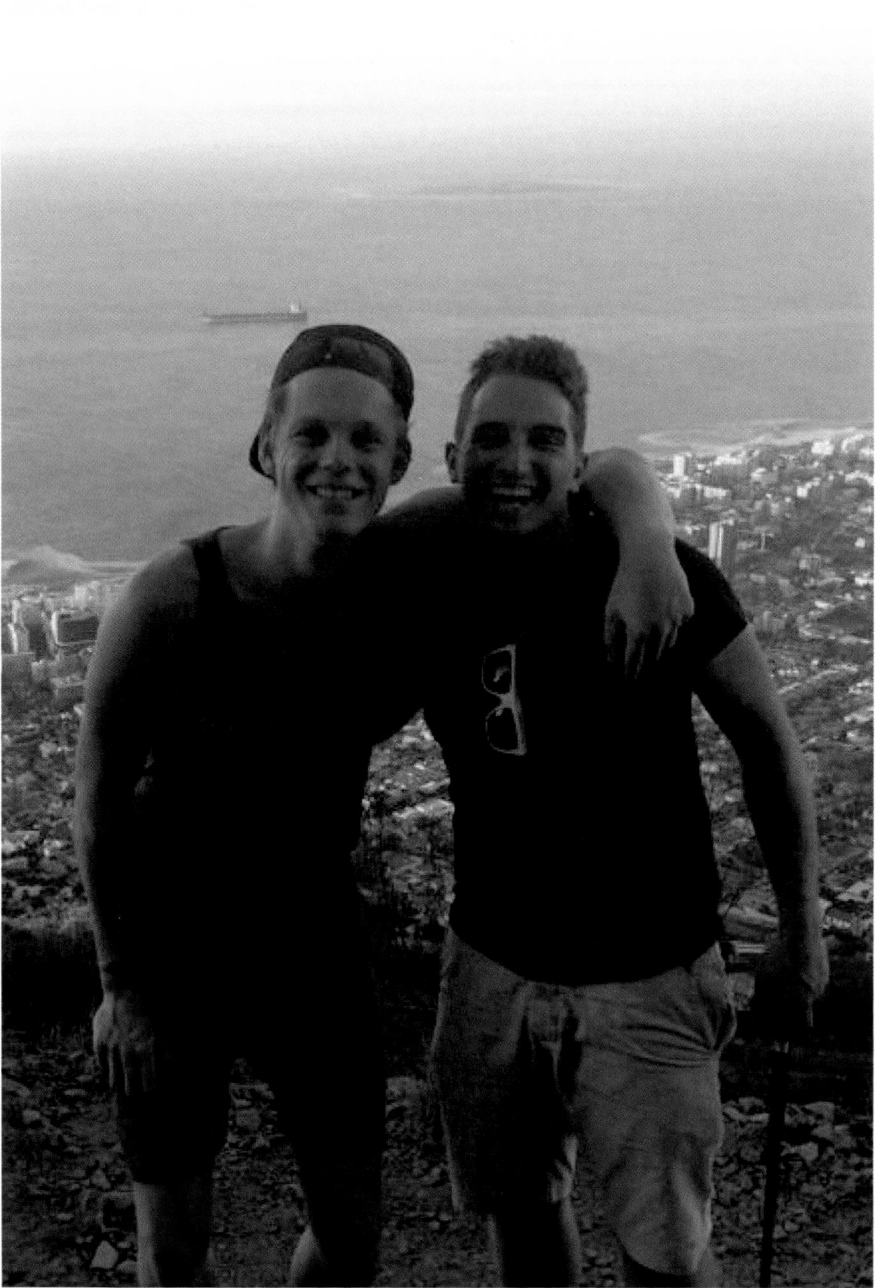

She opened up to me about how she was feeling and said that some nights she would cry herself to sleep, worried that she was going to lose her little brother to YouTube. She was clearly very happy for him, we all were, but it was a big adjustment for the family and we all had our different ways of dealing with it. The family dynamic was shifting. We had a star on our hands and we wanted to handle it the "right way", whatever that was.

I worried that Theo compared her own achievements to Caspar's unique success, but instead she was very supportive of him. To this day, she still loves helping him with his videos and she has her own channel with over 200,000 subscribers. Her decision to start a channel happened after university. She's always loved being creative on the internet and throughout her student days she blogged about being a drama student. So with additional skills and education in media and performance, and her ongoing love for video making, it seemed natural for her to follow this path on YouTube.

> We had a star on our hands and we wanted to handle it the "right" way, whatever that was.

We didn't like the thought of her being overshadowed by Caspar; we would hear of people saying that she was just "jumping on Caspar's bandwagon" which was very unfair. As it has turned out, she has managed to forge her own path, growing an audience through weekly videos that offer advice to teenagers on anything from depression to sexual health. She's very good at speaking openly about things and can often bring up the "elephant in the room" without making anyone feel awkward. So it's no wonder hundreds of thousands of viewers enjoy watching her videos. I am very proud of her too.

GO THEO!

Yeah, Theo, your videos are cool. It's great that people can turn to YouTube for advice as well as comedy!

The Matric exams came and went. Because of his Tourette's, Caspar got a special dispensation and was allowed to sit the exam on a computer, which suited him down to the ground. Caspar's not great with handwriting. Firstly, it's almost illegible, and secondly, he's rather slow with the pen. Surprisingly, he did OK, and well enough to study for a Bachelors Degree (BA) in the future if he ever wanted to, and he's quite proud of that fact.

I am. I know it may not sound like a big deal to a lot of people but it was important to me to prove that I could get into university despite my difficulties with academic learning.

I was going to have to say goodbye to my son, and let him go and find himself.

Towards the end of the year Grant Hinds, the gaming guru, became Caspar's manager in South Africa and got him a load of publicity. During this period, Caspar's YouTube mates were all signing up with a new management company in London called Gleam Futures, and he was invited to join them. He joined Gleam and announced to us he was moving to London.

CASPAR: "Mom, I've been asked to join a management company in London. I think it's worth doing, because everyone else is going with them. What do you think?"

ME: "Brilliant, darling, sounds fantastic!"

CASPAR: "But I think I'm going to have to move to London..."

ME: "What? I thought you were just going there for a visit?"

I was going to have to say goodbye to my son, and let him go and find himself. How on earth was he going to survive on his own in London?

CASPAR'; "I think I can afford it, Mom, and Alfie Deyes has offered to share a flat with me."

What happens if it doesn't work out? How will they find a place? I knew Alfie as a YouTuber, but I had never met him. Caspar was so young to be doing this. All these thoughts were going through my mind, but at the same time I knew he had made the right decision.

"OK, Casp, let's go for it," I said to him, my worries instantly floating out the window.

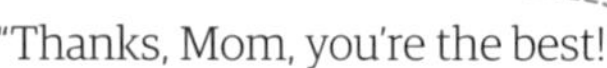

"Thanks, Mom, you're the best!"

#squadgoals

CHAPTER TWENTY FIVE

What Happens IN VEGAS...

As a parent, it's difficult to accept that your child wants to move away from home. I had encountered it with Theodora when she disappeared off to Stellenbosch University. I made it less difficult by driving approximately 300 miles every month to go and visit her. But with Caspar, it was going to be different. *Very* different. London was a very long way from Knysna, and the cost of visiting regularly would be difficult. So I very reluctantly had to let him go.

I didn't know how he was going to survive, other than that he had planned on sharing an apartment in Shoreditch with PointlessBlog's Alfie Deyes.

> I was immensely proud of that fact... that he could support himself completely, at the age of 18, in one of the most expensive cities in the world.

Caspar couldn't cook. He couldn't even boil an egg. He didn't know any basic survival skills. He also hated touching half-eaten food. **I don't think this is in any way weird, Mom.** I had been a bad parent in that respect, though I doubt it would have made much difference if I'd tried to teach him.

All I knew was that he had earned enough money on YouTube to start renting his own flat in London, and to survive financially on his own. I was immensely proud of that fact and found it quite astonishing that he could support himself completely, at the age of 18, in one of the most expensive cities in the world.

So after the final family Christmas holiday in sun-soaked Knysna, he packed his bags and left for freezing cold London in the middle of January. I don't think he realized quite how cold the English winter was going to be, and he got a bit of a shock, to be sure. The first thing he did was go out and buy the warmest duvet he could find, and luxury bed linen from The English Bed Company. Nothing but the finest white cotton adorned his new bed in London. *I'm worth it.* Apart from that, the only other thing he bought was a desk for his computer. It was now time to get to work.

how do I get this to turn into this?

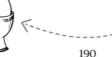

WELCOME
TO Fabulous
LAS VEGAS
NEVADA

Caspar with all the YouTube guys.

(Dinner)

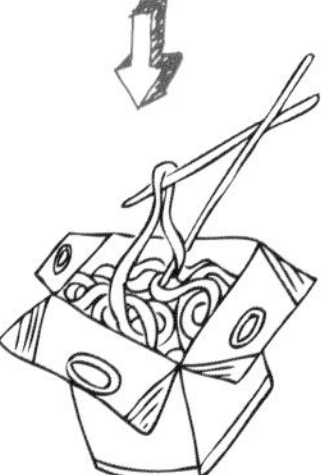

Living with Alfie was great fun, by all accounts. It was Alfie's first apartment as well, and Zoë Sugg often came to visit. I don't think any of them left the apartment very often because it was so cold. There were lots of photos of takeaways, *I had most of the local ones on speed dial! Still do.* and Alfie was quite keen that Caspar didn't leave a mess so he had to finally clean up now that I wasn't around to do it for him anymore. This was real growing up! *If by cleaning up you mean moving plates from the living room table to the dishwasher then yeah, I'm definitely a proper grown up now.*

Caspar was gaining so many fans it was hard to keep up.

The only time Caspar ever went out in those days (as far as I know) was to go clubbing a couple of times a week, eat at Nando's, or very occasionally visit his management company. Except, of course, that is, for the trips to America, of which there were quite a few. He'd go to YouTube conventions like VidCon and Playlist Live, which were growing into massive events similar, I suppose, to Comic-Con, but instead of comic book characters, real life YouTubers wander around. At these conventions, fans can watch their favourite YouTubers perform live on stage and queue in never-ending lines to meet up with them and get a signature and a selfie. Caspar was gaining so many fans it was hard to keep up. Sham, Theo and I were amazed, but not that surprised, at his rapidly increasing number of followers. Because of course, he'd been outwardly manifesting this type of success ever since he uploaded his first video.

"Mom, I know I am going to get big. Trust me," he'd say, shutting the door on us so he could edit his next video. It was like Caspar's life had been injected with a magic potion. Yet again, his manifestations had worked! *Everyone has their favourites on YouTube. The channels I watch most are Joe's, Alfie's, Ollie's and Josh's. I also like Adrian Bliss, Jacksgap and Kassem G, and I watch videos about hip hop gossip by this guy called DJ Akademiks. I find them really interesting for some reason.*

All for me!

Caspar made several trips to Los Angeles during his first year away from home, often involving meet-ups with fans. There seemed to be a wealth of opportunities there, and Caspar often thought he might move there one day. The climate was nice, and it felt more like South Africa than freezing London.

I found it hard to keep up with all his jaunts during his first year away from home. I do know that he was immensely happy and that made me equally as happy. I missed him a lot, and we didn't talk too much. I knew that if he didn't ring or communicate that everything was OK – the usual scenario with sons leaving home. He was so busy working and finding his feet at the same time that there wasn't much time for family.

OK, this makes me feel really bad. I honestly didn't realize you felt like that. You should have phoned/emailed/texted/Skyped/Facebooked/Tweeted/Instagrammed/sent a carrier pigeon. You know I always love talking to you.

Caspar knew this was the sort of news I hated – Vegas and poker, glitz and glamour – and he loved to wind me up, telling me how much fun he was having!

He'd always phone when he had really good news to tell. Like when he went on a road trip from LA to Las Vegas with his new friend Nick Hissom, and ended up playing poker at a luxury hotel, where he bumped into Wayne Rooney in the swimming pool!

Caspar knew this was the sort of news I hated – Vegas and poker, glitz and glamour – and he loved to wind me up, telling me how much fun he was having! It reminded me of when he was growing up, how he liked to watch all these dreadful celebrity programmes on the cable channel E!, about the lifestyles of Hollywood celebrities; I desperately wanted him to reject this rubbish and fill his mind with more cultural matters! *I learnt a lot of important life lessons from Keeping Up with the Kardashians.*

Hanging out in LA and London, Caspar was fast becoming a celebrity himself, and thankfully remaining unaffected by it all. In his eyes it was just a job, like any other job. Only his job was to make videos once a week, pose for selfies with fans and promote his "Caspar" brand across all social media. It was work he loved doing, and, boy, did he give it all he had.

Caspar also hung out a lot with all the other British YouTubers, including Alfie, Zoë, Marcus Butler, Jack and Finn Harries, and they became the centre of his social life. They worked together doing endless tours, they collaborated with one another, and they partied together – some more than others. Caspar was keen on clubbing and girls, and Alfie was not so keen, maybe because he already had a girlfriend (Zoë, of course). At home they often kept different hours; Caspar only emerging from the bed in the afternoon, when Alfie had already shot and edited a video, I expect. Caspar's never been a morning person, and I don't think he ever will be, clubbing or no clubbing.

He came home for Christmas, as he always does, and was so happy to be back in South Africa. Sunshine, his mates, his family – it was fabulous. And he was even more excited to bring his then-girlfriend, Gaby. She was a gorgeous young girl who was doing her A Levels in London. We really enjoyed having her to stay and she was such a fun person to have about. They went off to game parks together and did all the usual touristy things that Caspar himself had rarely done. It was great to see him so happy, and to be away from his computer quite a bit. She also managed to get him up in the mornings at a reasonable hour, which was quite a surprise for us all!

We noticed at Christmas that considerably more people stopped Caspar in the street asking for photos and autographs. Even people passing our house in their boats would shout out "Caspar Lee" as they cruised past. It was kind of surreal in the beginning, having fans waiting outside our house for Caspar to emerge, but now we take it as just part of his job. It's no big deal, really. He's the same old Caspar, and it's only work after all.

To be honest, Mom, it doesn't feel like work to me. I love it and it's so cool meeting people who watch my stuff and support what I do.

CHAPTER TWENTY SIX

French Fancy

Caspar returned to London after a glorious couple of months in South Africa and moved in with the Seale-Jones's in Crouch End, North London. I felt like it would be good for him to live with them because they were like our family, and it was nice for me to know he'd be looked after.

Caspar Seale-Jones and Emily Seale-Jones were also into movie making, so the house was a bit like a production office with everyone involved in their own projects. It all worked out well until Caspar bought a DJ kit and started making rather a lot of noise, and I'm sure this terrible music didn't make Trevor Jones a happy man. Caspar had seen how much the DJs in Vegas were earning, and for a brief while he thought he might turn his hand to that as well. Luckily it was short lived as it drove everyone in the house demented. **This whole thing about me wanting to become a professional DJ isn't true. I just really enjoyed playing around with the decks. I may have joked about doing it professionally but the reality was I sucked.**

Caspar decided to take [Gaby] to Paris for Valentine's Day.

Caspar continued dating Gaby, and decided to take her to Paris for Valentine's Day. I spent many wonderful hours helping him plan where they should eat and hang out.

I couldn't believe Caspar was actually going to go back to Paris again after our miserable freezing January holiday there. I was beside myself with excitement when I heard it was such a great success, and that he presented her with some make-up (I rather wished it was going to be an engagement ring - not really) Steady on, Mom! on the top of the Eiffel Tower, even if it was only for a promotional video!

Sadly, they broke up at the beginning of Gaby's school summer holidays. The break up was mutual. Caspar was doing a load of travelling at the time and he was scheduled to go to America for a month to shoot his guest appearance on *Web Therapy*, a show starring Lisa Kudrow from *Friends*, amongst other things. So it all seemed for the best.

Very original pose
there, Caspar

It's Phoebe from 'Friends'!

Shane is not doing what
you think he is doing

Web Therapy was just brilliant. To think here was Caspar being interviewed by someone from *Friends*! For people of my generation, Lisa Kudrow was quite a star. I'm not too sure whether Caspar was aware of her background or not, or had ever watched *Friends*, but he went with the flow, and stood his ground against this rather terrifying so-called psychologist. He was even given his own dressing room, a first, and was thoroughly congratulated on his performance by the producer and director. The irony of it all was that the show wanted to bring on Caspar to increase its online viewers, which they succeeded in doing. What giant steps he was making; it was fabulous to observe!

From America it was off to Italy to celebrate Tyler Oakley's birthday, and then straight after that it was back to South Africa to throw a big party in our house for all his school friends. Being a successful YouTube star is not easy in terms of maintaining relationships, and all the plane hopping it involves, unless your partner also happens to be a YouTube star. No wonder there are so many YouTube couples. It makes sense to be in it together, as it's virtually impossible otherwise to hold down a relationship outside of YouTube, especially at such a young age. It's the same sort of thing when you are at university. If your partner is not at the same college, or nearby, similar problems arise. Also, it's a strange life he's living and sometimes I guess it's easier to be with someone who's part of it and understands what it is. Sadly, this is true. I don't think it's impossible to go out with someone who doesn't understand the whole YouTube thing, but it would make it a lot trickier.

No wonder there are so many YouTube couples. It makes sense to be in it together, as it's virtually impossible otherwise to hold down a relationship outside of YouTube, especially at such a young age.

We had another wonderful Christmas – our penultimate one in Knysna – on Sally and Brendan's farm, with Sham and Theo, Hannah and Max and our collection of dogs. It was a truly South African Christmas, with a turkey on the braai (barbecue), a lot of tumbling on the grass with the kids, followed by a swim in the sea as the sun went down. No wonder Caspar was a bit sad at the thought of us all moving to Cape Town. He'd had such a happy time growing up in Knysna, and I don't think he saw the point in us moving. But he'll always have links to Knysna as many of his mates are still there.

After lightly denting an Audi (which Audi South Africa had kindly lent him), Oops! Caspar returned to London to set up camp with Joe Sugg in West London. I had never met Joe, but I'd heard he was Zoë's brother and had a similar following to Caspar. They seemed like a good match and immediately began to make numerous videos together. Joe has a great sense of humour, which was immediately apparent in their collaborations. Caspar did think briefly about renting a flat on his own, but I told him I didn't think it was such a good idea. Being on his own, in London, aged 20, would have made Caspar unhappy. He needs his friends around him.

Caspar living on his own would never work because he constantly misplaces:

A. His phone
B. His passport
C. His keys
D. Even himself!
E. Don't forget my brain, Mom.

Caspar needs somebody to keep his life on track, and Joe does a fabulous job of this. Caspar also needs constant company, and without Joe's kindness and somebody to bounce ideas off of, Caspar's day-to-day survival would be uncertain. **This is a bit dramatic. I am pretty self-sufficient these days.** The two of them also get on like a house on fire. I'm so thankful that Caspar's YouTube colleagues have turned out to be his best friends as well.

Joe is funny in his videos but he's even funnier in real life, and it's really easy to live with someone who's so easy to get along with. He's also such a kind guy and he hasn't changed at all since he's had all his success. He's had such a big lifestyle change but he's still so down to earth. I think it really helps that we've got each other and we can take the piss out of the craziness of it all. When something brilliant happens, like we get to go away somewhere amazing, we both get so excited. It reminds us just how lucky we are. We'll be on a plane somewhere and we'll look at each other and say: "How cool is this?"

> ... without Joe's kindness and somebody to bounce ideas off of, Caspar's day-to-day survival would be uncertain.

He also prefers to make videos with other people, having moved away from his solo performances in front of the camera. And collaborations always helped to appease the internal nagging and pressure of having to constantly increase your subscribers.

There were a lot of YouTubers coming and going from the flat. Though there were only two bedrooms, bodies would often be found all over the floor in sleeping bags, particularly after their Wednesday night soirees, which would begin with shots of Bombay Sapphire vodka **It's gin, Mom** and end up with free drinks from Buddha Bar in Mayfair. **What 21 year-old wouldn't want free alcohol?** This might sound a rather hedonistic lifestyle but these lads and ladies worked hard. It wasn't just one long party. There was a lot of boring, tedious slogging as well, just like any other job. Caspar still spent days on end in his room creating his next video, and often worried about how good it was going to turn out.

It kind of goes with the territory. And like I've mentioned before, I am a real perfectionist. I don't see the point in doing something just for the sake of it. I used to get questioned by some of my more conservative members of the family…

"Where will this lead? How long will it last? Surely he should have gone to university?" To which I have no answer other than, "Let's just see."

The growth of YouTube and social media is frightening the daylights out of everybody. Nobody knows where it's going, really, except that it has already surpassed TV's influence in such a short time, by a long distance. The prank and reality shows I used to watch as a child, like Candid Camera, have been replaced by YouTube videos made by modern celebrities such as Caspar and Joe. They're short and funny and easily accessible. They may be accused of being trite with shallow content, but it's what the adolescents of today are itching to watch. Teenagers, with access to sites like Vine and YouNow, now prefer to watch short bursts of reality-comedy online that they, and their friends, have made. Vlogging is the new reality TV.

The ideas for my videos literally just come from when I'm living my life. Every week is different so there isn't a particular format I follow. I'll come up with an idea either by watching loads of videos and getting inspiration, or seeing something random or funny. **Each video is completely different, but by the time I edit and everything it usually takes me around three days to make one that lasts around four minutes. It's not like I do three full 12 hours days though. It's quite draining so I break it up into half days. I take my laptop around with me pretty much all of the time, so I can make videos and edit them wherever I am. I love it and I'm learning new things all the time.** I'm not interested in becoming the best editor in the world; to me it's more about keeping my style and making sure things stay authentic.)

The most important thing that makes YouTube stars so popular is that they have a way of speaking to camera that makes you feel as though you're sitting next to them having a cup of tea. There's an intimacy there which doesn't happen with reality TV. When Caspar gets stopped in the street for a chat, the fan feels like they already know him. He's like a friend. Unlike movie stars or TV celebrities, YouTubers are accessible, and that's the key distinction. YouTubers constantly acknowledge their followers, are very grateful for their support, and that's how they continue to grow and grow.

We really are so incredibly grateful for the fans' support. They're the reason we do what we do and they make it ten times more fun. We're all really aware of how lucky we are that the viewers are so loyal and we love getting their feedback. I was making YouTube videos for about two years before I got 1000 subscribers and once I got to London everything snowballed very quickly. I dreamt of it being something I could do full time and the more my viewers kept growing, the more it seemed like it could become a reality. It sounds like things went from being very small to very big on YouTube, but it was a steady process. It still feels surreal that it's getting bigger all the time and I plan to keep working really hard on it.

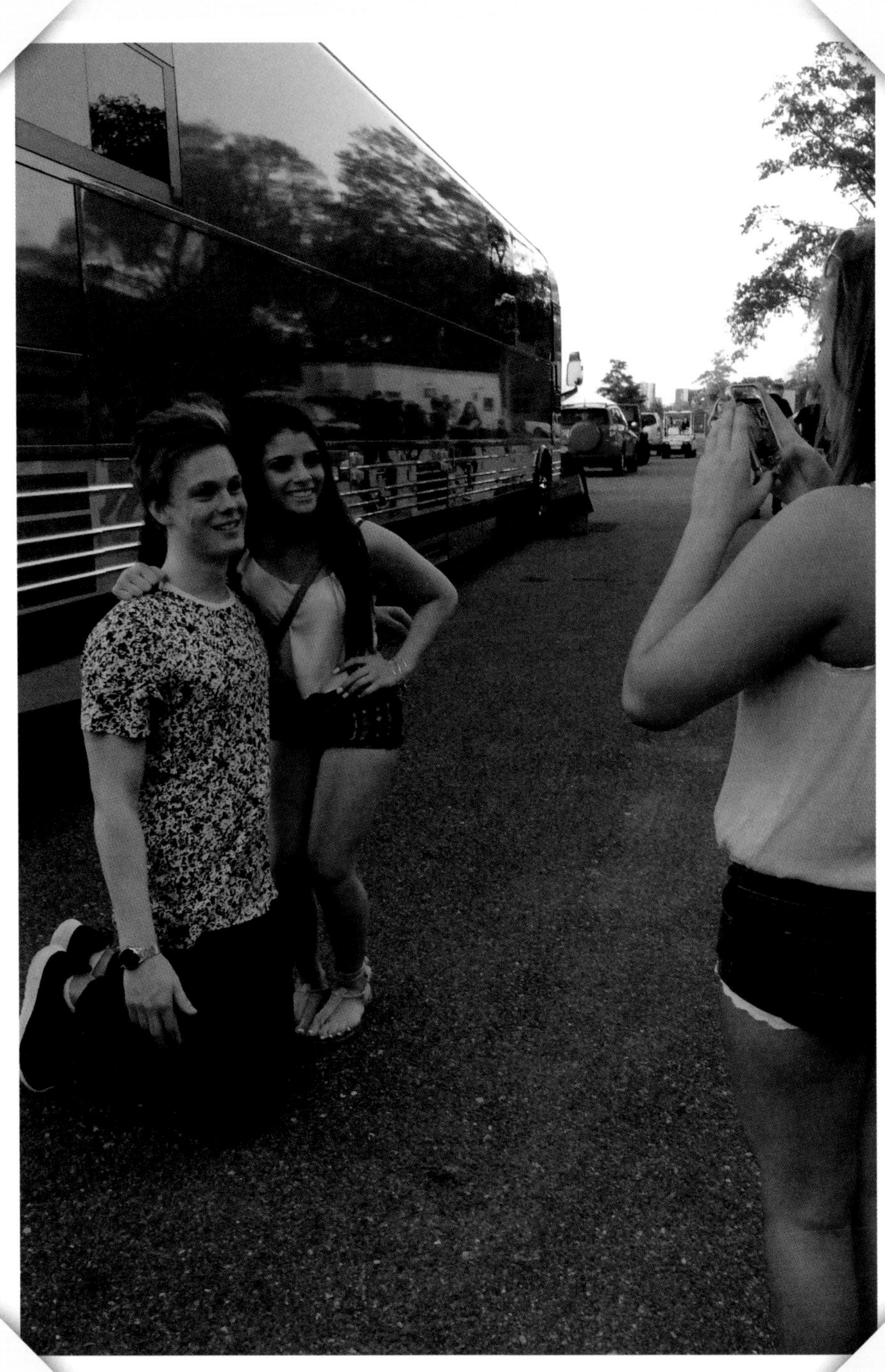

Caspar meeting fans at an event in New York..

CHAPTER TWENTY SEVEN

When Caspar Became A FILM STAR

Despite Caspar's huge success on YouTube, he was never averse to trying out something new. Similar to his enjoyment of different sports as a child, he was always quick to grasp a new idea, and to give it a bash. He's a natural comedian so after he hit three million subscribers he decided to celebrate it by trying to overcome his greatest fear by doing a bit of stand-up comedy.

He took some lessons from the great Russell Kane, and it resulted in his very own solo performance in a comedy club in Brighton called Komedia. In my mind, stand-up is the hardest form of comedy to crack. If you don't get the laughs or if the laughs are fake, it can be a total disaster. It also must be the most nerve-racking thing to do. But Caspar managed to remember his lines. He got the laughs, and vowed to do it again. We haven't seen any more as yet, but watch this space!

Caspar's next big event came as his very own radio show on BBC Radio 1. Caspar's ideas were really starting to diversify now. It was a one-off with the BBC trying to increase its listeners by importing a few YouTube stars to do some shows. Caspar was great, ever the natural. What a long way he'd come from the time he appeared on the Knysna local radio station as part of his school's work experience programme! I always love hearing his voice, and to hear it on the BBC was an incredible thrill.

2014 was a busy year indeed for Caspar. He was confidently building his career step-by-step, with a kind of exuberance befitting his age.

He's a natural comedian so after he hit three million subscribers he decided to celebrate it by trying to overcome his greatest fear by doing a bit of stand-up comedy.

Even I thought this was insane!

The way I run to my computer every time Troye drops a new song

Caspar as "Garlic" in Spud 3.

BBC
1

HMS BESTIVAL

There were radio shows, stand-up comedy routines and YouTube videos, which were becoming more and more inventive by the week. He knew his audience and there was no compromising. He met his fans at numerous Vid-Cons, and at Summer in the City, the UK's largest YouTube convention, held in London. And then there was the release of his first movie, *Spud 3*, in November 2014.

Spud 3 opened in Jo'burg to great success. I went with Caspar to the premiere and it was my first experience of watching Caspar get mobbed by fans. I couldn't get over the crowds, who were mainly there for Troye Sivan and his friend and fellow YouTuber, Connor Franta. It was my first time meeting Troye, his mum and his brothers. What fun we all had discussing the phenomenon of YouTube, and witnessing it first hand. I remember being surrounded by four security guards who had to make a path for us, through the hundreds of screaming girls, in order to get us from the venue to the after party in one piece. I found it scary, and Caspar held on tightly to me. It was totally crazy and unreal, and all I could think about was The Beatles. This was my first real introduction to Caspar's celebrity life, and it hit hard! If this was Johannesburg, what must it be like in London or LA?

Spud 3 opened in Jo'burg to great success. I went with Caspar to the premiere and it was my first experience of watching Caspar get mobbed by fans.

When the movie opened to the public, there were huge life-size cardboard cut-outs of Caspar in the theatre foyers.

It was quite surreal. Every time I went shopping at our local mall I'd bump into "Casper", spelt with an "e", much to his annoyance. **I'm over it now!** I knew that would always be a problem when I named him, but I still prefer the "a"! Caspar was one of the wise men, from the nativity, while Casper was a friendly ghost. Friends and fans started crossing out the "e" and replacing it with an "a" on the cardboard cut-outs! **And before you ask, no, that wasn't me.**

I'm Casper with an "e"

Caspar was having the time of his life and seemed to be permanently on the move between South Africa, London and LA. I don't really know much about what goes on in LA, except for what he tells me, and he particularly liked being there when Joe went along as well. He had good friends in LA; Nick Hissom and Alexa Losey, with whom Caspar shared a house in Hollywood for a couple of months. Alexa is great fun. She put up with no nonsense from Caspar. One of my favourite videos he's ever done is the one he made about sharing a flat with Alexa called "Living with Caspar Lee". It's Caspar in a nutshell – crazy, compelling and charming.

By this time Josh had moved to England to play cricket so he was around a lot too. Caspar enjoys his friends so much, and he really liked having Josh nearby. I guess Josh also gave him continuity of his childhood and growing up in South Africa. **That's true. I was so happy when Josh moved to the UK. Although now I can't seem to be able to get him out of my flat.**

Caspar started dating Emma Laven, who he had met at Bestival 2014, a music festival held every September on the Isle of Wight, and he brought her home to Simon's Town, near the seaside, just outside of Cape Town where we now live during the Christmas holidays. I really liked Emma. He was so happy when he was with her; they'd both leap out of bed in the morning ready for the next trip she had planned. Once again, Caspar was doing more outside adventuring and getting up at a decent time. The whole family even went horse riding on the beach. I couldn't believe it – Caspar was enjoying nature at last! Woo hoo! We also went swimming with the penguins at our local beach (Boulders Beach) and Caspar and Emma also went skydiving. *We went skydiving in Plettenberg Bay, which is really near my home town of Knysna. It didn't feel real – it's like you're in a massive air tunnel. It makes you realize how small you are in the world.*

I really liked Emma. He was so happy when he was with her; they'd both leap out of bed in the morning ready for the next trip she had planned.

After a jolly good Christmas in the sun, with a fun-filled trip to Knysna to visit Josh (most of it spent on the aforementioned music-blaring speedboat), what did Caspar do but hop on a plane to the Alps to go skiing for his very first time? Josh had been given a ski trip as a 21st birthday present from his parents, and off they went with another school friend, Alex Boomer. I had always wanted to take the kids skiing. It was on my bucket-list but we could never really afford it. Here Caspar was, aged 20, fulfilling all my dreams, and financing it himself. He took to snowboarding like I knew he would. *Snowboarding is the most amazing thing ever. It's something I want to do a lot more of. You don't even feel like you're exercising because you're having such a good time. It's hard to explain the feeling but flying down the mountain on my board made me feel like I was in a Bond film or something.*

It was the cold version equivalent of wakeboarding on the Knysna Lagoon and he said it was the best holiday he'd ever had! And it was another activity with him spending time in the Great Outdoors, I loved it.

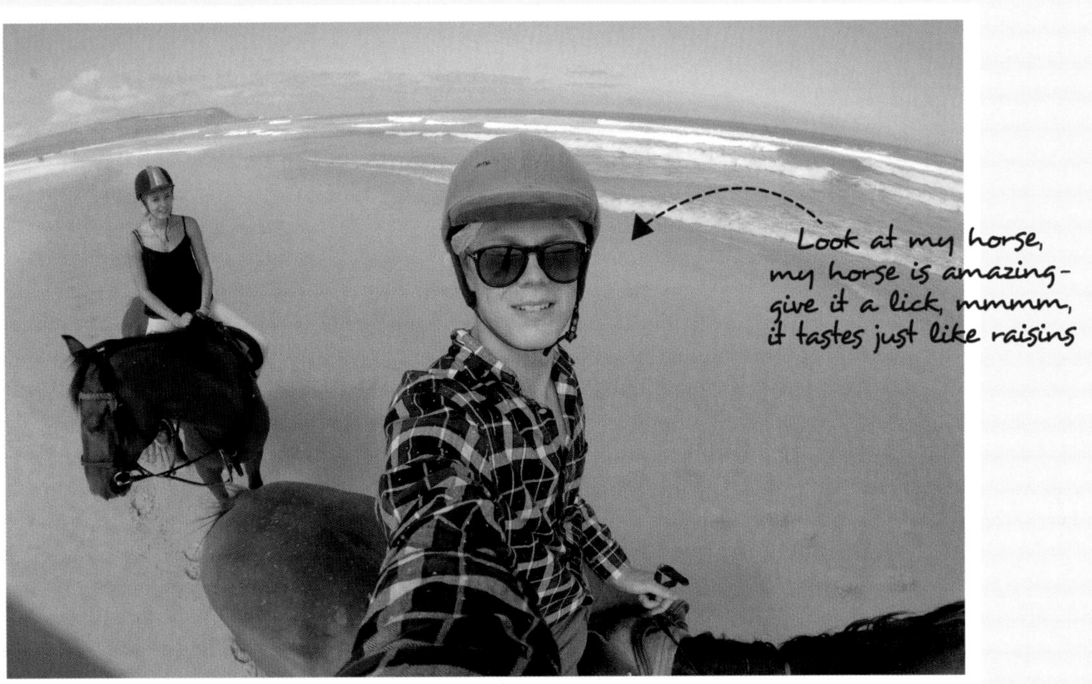

Look at my horse,
my horse is amazing-
give it a lick, mmmm,
it tastes just like raisins

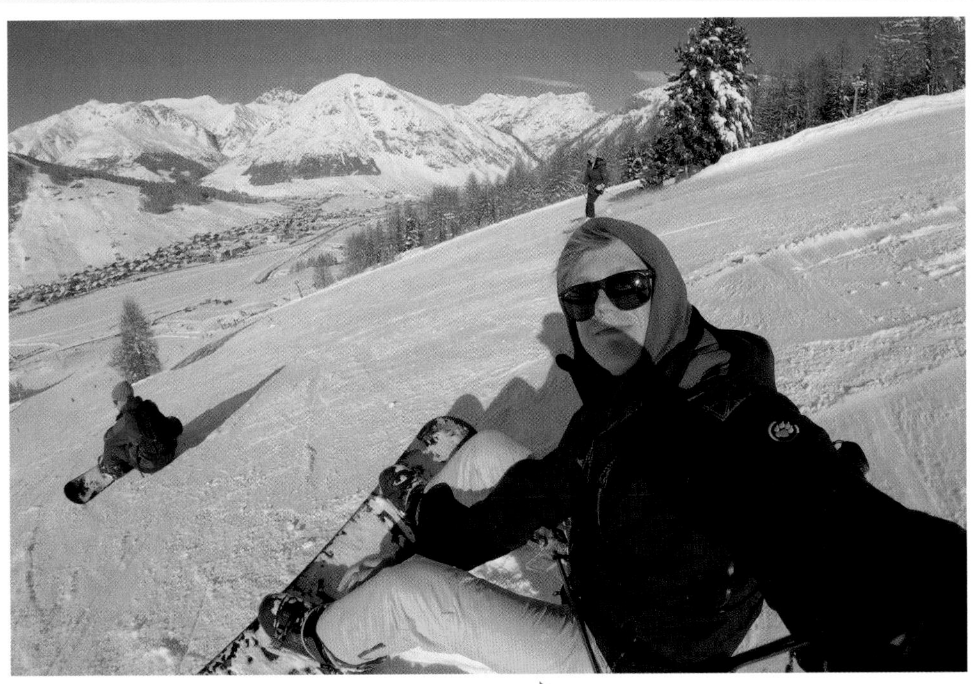

I went down the whole slope on my ass

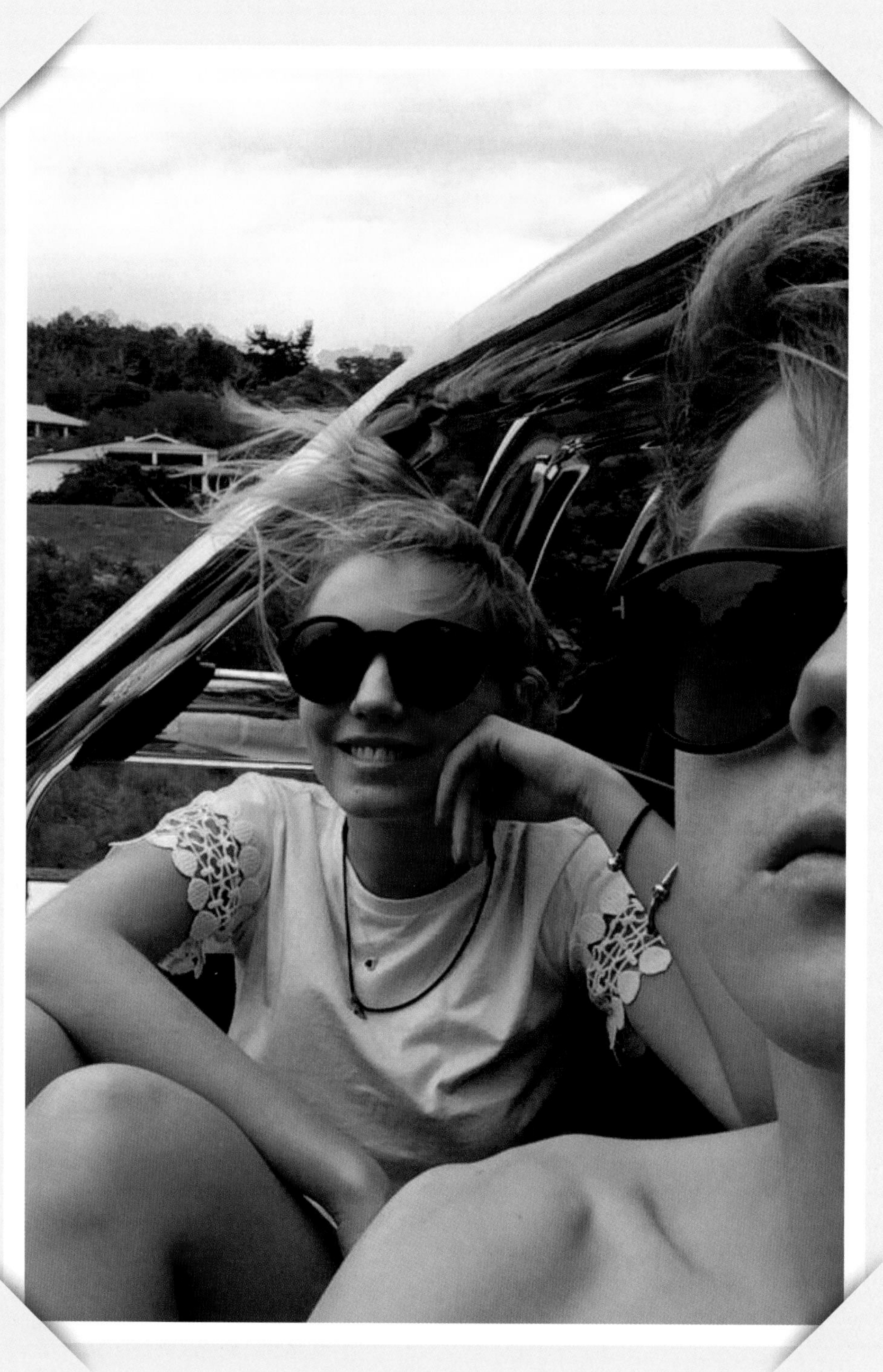

It's a bit creepy how similar
Emma and I look here

LOVE
THESE GUYS!

THE REAL YOU IS SEXY.™ #aerieREAL
I ♥ Summer
aerie
AERIE.COM
#JJSUMMERFIESTA

CHAPTER TWENTY EIGHT

Incredible Uganda

I'm proud to say not all Caspar's most recent life has been about fun-filled jaunts. He has worked immensely hard over the years and my proudest moment was in 2014 when he decided to board a flight to Uganda to do some work for the charity Comic Relief. I think it was inspired by Emma, who had gone to work in a hospital in Tanzania at the time, as part of her gap year. Caspar travelled to a very run-down hospital, which was being rebuilt with the help of funds raised by Comic Relief. Babies were born by torchlight from the nurse's mobile phone, which she held in her mouth, when there was no electricity. People were desperately poor and the hospital had few resources. It was a huge eye-opener for Caspar, and he set up a fundraising campaign on JustGiving. He realized that the stresses he has in life, such as bringing out a new video or waking up early, were nothing compared with what the people of Uganda had to contend with.

He announced to his followers that all he wanted for his 21 birthday was for people to donate to the hospital. His aim was to raise £21,000 – a thousand pounds for every year of his life. He announced on Facebook: "My new video is the most important I've ever made, together we can make a difference."

> Caspar travelled to a very run-down hospital, which was being rebuilt with the help of funds raised by Comic Relief... It was a huge eye-opener for Caspar.

He travelled around, larking about with kids who had so little compared to him, and he couldn't believe how happy they were. Though he had been brought up in South Africa, and encountered similar situations there, he had never really come across a situation quite like this before, where people in dire poverty did everything they could to help each other and kept their smiles on their faces.

Caspar spent a week there filming, and managed to raise the £21,000 by the end of it. It was, and still is, my proudest moment in Caspar's career, and I am the one now who is continually nagging him to do "more". Celebrities have amazing powers when it comes to fundraising, and for me it's one of their most important ways that they can give back to society. *This is definitely my proudest moment too. It was incredible to be able to go out there and help.*

After Emma had finished working in Tanzania, Caspar met up with her for a holiday in Zanzibar, before flying half way back to London, after being requested to attend a big compèring event in the city. But everything went belly-up on his way home. His flight from Zanzibar to Nairobi was delayed, so he missed his connecting flight to London. The airline lost his bags, which also contained his camera, and so all his videos and photos of his trip were lost. Worse still, as he waited in Nairobi Airport there was no food or water supplied while he sat up all night in a mosquito-infested terminal building. But Caspar bore it well, quickly overcame his disappointment, and turned the whole episode around by returning from Nairobi in the middle of the night, back to the hotel in Zanzibar to surprise Emma, who assumed he was already heading up an event in Leicester Square!

I believe Caspar learnt a lot from his trip to Uganda, and has done much more to support charities as a result, often with other YouTube friends.

My trip to Uganda was the most humbling experience: it really puts things in perspective. It was genuinely life changing. I don't get anywhere near as bothered about petty things as I used to, because I realize they don't really matter as much any more. I went there with a guy called Adrian Bliss, who also directs some of my videos, and it was a great bonding experience for us. We talked so much about what was going on around us.

The Ugandan people have very little – they have to use bicycles as ambulances – and yet, like my Mom says, they're always smiling. It's definitely inspired me to help however I can in the future. You think you know what it's like for people who live in extreme poverty from seeing it on TV, but until you experience it it's really hard to understand it.

I met so many incredible people over there who were working for various charities and are doing such amazing work in the face of so much adversity and danger, and it's mind-blowing how hard they work to help their fellow humans. They're out there volunteering and building clinics; they're the kindest people you'll ever meet. I'm not the most capable builder but I did help to do a bit of digging where I could. I met a great guy who was training to be a nurse, and he was saying that he knows it's a crazy place, but all he wants to do is help as many people as he can. I think about my time there constantly.

His aim was to raise £21,000 – a thousand pounds for every year of his life. He announced on Facebook: "My new video is the most important I've ever made, together we can make a difference."

Caspar with Adrian Bliss, his director in Uganda.

CHAPTER TWENTY NINE

The Name's Lee. CASPAR LEE...

Caspar's career took another giant leap forward in December 2014 when he started interviewing movie stars. With Caspar on four million subscribers at the time, it was a clever idea from the film companies to enlist Caspar to help promote their new movies in a fun and Caspar-esque way. Of course, Caspar acts the dumb interviewer, which brings a whole new dimension into the world of chat shows. Rather than be savvy or smart, Caspar plays the role of a befuddled host, who usually has to resort to hugs to communicate with his interviewee.

One of his first interviews of this kind involved taking acting advice from the pornstar Asa Akira. When I first heard about this I was flippin' terrified! I thought, this was it! He was going "over the edge". Definitely *not* suitable for a bunch of teen viewers. My son was actually hanging out with a pornstar. I gritted my teeth, opened up my laptop and thought I'd better watch it, before I impose judgement on it.

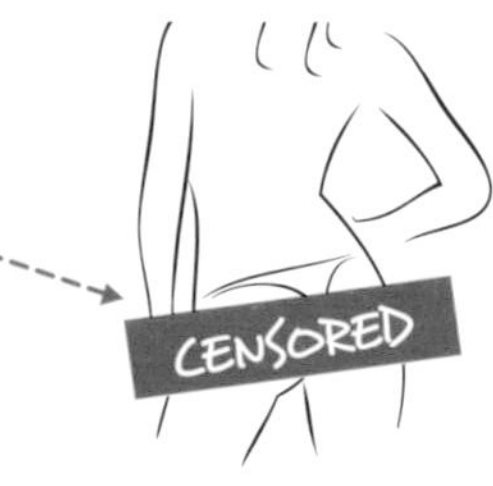

Caspar plays the role of a befuddled host, who usually has to resort to hugs to communicate with his interviewee.

Caspar got through it by acting like he was really nervous, and I have to admit, I did find it very funny. There were half a million beeps put in to cut out most of the sexually explicit bits, and then he proclaimed to Asa Akira, the pornstar (what a name!) LOL, Mom to watch out as his mum would be one of the viewers! The video ends in a rather awkward hug but thankfully the whole episode proved to be neither offensive nor inappropriate. Just Caspar, as usual, acting the nerd. Note the use of the word "acting" here please, everyone.

He used the same technique when interviewing the female stars from the latest Bond movie *Spectre*, *Lea Seydoux* and *Monica Belucci*, in a video called "My New Girlfriends".

The name's Lee... Caspar Lee.

F**K OFF JOE!

BEST BF EVER

It was very different from what a normal chat show host would do. He acts the nervous, loveable goofball, makes a fool of himself, and ends the video in a large group hug. Best. Moment. Ever. He never tries to be smart in these types of interviews – not that he's incapable of being smart! He prefers to go down the self-deprecating route, which results in a kind of comic pathos. The viewers cringe, at first, and then end up loving him to bits. I'm both offended and flattered by this sentence.

Hugs, friendship and love are big things in Caspar's life and unlike lots of boys his age, he is never shy in showing his affections, both privately and in public. In the interview with Chris Pratt (the handsome man from *Jurassic World*), Caspar hangs his arm over Chris and pretends to be his best friend, and tells Chris to tell poor old Joe to "f**k off"! Chris doesn't know who Joe is but is happy to do it anyway. I've got to meet so many cool people. I interviewed Mark Wahlberg and Will Ferrell for their new movie Daddy's Home. Will was great and Mark is like a big baby in real life. He was so funny and kind all the way through the interview. The comedian Kevin Hart told me to keep pursuing comedy and said that I really had something, which was amazing. Caspar gets into your heart with the small stuff, the everyday embarrassing moments, which we all go through, and invariably ends each conversation with a hug, or an "I love you!" no matter who it's with. I can tell you, however, it's wonderful to be on the receiving end of one.

In the interview with Chris Pratt (the handsome man from *Jurassic World*), Caspar hangs his arm over Chris and pretends to be his best friend, and tells Chris to tell poor old Joe to "f**k off"!

He deserved it

Caspar has a very open heart. His ability to read people has always been a strength and is probably why people are so easily drawn to him. He knows from first impressions how to act with people and make them feel special. Perhaps it boils down to the openness we tried to encourage in the family when he was growing up, or maybe it's just who he is.

Caspar never shies away from holding my hand or clinging on to his sister's shoulder and loves talking openly about everything, with such interesting insights and intrigue. It's hard not to fall in love with his persona and he's a treasure to spend time with. I know this rarely happens but I am seriously speechless. This is so nice. Almost too nice. I feel like I need to tone things down a bit so here goes... I once spread a rumour around school that Theo played with dolls until she was 15*.

*I didn't really.

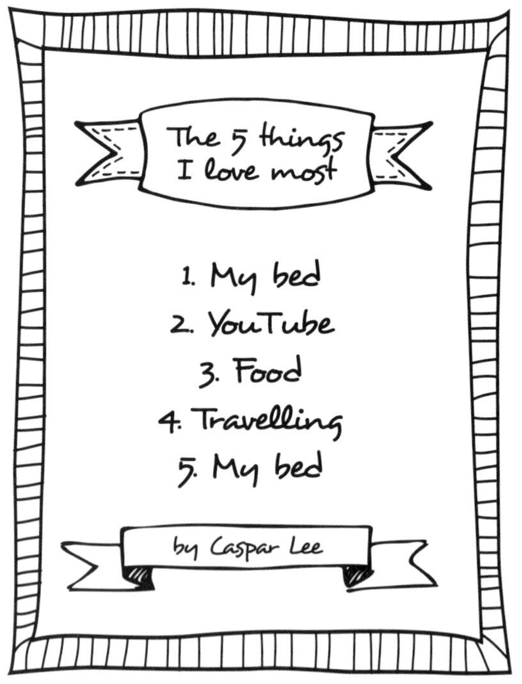

The 5 things I love most
1. My bed
2. YouTube
3. Food
4. Travelling
5. My bed
by Caspar Lee

Caspar became friends too, and made a wonderfully entertaining video in July 2014, with Maisie Williams from *Game of Thrones*. The video was the usual Q&A on the bed type stuff, and we all know how much Caspar likes spending time in his bed.

See list…

In the end there's an affectionate pushing and shoving off the bed, with Maisie ending up on the floor. I love Maisie and her fun, down-to-earth approach to YouTube. Caspar encouraged her to start her own YouTube channel, which she did in October 2015.

There was a lot of travelling in Caspar's 21st year and I could hardly keep up with all the plane journeys, and lost phones and interrupted Skype calls, that invariably went with it. Luckily when he went to Manila, in the Philippines, he had Joe and Olly White with him to pick up the pieces. Olly was a relatively new friend of Caspar and Joe's, and is also a very well known YouTube star. They often hung out together in the London flat and on this trip they made a jolly threesome. Their excursion to the Philippines to attend YouTube Fan Fest was a rip-roaring success with sold out shows all the way.

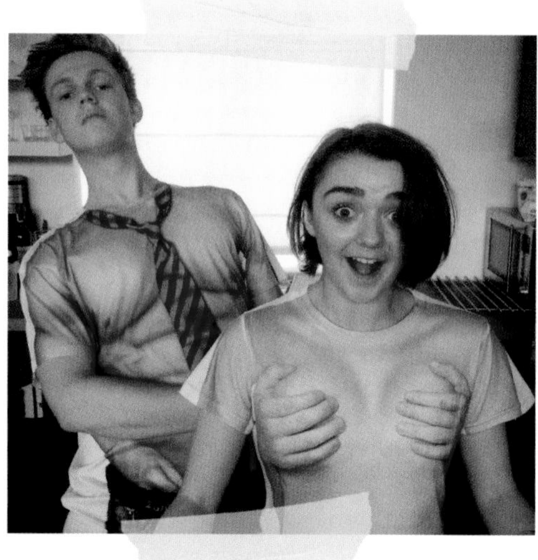

I love Maisie and her fun, down-to-earth approach to YouTube. Caspar encouraged her to start her own YouTube channel, which she did in October 2015.

Forgot my handbag

We got to travel around and appear on stage at various venues. We don't really perform when we're on stage as such; we just kind of talk and muck about and have a laugh. We went on a TV show while we were out there and the streets were so busy we had to get a police escort all the way. It was mad.

I was glad Caspar was travelling further afield than South Africa and LA, and had finally made it to the Far East. I was equally glad he was in the company of his best friends, if only because it meant that they each would share all the gifts they had been sent from their fans. The whole floor space of their hotel bedroom was literally covered in bags of mementos.

We were given so much cool stuff out there. Thanks everyone! I have a running joke about a baby doll called Emma in my videos so sometimes people give me dolls to be the new baby. It's hilarious. I get so many sweet letters, as well as a lot of pizza - my viewers are the best!

I was glad Caspar was travelling... in the company of his best friends.

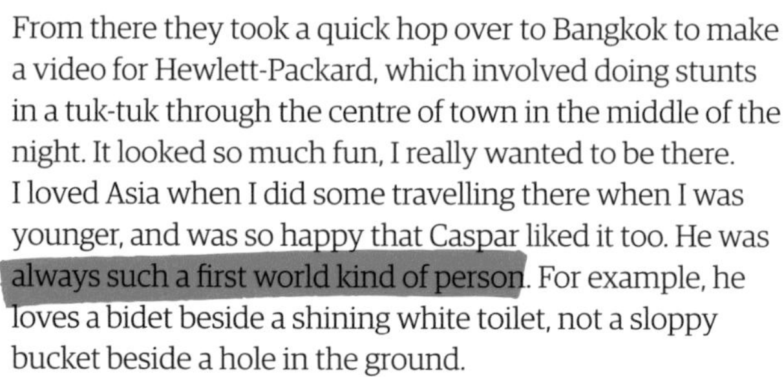

From there they took a quick hop over to Bangkok to make a video for Hewlett-Packard, which involved doing stunts in a tuk-tuk through the centre of town in the middle of the night. It looked so much fun, I really wanted to be there. I loved Asia when I did some travelling there when I was younger, and was so happy that Caspar liked it too. He was always such a first world kind of person. For example, he loves a bidet beside a shining white toilet, not a sloppy bucket beside a hole in the ground.

Bathrooms aside, his eyes were being opened. He was discovering the treasures of the East (including the amazing Whiskey Sours), and enjoying every new and unique moment. He hardly spent anytime in his hotel room. What a change from his days in Sri Lanka!

When they all got back from Thailand, Josh arrived in London for another go at the cricket. Caspar was really happy to have his old friend back and suggested to Josh that he could help him start up his online clothing store, in between his cricket matches. What a great idea it was. Now Josh had a real excuse to move to London. He loved London and couldn't see much of a future for himself in South Africa. So like a busy bee, he got to work.

I never worked out, and still don't know, how Josh survived financially

To be fair, I did give him a ton of free pizza and beer

but he carried on stoically, determined to make a life for himself in London and after a few hiccups - including a terrible bout of the kissing disease (glandular fever) - and lots of graft, managed to bring out a very fine range of Caspar Lee branded t-shirts and hoodies, available at casparleeclothing.com.

CHAPTER THIRTY

A Christmas CRACKER

Back in England, and its gloomy summer, Caspar launched his new online clothes store with another quirky video. I'd call it a bit daft, if I'm honest. Caspar ends up firing all his models, and accuses Maisie Williams of stealing his coffee. In the video, Joe Sugg suggests to him that having his name scrawled all over t-shirts had really gone to his head! A crazy idea emanating from one of Caspar's biggest worries – that fame will one day become too much, go to his head and change him into some kind of terrible egomaniacal monster. It would kill me if that happened. I never want me to change or get big-headed. I would hate it. I really hope people tell me straight away if I ever show any signs of doing that.

> He certainly hasn't lost himself in the jungle of celebrity hullabaloo.

It doesn't hurt to have a hangover every once in a while... they keep you grounded!

But luckily it hasn't, so far. I can vouch for that! And if it ever gets to that point, I'll be the first person on his case. I don't doubt it. In spite of his success, Caspar hasn't changed much. He's definitely happier because he's doing what he wants to do, but he certainly hasn't lost himself in the jungle of celebrity hullabaloo. It must be tough being stopped every five minutes, just for going down the local shop, but he treats it as part of the deal, and that's all. It also helps that he has absolutely no interest in drugs, and is not that bothered about alcohol either, apart from the occasional night out that I hear about.

Another "daft" episode was when Caspar came all the way from England to South Africa to visit me for one day. I had just arrived home from visiting Rick in Sri Lanka when he walked in the door, grinning from ear to ear. He had flown Josh from London to the "Rocking the Daisies" pop concert It's a festival, Mom as a surprise for Josh's 21 birthday. Rocking the Daisies is a kind of South African version of Woodstock.

Please note this outfit
IS NOT available on my online
clothes store

Caspar has always loved surprises… especially springing them on other people. Josh was beside himself with excitement, and when a helicopter arrived to take the two of them from Cape Town to the Cloof Wine Estate, the festival venue, Josh exclaimed, "Did you buy me a helicopter, Caspar?" I didn't. I nearly died laughing. Just the sort of thing Josh would say! Another impulsive move from Caspar. I never know what's coming next… Which is just the way I like it!

This incident reminds me of the time Caspar told me he couldn't come home for Christmas because he'd messed up on his flights.

"What do you mean you're not coming for Christmas? You always come for Christmas!"

He was "crying" down the phone, telling me excuses, I was so disappointed. On Christmas Eve, Theo's boyfriend, Andrew, and I went to the beach. Afterwards, I usually take a dip in our pool. As I was standing at the pool edge, with Theo talking about last minute Christmas presents, somebody came along and pushed me in from behind! As soon as I surfaced who did I see? It was Caspar who had jumped in with all of his clothes on, GoPro in hand.

I nearly drowned there and then with the shock of it all. I just screamed and screamed and repeatedly asked what he was doing in our pool. "I lied," he said, as he hugged me in his drenched clothes. "I wanted to surprise you." This still makes me laugh my ass off.

But that wasn't even his worst prank. There was also the time, not long ago, when he rang me to tell me he had got a girl pregnant. Now this was my worst fear come true… I really and truly fell headlong for that prank! I had happily finished a mammoth walk around Inishbofin, an island off the west coast of Ireland, when I got this phone call from him, so was clearly too exhausted to tell he was fibbing. He was "crying" (he's always been a very good actor, as I've said, and his fake cries always sound so real!) on the other end telling me the "trouble" he was in with this girl's parents. A baby, oh my gosh! I was the one trying to calm him down, when it really should have been the other way around. As it turned out, I had been pranked. Again!

But that wasn't even his worst prank. There was also the time, not long ago, when he rang me to tell me he had got a girl pregnant. Now this was my worst fear come true… I really and truly fell headlong for that prank!

To this day, Caspar still catches me out with his pranks, but he has to be a bit craftier about it as I am now wise to his lies. So, watch out, boy; I'm not as gullible as you think I am!

You are. That was definitely one of my best. I almost felt guilty doing it. Almost. Whatever will I think of next?

After being the ~~subject~~ *victim* of many of Caspar's pranks, I really enjoyed turning the tables and getting to pull a prank on Joe in July 2015. Caspar and I came up with a plan. I was to sit down with Joe and have a chat with him. I was to open up to him about my motherly concerns and what I really thought of him, bringing up things that were untrue and all part of the prank. So poor Joe had to deal with Caspar's horrible mother giving out to him. He was so nervous I thought he was going to pass out. I accused him of having a boring sense of humour with his toilet jokes, and that he should "grow up" a bit. Which was totally crazy because he is an amazing YouTuber. I personally quite enjoy his videos, and he's a great influence on Caspar. It went fairly smoothly, until Joe finally realized there must have been a hidden camera somewhere in the room. But we got him for a while, so Caspar got the better of the king of pranks, and we all had a great laugh afterwards.

Sorry Joe, but it was so worth it.

CHAPTER THIRTY ONE

Hitting the RED CARPET

The highlight of Caspar's 21st year has got to be the filming and release of *Joe and Caspar Hit the Road*. It was filmed by the Top Gear team and involved Caspar and Joe travelling to five European cities in a battered old camper van, trying to earn money for themselves. They were both pretty useless. Caspar, of course, faring a lot worse than Joe. Oi!

I saw little snippets of the film before it was released, which I thought were hilarious, but still beautifully captured the essence of these two boys and their close friendship. I loved the clip I saw of Caspar falling out of a gondola, and falling head first into the very dirty, and rather stinky, water of Venice's famous waterways. It was particularly funny for me because I know how much Caspar hates anything to do with dirt and bad smells. The stench was so bad. I feel like however much I shower I'll never quite be able to get rid of that smell.

I was so excited for them when I got the news that there was to be a red carpet premiere for their film at the Empire Theatre in Leicester Square.

I couldn't believe it when Caspar told me the DVD was the biggest first day pre-order on Amazon UK in 2015. Whoop! Things were really escalating, and there was a lot of hype surrounding the release. I was so excited for them when I got the news that there was to be a red carpet premiere for their film at the Empire Theatre in Leicester Square. Caspar and Joe were used to going to glitzy "red carpet" events, but one for their very own film? This was crazy. I never in my wildest dreams could have imagined this happening. I don't think any of us did! Making that movie and getting to travel with Joe is one of the craziest, and funniest, things I've ever done. I mean, who gets paid to travel around doing stupid stuff and having a laugh? Sometimes I really do think my life is a bit ridiculous.

Still can't believe this happened to us – we are just two planks

But Caspar was cool and took it in his stride. A couple of weeks before the London premiere, Joe and Caspar went on a promotional tour of Australia, with sell-out public appearances in Sydney and Melbourne. Caspar had never been to Australia before and completely fell in love with the place. It's so cool. The beaches were amazing and the people were so laid back and friendly. They were expanding their horizons again, and it was considered a huge success. I struggled to take it all in, to believe it was all real. What a time these two young guys (who more often than not would be just sitting in their bedrooms eating popcorn and making videos) were having. It was an adventure of a lifetime, for sure.

Caspar loved the idea of First Class travel so much, that he even thought of becoming a pilot, just so that he could travel up the front! What's more, as a teenager, he hated flying!

On their way home from Australia they somehow managed to get themselves upgraded to First Class. RESULT. Now this may sound very glamorous and all, but it's become a bit of a family joke that Caspar has always believed that he might one day get to turn left when entering an aeroplane. "In your dreams, Caspar," we always used to say, as we frogmarched him to the back of the plane where he'd have to sit next to a screaming child and remain painstakingly upright for the entire journey.

Caspar loved the idea of First Class travel so much, that he even thought of becoming a pilot, just so that he could travel up the front! What's more, as a teenager, he hated flying! On some of our early flights as a family, we would invariably get Caspar upgraded to Premium Economy section by explaining to the check-in counter clerk that he had a severe kicking problem due to his Tourette's. Worked like a charm every time. So here he was finally experiencing the real thing, by some lucky chance, and we've never heard the end of it. There was even a shower, apparently!

A day before the Leicester Square premiere, Caspar and I were talking on the phone about all the goings-on and I was wishing him all the best, when his voice went into a kind of whisper.

"Mom, I wish you were coming too. You should be there," he said.

I kind of knew what was coming, and why we hadn't thought of this earlier was typical. He was so busy will all the leadings up to the event that he completely forgot to invite his Mum all the way down in South Africa!

"Well, I'd love to come!" I said, laughing at his last minute invitation.

When I look at these pictures
I honestly think I'm dreaming

On holiday in Thailand with Joe Sugg.

Having an amazing time at the film premiere.
I still can't believe Joe and I made a movie!

A few minutes later I was packing my bags and heading for Cape Town International Airport. Here I was jumping on a plane to London Heathrow at the last minute to attend my son's premiere. It seemed kind of funny that we hadn't planned it earlier, but it really didn't occur to either of us until it was almost too late!

I got to London early in the morning in the freezing cold and was met by my old school mate, Victoria Seale. I was so happy that she too, my best friend, was joining me for this amazing event. The first thing we had to do was go shopping. Neither of us had anything suitable to wear, and we had the most wonderful time trawling the beautiful shops at the Caledonian Road flower market, in between eating almond croissants and drinking buckets of coffee to stay awake. I found a lovely red beret, which I thought would match the carpet, and that I was happy with. It had been a long 12-hour overnight flight, squashed in between two other people at the back of the plane. No upgrades for me, sadly! But the excitement of it all kept me going. I was pinching myself that I was actually here, in London, and off to my son's film premiere!

We went to a suite in the Westbury Hotel in Mayfair in the afternoon, where Caspar and Joe were busy getting ready. I hardly recognized them when I walked in, with their bow ties and tuxedos. Caspar was even having his make-up done. **Erm, it was manly make-up.** It was pretty surreal to see all this happening for my son, and he admitted to being quite nervous. He certainly looked it. Josh was there too looking very dapper indeed, with his jacket lined with a South African flag. These were no longer the two little boys from Knysna! I felt very small standing next to these two giants, who had grown in more ways than one. Olly arrived with his parents and little brother and there was a bit of a party starting in the boys' bedroom, which was good for relieving the nerves for all of us. Caspar and Joe headed off to the event first and arrived on the red carpet driving the camper van – with Joe driving, of course! It was such an incredible few hours. Hundreds of fans – many of whom had camped out overnight – were lining the streets, screaming loud, just to see the tiniest of glimpses of Caspar or Joe. Most were girls around the age of 14 or so, and some had travelled from as far afield as Singapore and the excitement could almost be seen in the misty vapour which surrounded them.

I was pinching myself that I was actually here, in London, and off to my son's film premiere!

CASPAAAAAAAAAAAAAAARGH!

JOE!!!!!!!!

Lots of British YouTube stars arrived soon afterwards and Jim Chapman, another famous YouTube vlogger, did an amazing job as compère. He did so many cool interviews, including one with the film's director Brian Klein, who announced he only expected four people to turn up for the premiere!

Turning up and seeing the crowds for the first time was unbelievable. My highlight was probably driving in and having that big adrenaline rush from hearing the screams of the crowd there to see us. It was so, so cool to see my parents there together too. I really hope I made them proud. I sat next to my Dad throughout the movie and he kept laughing and asking me questions - that was the best thing. Everyone was so happy and there was such excitement for something we'd had so much fun making. I don't get to see people watching me on YouTube, but obviously we were watching people watching us on a big screen and we could see how they reacted to the build up to the jokes and the pay-offs. It was a relief I wasn't the only person to find certain bits funny! I loved catching up with the crew and Brian, the director, because we all got so close during filming.

There were lots of autographs and selfies, of course, and I have to say it was the happiest occasion I have ever attended. It was also good to see Jon on the red carpet; we shared a proud parent moment, and enjoyed watching the spectacle unfold before our eyes.

By the time the screening started I was ready for a rest. It was almost too much excitement for one day. But when the film began I was back in the groove. What fun it was to watch the crazy antics of these two boys trying to work their way around Europe. My favourite bit was when Caspar tried to train as an opera singer. When he was a young boy I was forever trying, in vain, to teach him "Do-Re-Mi", from *The Sound of Music*, but I never thought this would happen! He should definitely be up for a "worst singer in the world" award. But somehow he did turn out to be an excellent pizza chef, which came as no big surprise to me, considering the amount he has eaten in his lifetime. I'll definitely have to test him on that one. I'm not sure I'll be making pizzas again anytime soon. Surely that's what takeaways are for?

I had such a great night. We all did. There was an after-party next door where I enjoyed meeting several of Caspar's new friends. I also chatted to one of the executive producers of the film, Paul Hembury, who spoke so highly of working with the two boys and said how down-to-earth and hard working they were.

I do hope we'll see Caspar and Joe doing more of these travel-adventure films together. They make a good Laurel (Joe) and Hardy (Caspar) combo, with their modern day slapstick humour and genuine chemistry. I'd like to see them properly roughing it on their next adventure and see what great humour will come out of that.

CHAPTER THIRTY TWO

What A Ride

A couple of days after the film's premiere, when we had all recovered, I spent an evening with Caspar and Josh at Winter Wonderland in Hyde Park. It's this enormous winter theme park with hundreds of rides and has a wonderful Christmas-feel to it. It was Caspar's idea- he's always loved that sort of thing - and I was game.

Caspar was so excited about going it was almost funny. It was like he was a little kid again, and the feeling was contagious. *Of course I was excited! There were cool rides and good food. It was absolutely nothing to do with Santa being there or anything. Honest.* As soon as we arrived I couldn't believe how pretty it was with all the lights and how huge and towering the rides were and I couldn't wait to go on one myself. There was even ice-skating.

We bought pizza, which I haven't tasted for about ten years, and it was delicious. Caspar bought chocolate and vanilla fudge, just like he used to when he was little. Then he made me eat it because he didn't like it, which is also a common habit of his.

Of course, Josh and Caspar hunted down the scariest ride, while I watched aghast, hoping they wouldn't throw-up afterwards like I saw numerous other people doing. But no, Caspar and Josh are made of stronger stuff.

They persuaded me to go on what they thought was going to be rather a lame ride, and I ended up screaming in terror and kept my eyes closed for most of it. I had a very sore rib afterwards because I was tossed about like a pair of pyjama bottoms in a tumble drier. It wasn't anywhere near as "lame" as they expected.

They persuaded me to go on what they thought was going to be rather a lame ride, and I ended up screaming in terror and kept my eyes closed for most of it.

FLOSS FACTORY
PROPER COFFEE

There's never any milk in the fridge - just champagne and mouldy old cheese.

Isn't every twenty-something's fridge like that?

It was such fun just hanging out with these young men, doing silly stuff like we used to as a family back in South Africa, all those years ago. A lot has changed in Caspar's life, but he's still a kid at heart. Amongst all the jingle bells and Christmas lights, Caspar turned to me and said, "Ah, Mom, I'm so happy you're here. This is what I used to dream about when I was a kid and it's so lovely that you can enjoy it with me too."

And so his life carries on, with its down-to-earth days in his London flat, where there's a deafening noise of overground trains going past - "klonk, klonk, klonk" every five minutes. **I'm so used to it now I don't even notice it anymore.** Rubbish accumulates, and piles of washing are stuffed into cupboards that won't shut. There's never any milk in the fridge - just champagne and mouldy old cheese. He lives a very normal life most of the time, with quick bites from Pret a Manger, and dinners at Nando's and Wagamama's. **Mmmmm.** I still haven't managed to instil my love of cooking in him, but it will happen one day...

So, there we have it; a remarkable life so far for a most determined young man, whose career path could have gone in so many different directions. He could well have been any of the following: professional poker player, lawyer, pilot, computer gamer, Olympic swimmer, professional hockey player... But I couldn't be happier than with his decision to become a YouTube sensation and entertainer **Me too!** and I'm so excited about his future and how it will unfold.

I have absolutely no concerns about where this "YouTube thing" is all heading. Caspar is very happy, thoroughly enjoying his life, and can look after himself very nicely. His future career is an open book full of many different and exciting opportunities, and for me this relatively unknown territory is a path of adventure and discovery. He's also exceptionally well looked after by Gleam Futures, his management company, who guide him on a daily basis through a myriad of work-related issues. In them, I have nothing but the greatest of confidence. My son is in good hands. He is an extremely lucky boy, who by pursuing his dreams, has made them all come true.

Writing this book really has made me feel like the proudest parent in the world and I've loved looking back at Caspar's brilliant life so far. He's happy, healthy and living his life to the full. What more could a mum ask for? *Awww, thanks, Mom! You really are the best mom in the world. I hope you know how much I appreciate everything you've done for me! Love you.*

As for me...

I split my time equally between Simon's Town in South Africa and Myrtleville in Ireland, and visit my Dad in Sri Lanka twice a year. I have a wonderful and very active life with Sham, and in between visiting our children and grandchildren we sail a beautiful old wooden boat. My children and step-children make my life rich and varied, for which I am truly grateful.

We also love daily swims in the sea regardless of the weather. I enjoy social media and keeping up with the times and I am genuinely looking forward to doing some more writing. More travelling to wild places is always on our agenda too.

Theo now lives in Cape Town with her boyfriend Andrew. She posts weekly videos on YouTube and is also a copywriter. I am forever amazed by her dedication to hard work and creativity. Caspar and Theo continue to have a close relationship and whenever they're together the older-sister-younger-brother dynamic is as funny as it was when they were children. They take good care of each other. It's very sweet!

Jon is an advertising copywriter and is happily married to Lindsey. They live in London and Cape Town, which allows them to closely marvel at all five of their children's progress.

Mini-Me, who has sat on my lap through the entire writing of this book, is still alive and kicking. Here's to many more adventures together!

Final Final Chapter

The 'Winning Shots'

...Well, it's not quite the end of the book.

My mom and her editor decided that they needed more pictures of me (apparently more pictures = more copies sold!) so they arranged a photo shoot. What follows are what are known in the business as the 'Winning Shots'...

Where the magic happens...

I literally have no idea who this is...

Caspar the Giant!

Equipment!

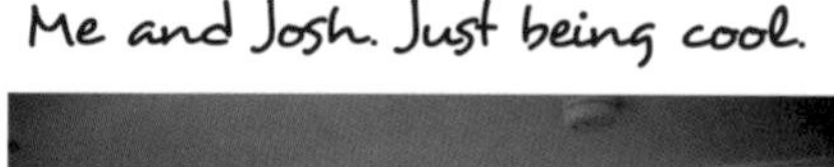

Me and Josh. Just being cool.

In case you've always wondered what my stairs look like. Ta-da!

A lot of you don't know this yet,
but I've just been revealed as the new face of
a well-known pyjama company

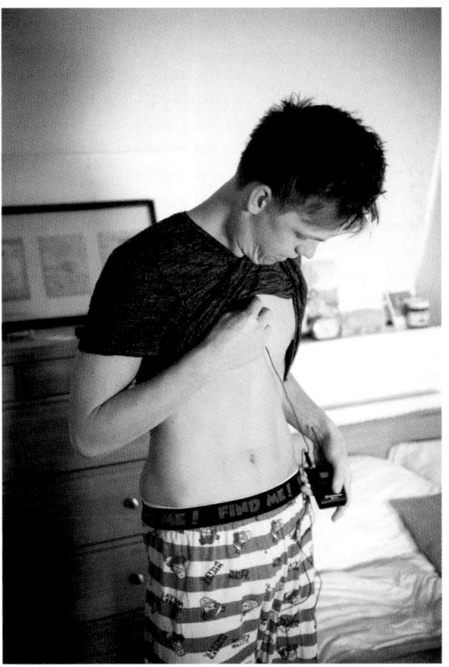

Oh, hi stomach

No honestly, Josh, they're size 11!

Those guys over there look just like us. Weird.

Where did Josh go? He was here literally a second ago!

On a quick Skype call to my palm reader

Josh's best angle

Look! I'm on a really tiny TV!

What do you mean I've got a bald patch????!

This is me working. No really, this is work!

Still working hard!

Seriously, Josh, I'm trying to work here.
I haven't got time for cats playing banjos...

Who am I trying to kid?
There's always time for cats playing banjos.

Time to jump on a tube to a photo shoot for this very book

Candy Crush Level 270. Really.

Would it be greedy to get one of everything?

Please note, this is not my dressing gown...
but that is my amazing hair

Is this button loose?

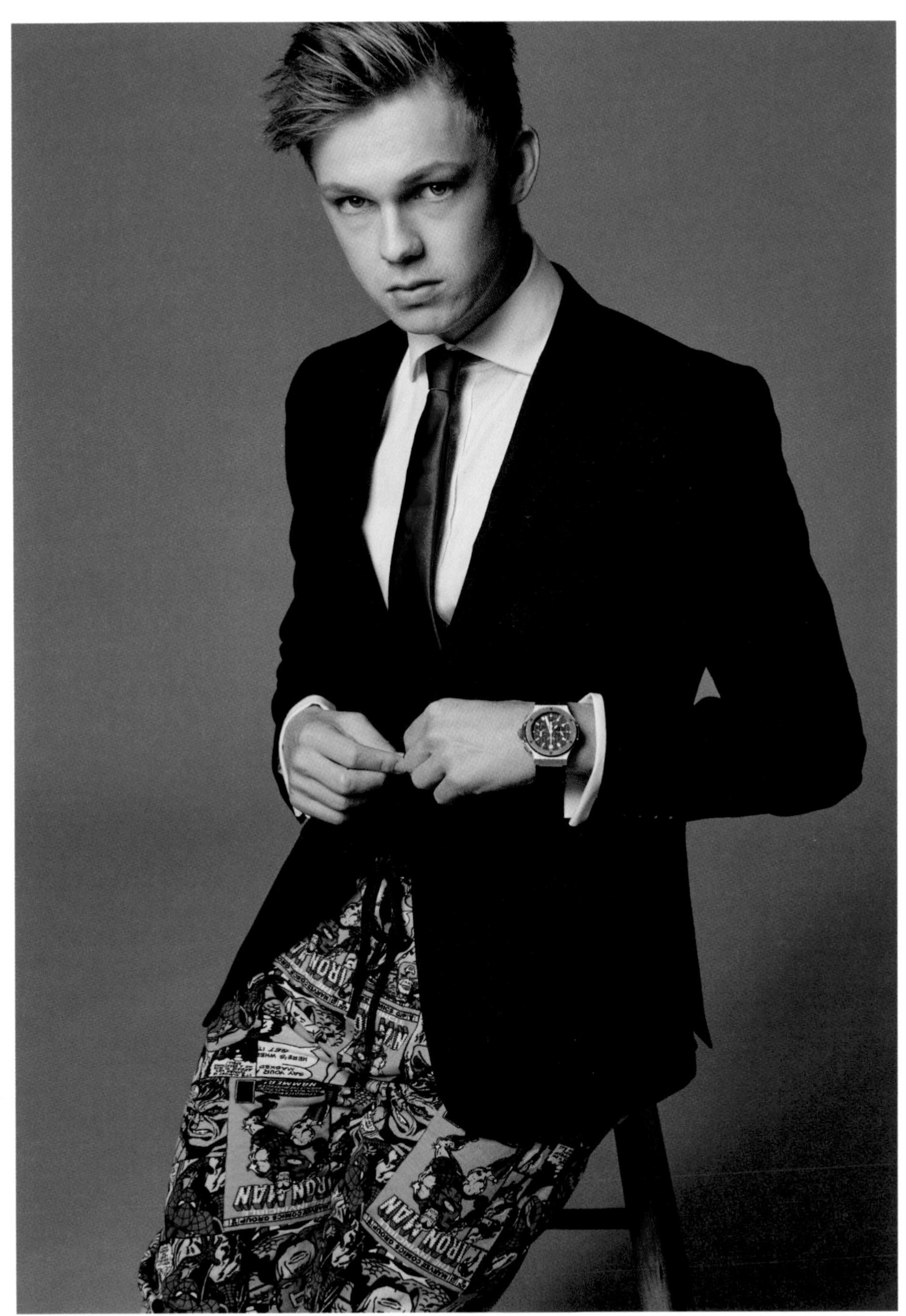
IRON MAN
IRON MAN

The blazer/pyjamas/sock combo is so this season

Someone really needs to fix this button...

Gigi and Zayn?

Noooooo...

It can't be true...

With a random fan. She insisted we took pictures.

She was VERY persistent

This is the September image for my 2017 calendar

Man, I loved that tree

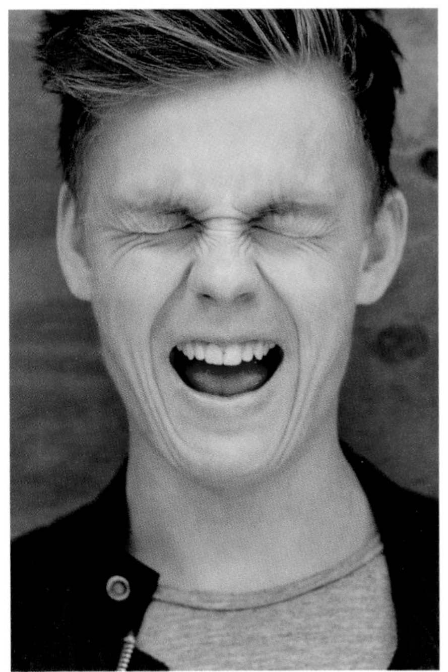

Shooting the cover

I always wear this outfit when I'm out jogging

I hope someone checked for dog poo...

In my spaceship

I sense aliens are trying to make contact

Clearly bored now…

The End (no, really this time)

Acknowledgements

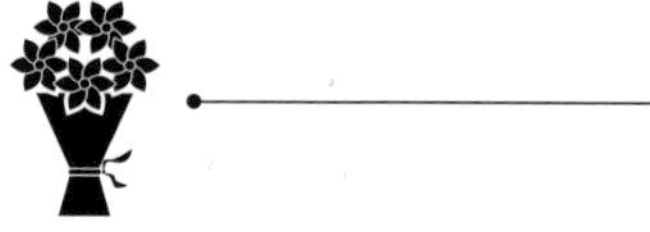

EMILY'S ACKNOWLEDGEMENTS

For all my family and friends.
In memory of my mother Patricia Avis, 1928–1977

"The old order changeth, yielding place to new."
Alfred Tennyson

I would like to thank Caspar for coming up with the idea, and for giving me the most marvellous opportunity, to write this book. I would like to thank my daughter Theodora, who was such a wonderful help to me throughout the writing process. I really couldn't have done it without her.

Many thanks to my best friend Victoria Seale for always being there for me. I thank my editor, Fenella Bates, for guiding a novice through this minefield. Huge thanks to Jonathan Lee for being such a great custodian of the family archive and for providing all the photographs.

Thanks to Pete Bishop and Josh Pieters for their input, and to my cousin Fiona Murphy and Liz Mellon for being ever so encouraging from the start. My thanks to Dom Smales, Amy Bryant-Jeffries and all at Gleam Futures.

Many thanks are due to my husband Sham, for all his patience and good humour throughout.

To all of Caspar's followers, or 'viewers' as he calls them. Without all of your support, his career wouldn't be what it is and this book would probably not be in your hands right now.

Thank you.

CASPAR'S ACKNOWLEDGEMENTS

A big thanks to my mom, dad and sister Theo, my brilliant friends Joe, Josh, Grant and Oli, and to Amy and Dom from Gleam. And, of course, a massive thank you to my amazing viewers for your incredible support.

HARROW COLLEGE
Learning Centre
020 8909 6520 (HH)
020 8909 6248 (HW)

177629